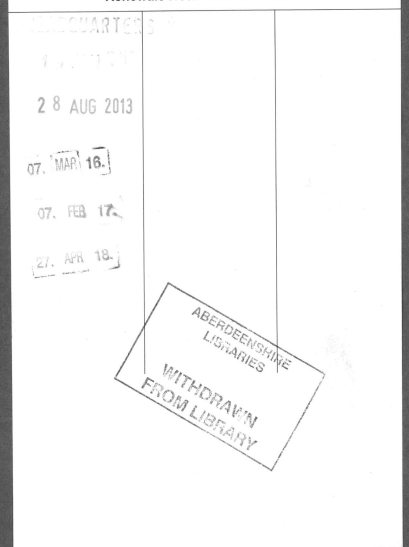

FISHING
WITH HARRY

a tale of piscatorial mayhem

FISHING
WITH HARRY

a tale of piscatorial mayhem

Tony Baws

Illustrated by Suzie Baws

Merlin Unwin Books

First published in Great Britain by Merlin Unwin Books, 2011

Merlin Unwin Books Ltd
Palmers House
7 Corve Street
Ludlow, Shropshire SY8 1DB
U.K.
www.merlinunwin.co.uk
email: books@merlinunwin.co.uk

B
BAW

ISBN 978-1-906122-32-4

Designed and set in 11.5pt Bembo by Merlin Unwin

Printed and bound by TJ International Ltd, Padstow, England

Contents

A Word of Thanks

Each week, in the UK alone, some 12 young people between the ages of 14 and 35, apparently fit and healthy, die suddenly of an unsuspected heart condition, leaving their loved ones and friends bewildered and devastated. One such loss among that staggering number is our darling son Gideon, at the age of 33.

Gideon was hugely talented, loving and lovable. He was fond of swimming, cycling and walking – in the May before he died he had swum 5 kilometres with a good friend to raise money for the Marie Curie cancer nurse charity. There was no history of heart problems. He was an entertaining drinker and a sensible eater, he was not overweight and he never smoked (beyond the usual college experiments!)

The charity CRY (Cardiac Risk in the Young) fulfils many important functions: it offers comfort and counselling to bereaved families; it acts to raise awareness by lobbying parliament and promoting an all-party group to keep these tragic deaths in the forefront of the minds of government. It sponsors clinical research through its dedicated units at the Royal Brompton Hospital and St. George's Hospital, Tooting.

CRY also supports cardiology screenings for the age group most affected. Arranged either nationally or by individual fund-raisers, staffed by medical experts in this highly specialised field, using equipment provided by CRY, the hope is to identify at an early stage those at risk and to advise them accordingly.

Author royalties from the sale of this book are committed to CRY; to raise money for their essential screening projects and to contribute towards their core funding. Thank you so much for buying it.

Tony and Suzie Baws
September 2011

This book is dedicated
to the beautiful life and memory
of Gideon Baws

CHAPTER 1

Wake up, little Suzie

'This above all: to thine own self be true
And it must follow, as the night the day,
Thou canst not then be false to any man.'
SHAKESPEARE *Hamlet*

The little I saw of Harry in the early days of my courtship of his stepdaughter was mostly his rear view: a broad back in a striped shirt, trousers riding high on elasticated braces. His hair was black, cut severely in a short-back-and-sides, parted in the middle and given an oily gloss by the liberal application of hair-dressing. Occasionally I could detect the merest hint of soap by an ear, which only served to amplify the overall impression that he was scrubbed clean to within an inch of his life.

This imposing figure was not much given to small talk. Some people found Harry threatening and I understood why he had this effect. I did feel some awe, but what I mainly felt was amusement.

I soon came to know Harry's routine. Every afternoon, as soon as he returned from his daily sales round in London, he commenced his paperwork. He put a lot of physical effort into his paperwork, did Harry. First a rickety, two-tiered wooden trolley, his mobile office of the day, was wheeled ceremoniously into its allotted position under the ceiling light, next to the oak gateleg table in the living room. On the top tier of the trolley were white customer record cards, yellow-pink-blue triplicate order forms and buff envelopes. In one corner sat a small, round tobacco tin, delicately decorated in brown on a yellow background, depicting female peasant-farmers in far-off lands, chatting and smoking as their crop was loaded onto mule-drawn carts. This charming container bore the evocative brand name 'The Balkan Sobranie'. It now held postage stamps.

A rubber band secured the bundle of customer records, and under this Harry had jammed a collection of pencil stubs, none longer than three inches. Alongside these sat a worn, grey eraser – a rubber sexton in a pencil graveyard. On the lower trolley shelf were piles of unused record cards and sheets of blue carbon paper. A battered leather briefcase with a frayed handle was placed, just so, next to the trolley. Harry pulled his chair up to the table. He was ready to begin.

In a practised blur, his hand disappeared into the briefcase and reappeared holding papers. These he smacked down onto the table. A pencil-corpse was selected from the assorted cadavers. Figures of quantity and price were transposed from the briefcase papers to the trolley-borne cards. The stubby pencil pressed down so hard that the table vibrated. Harry's knees shook, his feet tapped furiously and he emitted a high-pitched keening noise as he concentrated on his work. Every so often he would reassure himself with a few words of encouragement: 'That's that!' he would say out loud, 'that's that!'

Harry's regular steam train home from work was known locally as 'The Four O'clock Express' and it ran non-stop in 45 minutes from London to Leigh-on-Sea. A short haul down the line, past the cockle sheds and round the bay was Chalkwell Station. Here Harry would stir himself and get ready to alight. Sometimes, after celebrating a particularly large order, he might imbibe too freely of draught Guinness in the London station pub before the train departed. Snug in the warmth of the carriage, he would occasion-ally fail to notice his arrival at Leigh, or Chalkwell, or even Southend, but instead travel to the end of the line at Shoeburyness, there to be awakened in a befuddled state by a member of railway staff checking the train before it was shunted onto the up line for the return journey.

As our courtship progressed, I became a frequent visitor to Harry's house. 'Evening, Mr P.,' I would offer in friendly greeting, feeling that a formal mode of address was appropriate. I was only just restrained by Suzie from calling him 'Sir'. (By the time we went fishing together it was Harry or H. I never called him by his surname, whereas he would often call me by mine. I accepted this as a mark of affection even though it revived painful memories of school, where the use of a surname, bellowed by a master, would inevi-tably be followed by punishment, usually of the corporal variety).

'Hmmmm … Tony…' he would reply distractedly. It was the only acknowledgment of my presence that I would receive until he had finished his task. Eventually, the completed orders for Head Office were thrust into their envelope. A pen was grasped, an address scribbled, and the envelope glue licked extravagantly. A postage stamp was equally lavishly licked and pounded into place. His wife, Billie, would scurry off to the pillar box clutching the precious envelope. The day's work was done. Only then would Harry turn to face me, smiling, with eyebrows raised, and offer me his standard greeting to all and sundry men: 'How are you, boy?'

Harry's father, Henry, died in the First World War. En route from Marseilles to Egypt on New Years Day 1917 his troopship, the S/S *Ivernia,* was sunk by a German U-Boat off Cape Matalan in Greece. An almighty explosion wrecked the engine room and steering, leaving the ship floundering. A destroyer from the convoy came alongside to assist, but high seas, whipped up by a ferocious winter gale, smashed the two ships together. In the confusion many lives were lost. His body was never found.

Harry, born two years earlier and christened Henry after his father and his father before him, was raised by his mother. She would have preferred a daughter, and dressed Harry accordingly. Nevertheless, she always referred to Harry as 'Boy', to others and to his face, a nickname she used even when he was grown up.

Photographs of Harry as a baby and as a toddler indeed reveal a winsome child of uncertain gender. Clothes of the period were at any rate full of fandanglements and lacy embellishments. So keen was his mother to protect Boy's pristine condition that she continually washed every reachable surface in their home, fearful that her inquisitive offspring might touch something dirty and besmirch himself. According to family lore, the cleaning regime extended to the coal as well as the coal scuttle.

This fastidious upbringing no doubt contributed to Harry's adult preoccupation with the detailed maintenance of his person. Some might describe his rigorous washing and the subsequent application of cosmetics, humectants and unguents to various parts of his body and face as mildly obsessive. Other, less tolerant, observers of these ablutionary and decorative rituals called it a perversion.

Harry was privately educated and began his working life, courtesy of a family connection, at the Public Records Office at Kew, by the Thames in Surrey. There he acquired an interest in history and geography, subjects in which he had not shone at school, where, he confessed, he 'buggered about, went on the piss a lot, and achieved fuck all!' The post included a period of secondment to the American Library of Congress. The work was interesting and responsible, with a certain *cachet*, but poorly paid. He considered in later years that maybe he had been foolish to leave that privileged position, but, like many young men, he was envious of the salaries his friends were earning in their less demanding careers. Harry followed the money and chose a job selling insurance. Hertfordshire was his territory and he counted among his clients the barge families who traded along the Grand Union Canal, going aboard to collect premiums whenever the boats stopped over at Rickmansworth or Kings Langley. He enjoyed the time spent in the open air and the relaxed nature of his few appointments. 'Self determination, Baws,' he would frequently tell me, 'that's the key.' The Prudential continued to pay him even after he enlisted in the Army at the outbreak of the Second World War.

At the time I met him, Harry was a high-class salesman of high-class biscuits. His customers included Harrods, Fortnum and Mason and the Army Officers' messes in Chelsea and Kensington. Harry the Salesman played the part of the complete city gentleman: smart dark suit and overcoat, regimental tie, bowler hat, impeccably rolled umbrella and extraordinarily shiny shoes. He polished his shoes and cleaned his bowler hat with the same energy and vigour that he applied to his paperwork, but in place of a stubby pencil on paper, he wielded stiff brushes to attack his clothing. He did this so effectively that he eventually wore away the nap on one side of his best rabbit-fur bowler hat.

He caught the train from Chalkwell to Fenchurch Street in London at 6am Monday to Friday. This regime obliged him to rise at 3.30am, in order to give himself time to wash, pamper and preen to his satisfaction and still leave time to walk to the station, which he did in all weathers.

On the dresser in his small bedroom, Harry kept a large wooden tray which he used as a portable bathroom cabinet, containing a panoply of personal hygiene and cosmetic potions, lotions and equipment. Neatly arranged on the tray were a circular shaving mirror on a stand, a pair of tweezers with flat ends, an eyebrow pencil, his toothbrush, a flannel in a plastic dish, a tube of Kolynos toothpaste, a tin of Gibb's dentifrice, a deodorant stick, a bar of soap in another plastic dish, a tin of talcum powder, some cotton wool, a jar of Morgan's pomade and various brands of aftershave: Yardley's, 'Old Spice', 'Pasanda' and 'Cedar Wood'.

Then there were several bottles containing Bay Rum, Hungary Water and Eau de Cologne. Some of the packaging was exotic. My favourite was a bottle of Eau de Cologne, apparently made in England but bearing on the reverse of the label a mine of oddly translated information, both exhortative and cautionary, liberally sprinkled with asterisks:

* Invented about 1750 AD. A most refreshing toilet requisite
* Healthy * Hygenic [*sic*] * Used for after-shave * Hairfriction
* When having a cold, dampen your handkerchief
* Clean your face to take the make-up
* Few drops whilst cleaning your underwear
* Sprinkle sick-rooms or general cleaning
* But avoid polished furniture-tops
* A hundred uses feeling fresh – invigorating when using.

The main constituent of this Eau de Cologne was de-natured alcohol, contrived to dissuade the drunk, the unwary and the misguided from consuming it. De-natured or not, Harry, by his own admission was signally undeterred. At one particularly riotous Christmas party, held at a grand house in Tring, (the residence of a most important client), he had consumed half a bottle of this stuff, for a bet. Already drunk on 'Green Goddess' – a proprietary liqueur with a crème-de-menthe base, popular at the time – and feeling, as he put it, 'rather poorly and confused', he had sought escape

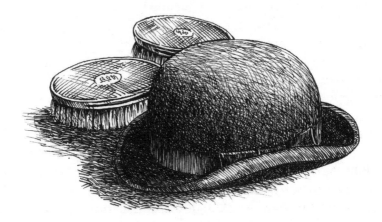

and refuge. The Yule log mercifully unlit, his unfocused eyes mistook the magnificent walk-in fireplace in the entrance hall for the cloakroom. Finding his exit barred, he attempted to climb the chimney, in the reverse fashion of Santa Claus. Exhausted in time by these efforts, he eventually collapsed in the grate. There he was found come the morning, suffering from an atrocious hangover and covered in soot.

Completing the collection on Harry's tray was a tube of Lavender Hair & Body Wash, a badger-bristle shaving brush, a tube of 'Old Spice' shaving cream, a Gillette safety razor, a packet of '7 O'clock' razor blades, a styptic pencil, some orange cuticle sticks, a nail file, a nail brush, a bottle of 'Man Tan' instant tanning lotion, a bottle of brilliantine, a tub of Brylcreem hair dressing, a bottle of Silvercrin hair tonic, a tortoiseshell comb and two silver-backed hairbrushes.

Every morning Harry carried this tray of preparations to a small table in the tiny kitchen of their flat above the tropical fish shop. There was no bathroom on the top floor where Billie and Harry lived, and he declined to use the one in the lower area of the flat occupied by his mother-in-law. There was a toilet, but even that involved a trip outside to a small, detached building on a roof terrace, accessible by a door from their cramped sitting room. The only heating in winter came from an open fire and a paraffin heater. There was no running hot water. He put two kettles on the gas stove and lit the rings. Placing a towel on the floor beneath the kitchen sink and warmed only by the paraffin heater, he stood on the towel and undertook his ritual cleansing and make-up for the next two hours, starting with a stripped-down-head-to-toe wash.

Liberally applied, the 'Man Tan' lotion imparted a somewhat orange shade, which contrasted sharply with the glossy black hair, black-pencilled, plucked eyebrows and trimmed moustache, giving him a strikingly theatrical appearance. Harry always maintained that a salesman's role was basically an act, but sometimes, when he had overdone the cosmetics, he looked more like a pantomime 'Baron Hardup' than the Errol Flynn lookalike to which he surely aspired. A final splash of aftershave, another dab of Eau de Cologne and Harry was ready to face the day.

If questions were ever raised about the time he spent at his washing and beautification, Harry could become agitated.

'You go to France or Germany, or anywhere in Europe,' he would respond, 'men there naturally take care of themselves, think nothing of it. It's only the Brits that are such filthy people, Baws,' he would rage. 'Look at them throughout history. We were wearing woad and animal skins when the Egyptians were already civilised. Elizabethans, Jacobites, Stuarts, Cromwell's lot, Reformation – they were all foul sods. Never washed, just covered everything up with powder and perfume. Fold them over and their pants would crack!'

Every Sunday without exception, Harry dressed in military fashion: khaki trousers, khaki shirt, khaki socks, brown shoes and a thin green woollen tie.

'I don't bother to ponce up on a Sunday, Baws,' he once explained. 'Of course, I still have a full wash down.'

14

It wasn't hard for me to fall in love with Suzie. Incredibly beautiful, with long black hair, green eyes, slim and delicate, she was intelligent, warm-hearted, talented and funny. And to cap it all, her name was a hit record by the Everly Brothers, one of my favourites. What she saw in me I will never know. She had a penchant for swarthy East European Gypsy musicians à la Django Reinhardt, and American tough guys Humphrey Bogart and Burt Lancaster (though she also swooned over a handsome blond-haired actor in some God-awful black-and-white Czech film – 'Ashes and Diamonds'). Maybe a dark, young, bespectacled, Jewish trainee accountant from Westcliff was just what she needed to satisfy her exotic taste until the real thing came along.

We had no sooner plighted our troth than Suzie was rushed into hospital with appendicitis. Visits were short, and Suzie was asleep for a lot of the time. Anxious for news of her progress, I spent an increasing amount of time at her parents' flat.

Suzie came home from hospital and our courtship blossomed. After her initial fright upon meeting the blonde, five foot nothing, impeccably attired, fierce woman that was my mother, the two bonded closely. Since we lived only a few roads apart, we spent a lot of time in each others' homes. Differences in our families and cultural upbringing were never a source of friction. True, Suzie's mum, Billie, (also five foot nothing), spoke in a refined voice and hated swearing, whereas my mother Lily, while well-spoken, could and did eff and blind with some fluency and to considerable effect.

Nor were religious differences an issue. Harry's first wife had reportedly been Jewish, although he rarely talked about her. Phyllis suffered terribly from depression and her condition worsened after the birth of their only child in 1946. Harry was forced to abandon a successful career at the War Office in order to care for her. Despite his best efforts and his frantic rescues of Phyllis after her several failed attempts, she eventually succeeded in committing suicide.

Unable to look after his one-year-old son by himself, Harry gave him into the care of close relatives. It was accepted that he would always recognise David as his son, but all agreed it would be best to keep contact between them to a minimum. By the time I met Suzie, Harry had not seen David for many years.

It seems that Harry was no stranger to alcohol in his younger years; on the contrary, episodes like the Christmas at Tring were fairly commonplace, (though he had learned his lesson with Eau de Cologne). The consumption of alcoholic drink might indeed have ranked as one of his major pastimes, both as a civilian and in the army. This compared sharply with me, who felt reckless drinking half a pint.

Often he regaled me with tales of mess-room drinking games, all of which demanded the ingestion of copious amounts of ale. One such was 'Cardinal Puff'. As far as I could tell, this involved reciting some mumbo-jumbo, downing beer and performing an arcane series of tapping movements with one's fingers in the correct order, all the while being closely observed by one's peers. If the strict rules of the game were not followed to the letter, the glass was replenished and the increasingly befuddled participant had to start all over again. Since prospects of eventual success diminished with each failed attempt, much drunkenness ensued.

By the time he met Suzie's mum, Harry was also drinking to obliterate the memory of Phyllis's tragic death. Billie was herself recovering from the trauma of a failed marriage to Suzie's father and living at the time in what she hoped would be only temporary accommodation with her young daughter. It happened to be close to where Harry's mother lived, leading to a chance meeting. Perhaps Billie's strait-laced attitude and teetotal lifestyle were the soothing balm, the antidote and the sanctuary that Harry desperately needed at the time. When questioned on this, Harry for his part, while expressing gratitude for her intervention, always maintained that 'Billie's big bosoms were the clincher'.

Harry and I gradually became more relaxed in each other's company, although conversation was still limited. Until one day he said to me, completely out of the blue, 'Ever go fishing when you were young, Tony?'

'Yes,' I replied slowly, 'I used to go quite a bit when I lived in Benfleet. Why?'

'Oh, just wondered.'

'I never caught anything of any size, Mr P. – Harry. Just tiddlers really. Used to take them back in a tin and put them in the pond in the back garden. What about you?'

'There used to be a place over by Lime Avenue, off the London Road in Leigh,' said Harry. 'Brush's Brickfields – it was called. Stacks of roach in there.'

'That's where they built Belfairs School isn't it?' I knew it well. 'I never went fishing there,' I told him, ' but I used to play football in the field the other side of the sand pits. All built on now, I suppose.'

We sank back into silence. Had someone interrupted us at that moment, had there been a knock at the front door, maybe both our lives would have been the poorer. Instead, Harry started up once more.

'Ever thought about going again?'

No, I hadn't. I went over the prospect in my mind. I liked the outdoors. I played rugby, football, cricket. I was even press-ganged into running cross-country for my school. The course followed the shores of a large lake which held huge carp. Spotting the basking fish on my way round took my mind off the boredom and cruelty of cross-country running. But I hadn't fished for years. I had no tackle, no appropriate clothing, and up to that point, no interest in fishing at all. The suggestion was crazy, but crazy ideas I liked.

'Why? Were you thinking of going, Harry?'

'Well, only if you fancy it, Tony,' he replied. Hang on I thought, I didn't start this. I should have bailed out at that point. But I ploughed on.

'Have you got anywhere in mind?'

'I was talking to old dog-face the other day. You know, whassisname, Old Clarke. Comes round with the shellfish cart on Fridays. He says there are huge carp in Priory Park but no one ever catches them. He reckons you'd have to fish at night to stand any chance.'

'We could go down and have a look on Saturday morning if you like,' I said cheerfully. Best not tell him at this stage that I had never fished at night in my life. I imagined from the confident way he spoke that he would be the one with some experience, the expedition leader. Oh, how wrong I was.

CHAPTER 2

The Priory

'Footsteps coming down the stairs!
Who should it be but the maiden's father
With two pistols in his hand,
Looking for the man who shagged his daughter!
Jig-a-jig-jig, jig-a-jig-jig
Balls an' all — jig-a-jig-jig très bon!'

In the distance I could hear Harry's strange song, sung purposefully to his marching footsteps. He never would say where the song came from. Maybe army days, maybe drinking days in Ireland. Whenever I asked, he just grinned and carried on singing:

'It... suddenly came upon my mind
To shag Old Reilly's daughter ...'

Billie was not in favour of swearing. 'Harry, please!' she would scold, whenever Harry voiced what was for him a mildly rude word. He did it to annoy her, and giggled like a naughty boy. Billie had been brought up in the Anglican Church and she never failed to reprimand Harry for his swearing and blasphemous outbursts. This only made him do it all the more, drawing from her ever greater reproach, much to his amusement. I wasn't particularly foul-mouthed or blasphemous until I met Harry. Somehow we sparked off each other. When fishing was quiet we often made up obscene limericks or spoonerisms or just streams of blank verse swearwords, seeing who could make up the longest unbroken chain.

The singing changed to a loud humming and the footsteps drew closer. I edged out of the door into a warm and gentle May night. Silent, except for Harry. I could make out his beaming face in the half-shadow of the street lights down on the main road.

'Is that you, Tony?'

'No – it's the Archbishop of bleedin' Canterbury, you daft sod!'

'Hello Baws. Smashing night. You going to float fish?'

'Probably.'

'Flake?'

'Yes.'

'Got some bread?'

'YES! Come on………….'

It soon got to be like that with Harry. He would ask question upon question. I would become short tempered very quickly and he would stop for a while, but soon start up again. 'Looking forward to it, Baws?' asked Harry. From that vague discussion some months ago of how we had gone fishing in our childhood, we had now worked ourselves into a state of extreme excitement and anticipation. From the moment we had decided to go fishing we had talked of nothing else, thought of nothing else. The fishing drug was in our blood, and it was to stay that way forever.

There was no one else around, which was just as well. We were a strange and lawless-looking pair. Harry, who during the week was immaculate in pinstripe suit and bowler hat, was wearing for this occasion old corduroy trousers, tucked into wellington boots and done up round the waist with a long woollen scarf. Over a purple jumper he sported an ex-army leather jerkin, and on his head was a knitted army hat, with a pheasant feather stuck in it at a jaunty angle. His application of tanning lotion imparted a particularly stage-like appearance under the street lights.

I was still in my Buddy Holly phase, all thick rimmed glasses and dark suit. But for fishing I had acquired a camouflage outfit from the local Army & Navy surplus store, and so with the rod bags over our shoulders and in the dim light we looked like mercenaries in search of a war.

Prittle Brook in Essex runs down from Daws Heath, through Hadleigh Great Wood and Belfairs Wood and on to Rochford where it joins the River Roach. Leaving the north part of Southend it passes through Prittlewell. Here in the early 12th century, Robert de Essex gave a grant of land for the establishment of a Cluniac Priory. This survived with various alterations and additions until 1536, when, during the dissolution of the monasteries by Henry VIII, the buildings fell into disuse. Importantly for us, however, the monks had established fish ponds for their carp stocks, and incredibly these ponds still remained.

At Prittlewell, the brook is culverted under the road before emerging into the park – 'The Priory'. Close to the ruins of the monastery are the two ponds, divided by a strip of land about four yards wide, accessible from one end (but still referred to as 'the island'). These were nominally club waters but, being a Corporation property, day tickets were available to the public, and the area was jointly patrolled by club bailiffs and corporation 'parkies'. But there was definitely no night fishing, and fishing out of season was not even considered. Doing the two together was probably a hanging offence.

We shinned down the banking before the concrete culvert began. I was just 20 years old. Harry was 45 and fairly fit, in spite of the disdain he always expressed on the matter of physical pursuits. However inept he made himself out to be, some of his reluctantly acquired military training must have stuck.

Bending nearly double, we crept under the long road bridge, trying not to step into the shallow brook. Once in the park, we kept in the brook cutting until we felt far enough away from the street lighting. Up onto the bank, we walked silently along the grass edging to the dog-leg fence which protected the edge of the first of the two ponds. We paused at the fence, listening for any human noise. No clicks or rustles, no hiss of line on reel. No lights.

'What do you reckon, Tony?' whispered Harry. It was the first time either of us had spoken since we entered the park.

'Let's make our way onto the island,' I whispered back.

The island seemed to be more overgrown than I remembered it from the single daytime recce. The rods and the tackle, not to mention Harry, did not make things easier. Five paces forward and I was stuck. We shuffled back the way we had come.

'Look, you wait here, Harry, and I'll go and check the swims.'

My eyes were now accustomed to the dark, and by a slightly different route I came out to a fishable swim about half way along the island. Alongside, separated by an overhanging hawthorn bush, was a spot for Harry. That became the way of it over the years. I would lead the way, find two adjacent swims, mine and Harry's. He was always so good about it, never complained when I had first choice and took the more promising place. We always fished side by side, only as far from one another as a stage whisper would carry in the silence over the water. I went back for Harry and cautiously we threaded our way through the overgrowth to the two swims.

There was not much headroom to tackle up, but we both had only two-section rods and centre-pin reels. I had mastered one single knot because it was easy to tie in the dark. With the rod silhouetted against the night sky I threaded the line and tied the hook. I had the choice of two floats, both of them the kind that boys used to buy. Bright and bulbous, they took about an ounce of lead to cock them. I put one up the line and went round to give the other to Harry.

'This one be all right, H?' I showed him the float in the light of the torch.

'No, it's okay, Tone. I'll just sit and watch you. Feeling a bit gutty.' Poor Harry. Fit as a flea really, but he was obsessed with the minute-to-minute condition of his bowels and his snout. The first he put down to a bad case of dysentery when he was in the army. Fair enough, but I felt that the situation was not helped by his huge appetite.

Billie, long-suffering soul, had prepared for us two identical boxes of food to take on this, our first fishing trip; hard boiled eggs, sandwiches, biscuits, fruit, and so on. Foolishly, I had left both boxes in Harry's care.

'Harry – where's my food?'

'Don't know, Baws. Isn't it there?' Greedy sod. 'No Harry, it's not effin well there. Have you scoffed it?'

'I haven't had it, Tone.'

'Well, there's none left.'

'Oh. Well, I only ate mine!'

It was useless to argue with him. He ate like an automaton. Or a bison. He had grazed away until it was all gone, mine included. As to his snout, as Harry often remarked, nasal distress was an affliction we British shared with the Romans on account of our changeable and dampish weather. 'Bastard climate,' fumed Harry, 'saw off Julius Caesar – soon went pissing off back to Rome. Couldn't stand it!'

So Harry settled himself in just behind me, on one corner of the ground-sheet. We had no chairs, but the bank was level and sloped gently to the water, making a natural seat. A rod rest I cut from the bank-side branches. Eight inches from the hook I nipped enough shot to sink the *Bismarck*. I pinched on a bit of bread flake and cast out into the searing spotlight of my brand new Ever Ready 'Space Beam'. The float sat dumpily in the water, brilliantly yellow in the light of the torch.

A brisk breeze had sprung up and it had become chilly. The branches of the trees swayed and the float drifted out of view. I swung the torch beam across the water and found the float again, but a sudden eddy of wind pushed it back the other way. Back and forward went the float like a leaf in a storm.

'Pack it up God!' moaned Harry (who, as a devout heathen, still believed in divine intervention if one's plea or complaint was expressed with suffi-cient vigour). 'I'm beginning to feel dizzy watching the bugger!'

Forward and back went the float for what seemed like an eternity.

'Those monks, Tone,' observed Harry, 'relied on this pond for their scoff. Bugger that. Must have been thin bastards.'

Every time the float changed direction Harry asked if it was a run. 'No Harry, it's just the wind,' I replied each time, with increasing frustration. I hadn't used a plummet. I had just guessed the depth and set the float, so it was free to travel along like a boat. Then suddenly, the float just carried on and on into the darkness. I struck, and felt resistance. I stood up, and put a foot in the water. I pulled back, and fell on top of Harry. The line zinged out against the reel ratchet as I struggled to keep the rod upright and to regain my balance.

'I'll get out of your way,' offered Harry, in the manner of Captain Oates.

'Jesus, Harry!' I yelled, 'just grab the net and shine the torch down by my feet.' I was panicking and Harry was dithering.

'All right, Baws,' he soothed, 'keep calm.'

I had lost all contact with the fish and was merely flailing about, but I began to retrieve line. Then the resistance again, to my left, as I judged, about ten yards out. Slowly I made headway and could make out the outline of the float on the taut line. The fish surfaced and swirled, and Harry slid the net under my first, and last, Priory Carp.

Harry and I faced each other, and we hugged and we laughed and we jigged up and down. It was a tiny fish, by carp standards even then: about two pounds, I guess. But it formed a covenant between Harry and me and fishing and friendship.

We fished the Priory all that summer and never had another bite.

CHAPTER 3

Cunning Men

'Whenever the moon and stars are set,
Whenever the wind is high,
All night long in the dark and wet,
A man goes riding by,
Late in the night when the fires are out,
Why does he gallop, and gallop about?'

ROBERT LOUIS STEVENSON *Windy Nights*
(from *A Child's Garden of Verse*)

Who would have believed that the obsessive, kempt Harry I met at his home and the relaxed, rakishly-attired Harry who fished with me that first night at the Priory were one and the same man? Now he was apparently untroubled by the dirty hands and the grubby clothes acquired after a night spent on the banks of a muddy pond; blemishes which his City persona would never tolerate. His voice too had changed; the strident vocal delivery which was so noticeably clipped and formal when Harry was dressed in his City suit, or kitted out in his khaki-for-the-weekend army wear, had mellowed to become friendly banter and brisk repartee.

His grandiose self-image however, remained unaffected. Harry, in his general demeanour, was confident of being instantly recognised as a member of the gentry. Whilst in no way a snob, he expected to be accorded all due rights and privileges of that curiously intangible and diminishing class.

Harry was an avid reader, often using his choice of reading material to bolster his expectations, as if by some strange alchemy or osmosis his mere contact with the written word would serve to reveal his true class identity to the *cognoscenti*. He mainly sought out non-fiction works and historical novels of the Georgian era, particularly the Regency, as the period with which he identified most strongly. But he was equally fascinated by tales of notable English eccentrics and the history of ancient Egypt, with the unsettling result that one moment he was identifying with a Regency dandy or a famous English eccentric or a member of the Hellfire Club, and the next he was insisting that he might well be the reincarnation of an Egyptian Pharaoh.

Even if he had no substantial claim to an actual title, he believed that the reward of land and wealth which were due to him by grand design would somehow be duly granted. Until the arrival of that happy day, Harry, reluctant gentleman-in-waiting, would continue to dispense a certain *noblesse oblige*. This mainly took the form of large tips for serving staff and extravagant expenditure on rounds of drink in pubs until his money ran out – behaviour generally accompanied by much patting of his wallet pocket and cries of 'This one's on me, boy!'

Harry had plotted out for himself two potential routes to his inevitable elevation. Firstly, there was mention of a family tie to a rather grand and ancient firm of crystal glass makers, holders of a Royal Warrant, (as if this connection was ennobling in itself).

Of possibly greater substance was a rumoured family relationship to a certain Canadian who, while having a background 'in trade' (like Harry), was nevertheless granted a baronetcy, in recognition of his business acumen and military success (or it might have been the other way round). This personage was at one time possessed of a considerable tract of real estate in Canada, including a magnificent Gothic castle. Any remote hopes of inheritance that Harry entertained in his fantasies were frustrated when swingeing taxes plunged the unfortunate baronet into debt and near bankruptcy.

'The man was a bloody fool!' declared Harry unsympathetically. 'Like owning a Rolls Royce and not knowing how to drive.' This was an expression he employed quite frequently. He used it to describe anyone who, blessed with opportunities and/or qualifications, (either or both of which, in his opinion, led automatically to wealth and success), failed to take full advantage of them. Not that Harry was expressing envy, (he said), just stating the obvious. Namely, that he would have made a resounding success of things had he the good fortune to be in that position himself.

Walking home that mid-morning from the Priory, our talk was of nothing but fishing and the events of the previous night. We began again to mull over venues of our youth where we might still go fishing. One such spot was Greenacres, a farm pond in Hadleigh where I had often gone as boy. Not too far away, it was still well-known locally as a day ticket water. The rumour was that the owner was thinking of selling up soon and so he was not currently too particular about the presentation of fishing licences or the observance of the closed season. I mentioned this to Harry.

'You want to be careful there, Tony.'

'Why, Harry, you're not worried about poaching again after last night are you?'

'No, Baws, not likely. Adds to the fun. Still, I'd be careful if I were you.'

'Greenacres isn't a dangerous place to fish is it?' I asked. As I recalled, it was not very deep and there were firm, easily accessible banks all round.

'No, nothing like that,' said Harry measuring his words. I was too exhausted to be teased and Harry's mystery was beginning to annoy me.

'What have you heard about it then? Hooligans? Trouble? Come on, what's the problem?'

Harry paused before answering.

'Did you ever hear of 'Cunning' Murrell',' asked Harry, 'the 'Wizard of Hadleigh'?'

I tried then to recall what people in Hadleigh had looked like when I was a boy. Faces came back to me: sinister, brooding men in dark clothes and hats, and women with small eyes, hooked chins and facial hair. I had always thought these people were normal in a small country village.

'No, I don't think so.'

'He lived in a cottage opposite Hadleigh Church,' continued Harry. 'There were witch families in Hadleigh and Rochford and Canewdon. James Murrell, 'Cunning' Murrell as he was known, was their master. '

'You're pulling my leg, Harry.'

'No, honestly Tony. I'm not joking.'

'Harry, leave off!' I could see that he meant it though. 'Okay. What did he do then, this wizard?'

Harry paused again, savouring the capitulation of his audience before speaking.

'His main business was making potions. He used to brew them up from people's hair or skin or nails, mix them with the juice of wild plants and then have them sealed in iron bottles by the local blacksmith. 'Witch bottles' they were called.'

It sounded foul, but there was a blacksmith's forge in Hadleigh, that much was true.

'And what did he do with these iron bottles?'

Harry started to explain. 'Well, say someone came to Murrell and told him that they were under a spell or a curse...'

'What sort of curse?'

'Oh, I don't know – failed crops, ugly wife, cow with the shits – that sort of thing. Anyway, people would collect this stuff from whomever they said had laid the curse and Murrell would make up one of his witch bottles.

Then he would go round to the house of the guilty party when they weren't at home, and put the bottle in their fireplace.'

At this point, Harry's face took on a slightly demonic look. 'Next time they lit a fire, whoosh! The bottle exploded with the heat and all this boiling stuff shot out.'

'And?' I asked, intrigued now.

'It would break the spell or lift the curse,' replied Harry triumphantly.

'Must have made a mess of the living room, eh?'

Harry came over all serious, and gazed into the distance. 'I wouldn't joke about these things Tony,' he observed darkly. 'You never know.'

I had the feeling that if Harry did believe in anything supernatural, it would tend towards Hell rather than Heaven. Best to move on.

'So what else did he do, this wizard bloke?'

'Well,' said Harry, smiling again, 'he had a magic mirror. He could find things and tell the future. And he had a magic telescope that could see through walls.'

'That would have made the neighbours careful,' I mused, 'especially the women.'

'Baws!' said Harry in mock seriousness, 'I'll tell Suzie.'

'So, this wizard, Harry. Anyone seen him recently?'

'Oh yes. People say they still see him sometimes in Hadleigh. He rides around at night on a black horse, whistling up witches.'

Harry's tale conjured up images of a song they taught us at infant's school, about a mysterious mounted man galloping through the night, and how it used to terrify me. As a small boy I lay in bed in the dark of winter at our house in Hadleigh, listening in fear to the wind rattling the windows, watching the rain lash down and the clouds scud across the moon, my ears pricked for the sound of beating hooves.

'It's a load of old cobblers, Harry.'

'Well, he was a shoemaker to start with!' Harry grinned.

'Come on, it's all nonsense.'

'Don't you be so sure, Baws. There are lots of thing we don't know about. Ask Suzie, she's fey.'

'What do you mean, 'fey'?'

'She's fey, Baws. I can tell.'

Was Harry really telling me that his stepdaughter, with whom I had fallen deeply in love, was a witch? Undaunted, I decided we must give Greenacres a try sometime soon: gallopers, cobblers, wizards or no.

My father was still alive when I was a small boy in Hadleigh. He was for a time, like Harry, a travelling salesman. He began by selling furniture and later cosmetics. But that work dried up as war loomed, and he found himself reduced to working in the small, dark, damp, clothing factories of the East End of London – the sweat shops. He became a garment presser. The steam, the poor sanitation, the heat and the constant wielding of the heavy pressing irons and Hoffman Press dragged his health down. He contracted tuberculosis before the outbreak of the Second World War and was declared unfit for military service. He died of the disease in 1944, aged only 29.

As my father became progressively unwell, and with a small child to raise, an escape to the countryside away from the grime of London must have seemed like heaven. Fresh air and rest were all that were on offer at the time to combat TB. Somehow enough money was found to make the move and pay the rent. After short stays in New Bradwell in Buckinghamshire, then in a house on the outskirts of Peterborough, we ended up in Essex.

My Dad was archetypically tall, dark and handsome before illness ravaged his fine body. He was a good swimmer and an amateur boxer at club level. For a short while he even served in the City of London Police force as a volunteer, until he was too ill to continue. Those who 'stayed at home' during the war, but were not involved in reserved occupations, were accepted into voluntary auxiliary services fairly readily, without much scrutiny of their past records, medical or otherwise. The Government welcomed them into the war effort to help in any way they could.

On the other hand, non-serving male civilians were sometimes vilified for a wrongly-perceived lack of patriotism. 'Why aren't you in uniform? Why aren't you out there helping our boys?' That kind of remark was commonplace. Being Jewish, we were also subject at times to a degree of anti-Semitism from these short-sighted bigots, a double blow for my father. But most people were kind and helpful and welcomed us into the local community.

Hadleigh back then was a sleepy village. Most of my young days were spent playing in open fields or woods near home. At the bottom of the road ran a tributary of Prittle Brook, that very same stream which had provided the entrance route for Harry and me on our furtive nocturnal foray into the Priory.

The water at this spot meandered along the bottom of a deep channel. To us youngsters, it might as well have been the Grand Canyon. The challenge was to ride your bike down one bank, across the brook and up the other side without stopping. Getting wet was an acceptable hazard, but avoiding contact with the vicious waterside stinging nettles which grew on both sides of the banking – that took real skill.

Here – before the road was metalled and extended and the houses and shops sprang up and the brook was diverted along a deep concrete cutting – was a small field. Flanked by birch, oak and hazel trees and edged by tall bracken, a footpath led northwards to join a bridle path.

At the junction of these two paths was a pond and here we boys fished for Great Crested Newts. The method was simple. All you had to do was tie a small worm securely to a length of thick cotton braid, with a match-stick tied further up the 'line' as a rudimentary float. The newts gorged the worm and they could then be lifted gently from the water, stubbornly refusing to spit out the worm until it was retrieved from their gullets with a firm pull. I was so successful at this form of 'fishing' that not only did I stock the pond in my back garden with newts, but I was able to sell the surplus to local pet shops to supplement my pocket money. My mother was forever retrieving newts that did not take to pond life and had emigrated to the house. Here she found them; in the pantry, under the carpet or behind the kitchen cupboard.

Towards Hadleigh the bridle path ran parallel to an unmade road – Scrub Lane. Halfway along lay Greenacres, a small-holding owned by Ken, a young farmer who lived there with his wife in a rambling house, surrounded by pigsties, barns, sheds and semi-derelict outbuildings. On the other side of the road were two arable fields which Ken also owned, and behind the farmhouse lay Greenacres Pond. I remembered going there as a boy, not to fish, but just to hang out with the older kids, and in particular with Ginger Padmore, a local hero.

Now that there was a prospect of revisiting Greenacres with Harry, memories of Ginger flooded back. Ginger was a master of many skills: groping, smoking, fishing, thieving and football. A small boy could learn a lot from Ginger. I once saw him steal a football from a local shop by the simple expedient of stuffing it up his jumper, turning on his heels and walking out. His approach to girls showed similar finesse; full-on groping and boasts about how he had felt Jenny's or Jane's 'this and that'. I had no personal experience at my tender age of what 'this or that' truly were, but I knew they were infinitely desirable.

I remembered how Ginger would fish, standing in the shallows of Greenacres Pond on bright summer days; trousers rolled up to his thighs, a cigarette in the corner of his mouth, catching small roach and gudgeon. These he placed in a half-submerged butler sink which had somehow found its way into the water. With the plug hole stopped up with clay, it made an excellent short-stay aquarium. If I was indeed to make it back to my childhood haunt, this time in the company of Harry, I half hoped that the old butler sink would still be there.

CHAPTER 4

A Pig's Breakfast

'Singing hey piggy-pig,
Do a little jig,
Follow the band,
Follow the band all the way.'

HARRY (after WW2 squaddie song)

When I arrived at the flat, Harry was still busy beating up that day's paper-work. Waiting until he had finished, I broached the subject of the fishing arrangements. It was a glorious late Friday afternoon in early May. Our rekindled enthusiasm for fishing had continued to grow apace. The warm, settled conditions only served to stoke the fires of our mania. Where others might long for a swim or a sunbathe after work in this splendid weather, all that Harry and I yearned for was the spell-binding sight of a still float on calm water.

Suzie and I had planned to go out that evening, and Harry also had things to do, but all he and I could really focus on was fishing. We agreed to meet at Greenacres Pond early the next morning. I was to go by bus, while Harry announced rather grandly that he would book a taxi to take him there in the small hours. I thought it tactful not to mention that, if Harry's planned fishing attire for the journey to Greenacres was anything like the outfit he had sported for the Priory mission, a cautious taxi driver might just refuse the fare.

Billie again offered to prepare some food for both of us.

'Remember, Harry,' she cautioned, having learned of the 'Great Priory Park Provisions Disaster', 'leave Tony's food alone this time! I'll make up two separate boxes. There'll be plenty for both of you.'

I was not totally convinced.

'There'll be a full moon tonight, Tony,' said Harry.

'Should be good fishing then. Can't wait.'

'He used to have a dog,' said Harry.

I was stumped by this *non sequitur.*

'Who did?' I asked

'Cunning Murrell.'

'Oh him. What was it called then?'

'Black Shugg.'

'What breed was it ?

' A cross between a sheepdog and a pug' said Harry with a straight face.

'Hmm,' I mused aloud, 'sounds familiar.'

'Oh very good, Baws! Actually most witches and wizards had cats as their familiars. '

'I'll let you know if I spot him Harry,' I promised. 'See you later then. 'Night Mrs P.'

Suzie and I went off to catch an early performance at the cinema in Southend. During quiet moments in the film, I would close my eyes and my mind would wander. 'What are you thinking about at this moment?' Suzie would ask softly, the way young lovers do. I could not confess to her that in my mind were images of a rod in its rest, and a float on calm, green water; a beautiful, still float.

After the show, I escorted Suzie back to the flat, holding her hand and feeling very much in love. But instead of coming in for a coffee and a goodnight cuddle as usual, I briskly kissed her goodnight and rather unromantically scuttled off home to change. Picking up my fishing things, I caught a bus to Hadleigh around half past ten, aiming to relax at Greenacres until Harry arrived. I wasn't going to start fishing without Harry.

I called at the farmhouse to pay Ken and try to sort out somewhere to sleep.

'You're welcome to stay in the barn, just beyond the sties,' said Ken. 'But no smoking in there, mind!'

I explained that Harry would be arriving later, paid him for the two of us, thanked him and wished him good evening, stubbing out my cigarette ostentatiously on the ground in front of us. I made my way past the sties, patting the pigs as I went. It was a perfectly still night, illuminated by a huge, bright, white, full moon. I could hear low voices from the far side of the pond, but there was no one on the side where I was hoping to set up with Harry.

Tense and excited at the prospect of the night's fishing, I entered the barn. It was the first time in my life that I had slept on straw. I had often played in and around the stacks as a kid, and sometimes thought how great it must be to curl up and sleep in a barn. I arranged some bales, set my alarm for a quarter to three and tried to settle down.

I thought I could hear rodent rustles in the straw. My ears were pricked. The mice or rats might as well have been the size of dogs! A song started to go through my head: 'Whenever the moon and the stars are set, whenever the wind is high...'

I listened to the sounds of the night, but thankfully there was no sound of hoofbeats. Eventually I began to doze off.

I must have been blissfully comfortable for all of thirty seconds. It had seemed such a perfectly rustic thing for a nature-loving, country living boy to do, to sleep under the haystack, just like Little Boy Blue in the nursery rhyme. Even if technically it was not hay, but straw. Well, you lucky, lucky sod, Little Boy Blue! You may have been an incompetent halfwit, letting the cow in to trample down the corn without blowing up your horn. But at least you were immune to harvest mites or whatever the hell was assaulting me. At least you managed to fall fast asleep.

I felt like I had been covered all over with those hairy seeds found inside rosehips, the 'poor man's itching powder' we used to put down the back of other kids' shirts to drive them insane. I tossed and turned and itched and scratched until I could stand it no longer. In irritation, rage and panic, I gathered up my things and went outside. Another nursery rhyme occurred to me as I sat on a tuffet and smoked a cigarette. Fortunately no spider arrived.

The moon was still up. The air was heavy with the smell of pigs and warm straw. Every now and then there was the sound of water splashing, as fish surfaced or rolled in the shallows. The itching gradually subsided and I grew drowsy. Pulling my jacket up over my head, I rolled into a ball on the grass and was soon asleep.

I awoke to the click of the alarm clock as it prepared to ring. I took a swig of coffee from my flask and tried to bring my eyes into focus. The moon was gone, but dawn was still a little way off. The reed-and-bulrush-edged pond was shallow, probably only four or five feet even in the middle, with no deeper holes as far as I could remember. The bank around the pond was flat, and the topography resembled a water-filled saucer. I placed my rod and bag in a swim where there was a break in the reeds. Another break further along would be a fine swim for Harry.

Just then I heard a car pull up. Muffled voices and a car door shutting surely heralded Harry's taxi. Unlike me, Harry did not have good night vision. I could hear him curse and saw the strong beam of his torch weaving about in the night sky, bright as a searchlight hunting for enemy planes. I went to welcome him.

'Hi, Tone,' he greeted me. 'You okay?'

I wanted to say that I'd been having a wizard time, but I held my tongue. Besides, confident as I was, a night in the open listening for hoofbeats can unsettle the bravest soul.

'Fine, Harry,' I replied, 'I was just waiting for you.' I would like to say that I followed this with 'I've been itching to start' but that would be lying.

Harry again looked nothing like his weekday or weekend self. For this, our second outing, he wore the same baggy corduroy trousers he had worn at the Priory, but this time fastened with a yellow and red striped canvas belt. His ex-army leather jerkin was now worn over a lurid orange jumper. On his head in place of the woollen hat was a black beret with a chevron black ribbon hanging from it. Black wellingtons, (which Harry always insisted on calling water boots), completed the *ensemble*. He held in one hand the two sections of his fishing rod, and in the other a brown plastic shopping bag containing the rest of his tackle and the food which Billie said she would prepare – the food for Harry and me. I led the way to the swims.

'Come on, Baws,' said Harry, in an excited stage whisper, 'let's get in the water!'

We tackled up in silence. I was aware of the wide sweep of the beam from Harry's torch, intermittently illuminating the pond and the surrounding area as he tried to locate and assemble his rod and reel and thread his line. A steady stream of *sotto voce* swearing accompanied his efforts:

'Come here, you bastard!' he gasped. 'Where the fuck has that fucking float gone now?'

'You okay, Harry?' I asked, more in encouragement than enquiry.

' Yes, I'm fine,' he replied 'You just carry on, Baws. I'll be okay.'

I had gradually learned that Harry's Captain Oates-like optimism and implied self-sacrifice were usually unfounded. Now I opted for early intervention, rather than risk Harry fuming and cussing over an increasingly unravelable bugger's muddle in the dark. I went round to his swim to offer help.

Harry hated manual labour. He couldn't use a screwdriver or hammer to save his life. No one could appear to be as useless with his hands as Harry. How did he manage it? Here was a man who served in the Army throughout the Second World War. Basic training alone must surely have imparted some manual dexterity?

Harry had originally been enlisted in the Beds. and Herts., an infantry regiment, whose home base was close to where he lived at the outbreak of hostilities. A series of home and overseas postings then saw him attached or transferred to various Irish rifle regiments: the Royal Ulster Rifles, the Royal Inniskilling Fusiliers, the London Irish. As far as I knew, Harry had no Irish blood nor Irish connections but then there was always something mysterious and elusive about his wartime exploits, which he alluded to from time to time, but never fully explained.

The question was, how could you successfully maintain and fire a Lee Enfield .303 rifle, say, without a modicum of hand–eye coordination? Recruits were taught to strip and reassemble the ruddy thing with their eyes shut! Harry often amused me by reciting some of the mantra-like army procedures. Firstly the Drill Corporal:

'Check bolt number with rifle number! To remove bolt, raise back sight, push safety catch forward, press down bolt catch, pull back bolt, turn bolt, withdraw bolt, lower back sight!' Then he would play the officer, berating some poor unfortunate who had dropped his rifle: 'Corporal! Put that man on a charge!'

It was from these recitations that I learned the origin of terms such as 'pull-through' and 'half-cock', phrases which Harry of course put to suggestive and bawdy use whenever the occasion presented itself. But put a fishing rod and reel in his hands, and chaos ensued.

Surveying the scene, I could not believe what a mess he had made of his fishing tackle in so short a time. Somehow he had contrived a large knot of line just beneath the top rod ring, with the float hanging upside down below that. He hadn't got as far as hook or shot.

'I don't know how that happened, Tone,' Harry half apologised. He was so childishly contrite that there was no point getting cross with him.

It took patience but eventually the tangle was freed. I attached his float and sufficient shot to cock it nicely. Using a plummet, I adjusted the depth and handed him back his rod.

'Thanks, Baws,' said Harry quietly. 'You get back to your stuff now. I'll be fine.'

Although Harry's cleanliness fetish was partially suspended on fishing sorties (he could end up with filthy and disgusting clothes, face and hands, provided he was pristine as always beneath his clothes), I do believe that the fastidious manner in which he lifted and gripped things, as though anything and everything he touched would sully him, played an important part in his sheer uselessness at all things manual.

I had invested in a new invention for this trip; braided terylene line – the very latest in fishing tackle development. Its great advantage, so ran the advertising copy, was elastic strength and non-kink casting. What the manufacturers failed to mention was that the braid unravelled when cut. At 4lb breaking strain, it was an absolute pig to thread through the eye of a No.14 hook, especially in the dark. Furthermore, once cast, the line floated morosely on the water. Even in these calm conditions it slowly drifted, acquiring an ox-bow profile. It would take a vigorous pick-up to straighten it out if I had a bite.

Float fishing at night requires some source of light. Some anglers maintain that a dull light disturbs fish the least but I went for maximum intensity with my 'Space Beam'. I could usually see to attach a hook without artificial light, except on the darkest of moonless nights, and I could tie a basic turle knot by feel alone, but no one can see a float in total darkness. The 'Space Beam' was a particularly good accessory, since it had a stable, broad base and an adjustable head.

I could see the steady, red tip of my float clearly in the torch beam. As Harry would say, 'sitting there like a dog's prick'. On the third cast, the float wavered, dipped and disappeared from view. I grabbed the rod and lifted it smartly to pick up the floating line. I was into a fish. Relying on the manufacturer's promises of elasticity and strength of my new line, I refused to give way to the fish and started reeling it towards me in a heavy-handed manner.

'A mighty beast is it, Tony?' enquired Harry jovially from the next swim, hearing the reel ratchet, 'or just a tiddler?'

The fish, perhaps taking offence at this enquiry as to its calibre, put its head down and charged for the reeds. Again I dragged it back. This time I managed to position my landing net under it and lifted it clear of the water.

I was soon joined by a couple of local lads who were fishing a few swims away and had been attracted by the raised voices and the splashing. Harry also had hurried round to see the 'mighty beast'. This was a fish of about 4lbs, but what species of fish it was, I had absolutely no idea. It was dark and smooth, with a row of large scales on the flank. I had never seen anything like it before.

'What the hell is that, Harry?'

'Buggered if I know, Baws!' exclaimed Harry, forgetting for a moment that we had the young lads for company.

'Don't you know, mister?' offered the younger boy, by way of explana-tion, apparently untroubled by Harry's language. 'It's a sea bream!'

I looked at the boys in the torchlight. One was about ten, the other around sixteen. Both had ginger hair. No, couldn't be. Too young to be

Ginger's kids. The same cheeky attitude though. Brothers of his, perhaps?

'Well, how the hell did that get in here?' I asked, not unreasonably I thought.

'Dunno,' answered the older boy, stifling a chuckle. 'Someone must have caught it off Southend Pier and brought it over.'

I must have been about eight or nine when I innocently asked a grown-up what he was fishing for in a local fresh water pond. 'Cod,' he replied brusquely, and I believed him, without question. Now I believed these youngsters at Greenacres too. (It was some time before I came to recognise the 'mighty beast' as a small mirror carp). Perhaps the tale of the Loch Ness Monster began this way – maybe it's only a goldfish? It is a fallacy to say that all fishermen are good liars. We are all innocents, beguiled by the fantasies which engulf us on dark nights in mysterious places. I just happened to be very gullible as well!

As dawn broke, the air temperature dropped and the water became shrouded in mist. Harry called to me from the next swim.

'Had any more bites, Baws?' he asked cheerily.

'No, not a thing. What about you?'

'One or two little knocks, Baws, that's all. Probably gudgeon.' He ruminated for a while.

'Would you like me to sing you the Celtic Song of the Dawn, Baws?'

'Go on then. There's nothing else happening.'

Harry began to intone an extemporised cod-Celtic ode:

'*Un fair ta snoo, y porric tre,*
A nith yn durri spuket.
Fra noor da kerr an mather tro,
Ta goor ti bec un fuket'

'Well that should liven things up!' I said appreciatively.

I pulled my line from the water, securing the hook in the cork of the rod handle, and went round to where Harry was sitting.

'I'm starving, Harry. Where are the sandwiches?'

'In that bag, Tone. Bill made some up for both of us.'

'Where's that, Harry?

'In the brown bag, Baws.'

I peered into the bag. There were the two identical boxes. I opened one – nothing. Fearing the worst I opened the second.

'You've scoffed them all again, haven't you?'

'No Tony, I only had mine. There's some bananas as well.'

'No Harry. There's no sodding sandwiches and there's no sodding banana either.'

'Hmm,' said Harry, 'I could have sworn there was one left!'

I couldn't believe it had happened again. The greedy, greedy bugger! I lit a cigarette, to take the edge off my hunger and to try to calm down. Fishing was meant to be calming – good for the nerves they said. Whoever 'they' were obviously hadn't met my future father-in-law, 'Harry the Hog Scoffer'. Furious that my nosh had been nobbled for the second time, I had to move about or I felt I would explode.

'I'm going to take a look round,' I muttered through clenched teeth.

'Okay, Tone, I'll still be here.'

The pigs had awoken with the daybreak and were now squealing and grunting noisily. I walked around the pond until I came to the sties. I like pigs – I find them amusing. They are said to be quite intelligent, although they don't often get a chance to display their intellectual prowess before the slaughterman calls. In China they even arrange pig sports days and porcine swimming events. I don't mind the smell either, and reached out to pat a couple of them firmly on their bristly backs.

Pigs are not fussy eaters but Ken's pigs dined like kings, on a well-balanced diet of proprietary pig feed enriched with fruit and vegetable scraps from the farm. They jostled each other, noisily snaffling up everything under their snouts.

On the floor of one sty, within arm's length, was an object I recognised. Despite the fact that it was begrimed with pig ordure after all these years, my heart turned over. I was looking again at the white butler sink that Ginger used to keep his catch in. Except now it was a food container, piled up with apples, the porkers' *plat du jour*. I gazed fondly at the old sink, and even more fondly at the apples. I reached for the least-damaged looking pair of them, wiping one on my jacket and putting the other in my pocket. I bit into the ripe red fruit and it was the sweetest, most juicy apple I have ever tasted in my entire life.

CHAPTER 5

Waiting for the Tide

'There is a tide in the affairs of men,
Which, taken at the flood, leads on to fortune;
Omitted, all the voyage of their life
Is bound in shallows and in miseries.'

SHAKESPEARE *Julius Caesar*

It was Chris who first suggested that we try Star Lane. He told us that Southend Police Angling Club had been trying to lease the fishing rights for a while. Their members regularly patrolled and 'came on a bit strong', as he put it, but so far it was legally a free water, open to anyone.

We had got to know Chris at the Priory. He was a skilful fisherman, about the same age as myself. Chris fished in a very precise manner, using a running float method where the float was free to move until it was stopped by something fixed to the line, usually a small piece of knotted elastic. He had made his own elegant modification to the basic tackle and used a small glass bead above the tiniest dust shot to stop the float.

Chris was not that interested in the large and elusive Priory carp, but instead concentrated on the fine stock of roach in the north lake. As far as Harry and I were concerned, these were just as elusive as the carp. The fact that Chris could catch them in good numbers, and in summer too, impressed us both. We night-time poachers in the Priory were few and there was an immediate bond between us. We never arranged to fish with Chris but we often met up.

'Is that you Harry?' a voice would whisper through the darkness.

'Yes – that you Chris?' I would whisper back.

'Hi Tony, how you doin'?'

We booked a car for 2am from Tiny's Taxis and assembled outside Harry's flat with all our stuff. The name of the cab firm was the owner's joke – he was a huge man, hardly able to fit in a car seat. We were expecting to be driven by Tiny himself at that late hour. He would always turn out personally if there was any hint of trouble on the horizon, or if it was after midnight. No one was likely to argue with Tiny or try to escape without paying the fare.

A taxi duly arrived, driven by Mrs Tiny, who was no wilting flower herself. It was still pitch black.

'Where to gents?'

'Star Lane, please. Off Poynters Lane in Wakering?'

Mrs Tiny surveyed the equipment assembled on the pavement and looked us up and down quizzically.

'I'll come round and open the boot,' she said ruminatively.

Harry was dressed in his usual flamboyant style; hat with pheasant's feather, leather jerkin and bright cravat. We both wore black wellington boots. I had recently bought an American ex-Serviceman's jacket with the name-flash Wizniewski stitched above the right breast pocket. It was ideal for fishing; dark green, double-lined and with plenty of room. I was immensely proud of the fact that it had what appeared to be a bullet hole in the right sleeve, surrounded by charred material. The pockets I had mainly filled with fishing necessities: packets of hooks of assorted sizes, a container of lead weights, a plummet, a disgorger and so on.

But in the lower right pocket I kept a small, green-handled flick-knife. I forget now how I came by it. I rationalised that it would be useful for cutting line and such, but basically I just liked the feel and action of it. Harry had got quite the wrong idea, and on a tit-for-tat basis he now always carried a brass knuckle-duster. I have no idea where he got that either. 'Just in case, Baws,' he would explain furtively. 'You never know.'

Lord alone knows what Mrs Tiny made of us. In the shadow of the street light our rod bags were easily mistaken for gun slipcases, while the lingering smell of Harry's Eau de Cologne might also have made her pause. Thankfully she didn't ask what we were up to and we didn't volunteer any explanation. We put our bags in the boot and, after a struggle, managed to get the rods and ourselves in the back of the car. Not another word was spoken and off we went.

Star Lane Works lay on the edge of a tiny hamlet of farm buildings and workers' cottages. It was a fully functioning gravel pit and brickfield. Grab buckets worked two active pits all day, while huge revolving cascades sorted, washed and graded the aggregate. Despite this, the raw materials for the bricks were mainly brought in, delivered by tipper lorry, to be fired in the on-site kilns operating 24 hours a day, seven days a week. Older, original pits had been left untouched once they were worked out, allowing time and nature to take over, covering their tops with grass and filling their depths with weed. According to Chris, these disused pits carried a fine head of prime rudd, sizeable tench and the odd carp.

The brickworks still offered employment to a large, mainly casual work force. Workers were needed to operate the kilns and to move the raw materials in and the finished bricks and graded gravel out. There were also some permanent staff; maintenance men and one or two administrators. Employees were catered for in a large outbuilding, which included clean toilets and a wash-room as well as a snug cafeteria, open round the clock.

It was a very cosy, almost luxurious, venue. If one could avoid being rumbled as a fisherman and simply blend in with the ever-changing team of manual labourers, the catering staff were happy to serve you. This was extremely handy for me, in view of Harry's light-fingered and cavalier attitude towards the food that was rightfully mine.

The worksite was illuminated at night by floodlights, the glow from the kiln chimneys visible for miles. Approaching the spot, I asked Mrs Tiny to slow down.

'The next corner will be fine, thanks.'

There was a brief silence before she spoke.

'It's bleedin' miles from anywhere, this is,' she said at last. 'What do you want to be out here for?'

Harry cleared his throat and spoke out.

'We're going fishing, actually.'

I could practically hear Mrs Tiny rolling this statement over in her head.

'At this time of night? There's no bloody water out here neither.'

This was getting tricky.

'Ah,' said Harry, 'we thought we'd get here early, before the tide comes in.'

I cannot believe she swallowed the tale, since Star Lane is many miles from the sea. Maybe business was slow and she did not want to accuse us outright of lying.

'Just here do you, then?' she asked resignedly.

'This'll be fine, thanks,' I snapped, eager to get out and avoid further interrogation.We struggled out with our rod bags and recovered our stuff from the boot.

'That'll be two pounds seven and six, please.'

Harry counted out two one pounds notes and a ten shilling note and handed it to her, adding grandly, 'And keep the change.'

'Do you think you could pick us up here about 11 o'clock this morning, please?' I asked politely.

'Okay, dear, see you later. Good luck!' And off she drove.

Waiting until the taxi was out of sight, we made our way to the site entrance. This was the exposed part of the mission, where we were most likely to be challenged. We moved briskly across the yard where the tipper lorries turned. Thankfully the gravel here was so impacted and scoured that our rubber-booted footsteps made little noise.

Soon we were shielded by the outbuildings from the harsh glare of the artificial lights. Swiftly we climbed down into a grassed depression, formed by the banks of an abandoned excavation. The bottom was full of water. We made our way gingerly along the path set into the side of this narrow pit.

Chris had given us a mental plan of the site covering the present gravel workings and the fishable lakes. Despite this meagre intelligence, the first visit in the dark was a scary business. I didn't want to start flashing about with a torch – we were still too close to civilisation. Besides, I could see quite well. Harry unfortunately could not.

'Fuck me, Baws,' he whispered behind me. 'It's dark as arseholes. Can you see where we're going because I'm fucked if I can.'

'Don't worry, H,' I sought to reassure him. 'Just stick close.'

The path rose steeply at the end of the pit. Half submerged in the water, rusted remains of abandoned machinery formed skeletal, grotesque forms, eerie and menacing in the dark. I was pleased to be past them. We scrambled up to the top of the pit onto a narrow ridge which served as a divider between new workings directly ahead of us some twenty feet down and the worked-out pit we were now leaving.

I thanked our luck that it had been dry for several days and that the ground was baked hard and offered good footing. Standing upright, I paused for a moment to reflect on this and to take my bearings. It almost cost me my life.

I remember hearing Harry ask, 'Okay, Baws?' the second before his head piled into the back of me and sent me tumbling down the bank.

My duffle bag slipped off my shoulder and my rod bag was trapped under me. These slowed my descent but I continued to slither downwards, desperately trying to dig my feet in and get a grip with my hands in the dry clay. Nearly at the water's edge, my feet jammed against something solid – the coil of a suction pipe. This too began to move downwards but it had slowed my fall sufficiently for me to cling on to the steep bank for dear life. Two feet from the water I came to a halt. On a wet night it would have been next stop Davy Jones, (or whatever his fresh-water cousin was called).

'Is that you, Tony? Harry?' There came a voice from out of the dark.

'Christ!' I answered, startled. 'Hello Chris!'

Harry spoke after what seemed an eternity.

'Are you all right, Baws? Do you need a hand?'

'No, it's okay, Harry. I was just testing the depth. Thought we might set up here.' The irony was lost on him.

'Whatever you say, Baws. That's fine with me.'

I slowly struggled up the bank to join him. 'Come on Harry.' We continued to make our way along the ridge. I was moving more cautiously after my tumble, but the excitement of fishing a new water soon allayed my fears, especially since my eyes had adjusted fully to the dark and I was able to make out the topography more clearly.

On our left was a broad expanse of open water. Reed-fringed spits of gravel reached into the dark and curled back upon themselves, forming small bays and islets. Ahead of us the path turned abruptly left to skirt a field of wheat. This marked the southernmost limit of the lake and it was here we found Chris, chuckling to himself.

'Okay you two? Making a bit of a noise weren't you?'

'Sorry Chris. How's it going boy?' asked Harry cheerfully. 'Caught anything?'

'Had a couple of decent rudd earlier on, before it got dark. Nothing much all night though, apart from a couple of knocks. I've gotta shoot off early anyway. Where were you thinkin' of tryin'?'

'Somewhere we don't fall in would be good, Chris,' I muttered. 'Any suggestions?'

'Just along from me the way you're going,' said Chris. 'There's a wide bank along the field, plenty of reed cover.'

'We'll give that a go then. See you later.' And off we plodded.

'Nice bloke isn't he, Tone?' observed Harry. 'Reminds me a bit of someone out of Dickens.'

'Who – the Artful Dodger perhaps?'

'No, more like Pip. You know, John Mills in the film *Great Expectations*? Deep-thinking boy, is that young Chris.'

This was praise indeed from Harry, to be referred to as 'deep-thinking'. I suspected that many of his 'deep-thinkers' simply had their lights turned off, but I could see what Harry meant in the case of Chris. All he needed to complete the picture was a top hat, waistcoat and moleskin breeches.

We arrived safely in the area Chris had suggested and laid out our things on the wide, level bank. I helped Harry tackle up and then went to look for two swims. Soon we were settled and content, the earlier trauma of near-death a fading memory.

Dawn broke fresh and clear, with an early sun promising a warm morning following a chilly, bite-less night. The swims which had looked so inviting turned out to be rather poor, too shallow in patches where reed debris had built up over time. The reeds themselves were home to an infuriating number of moorhens who snagged the line regularly as they scuttled about.

'I'm going to try a bit further along Harry.'

'Good idea, boy, I'll pack up and come and watch you. Sod all happening here.'

I gathered up my rod and landing net, hoisted the duffle bag onto my shoulder and started walking. Soon I came to a broad, straight section of bank, backed by a wheat field. In this spot too the lake edge was softened by reeds but here they began growing a yard or so out from the bank, with shallow water washing between the reeds and the shoreline. I edged cautiously towards the water.

I could make out activity in the reeds, probably carp nosing about for breakfast. Picking up my rod, I slid the float down the line in order to suspend the bait and present it some 18 inches below the surface of the water. I attached a modest pinch of bread flake onto the hook and cast in.

My float had hardly time to settle before it disappeared under the water. The line fairly zinged out and I could feel a delicious solidity on the business end as the fish surged away. Although there was plenty of open water and the fish put up a decent fight, I was soon able to steer it towards the bank.

'Hey, Harry!' I yelled, more loudly than was wise, 'come and see this.' An excited Harry arrived just as I slid the landing net under the swirling fish.

'Look at that, Baws,' he chortled. 'Biggest you've ever caught, isn't it?'

I guessed it was — a lovely looking fish, about 10 pounds. I laid it gently on the bank, still in the landing net, and carefully removed the hook from where it was lightly caught just inside the carp's cavernous mouth.

'I must go and tell Chris.'

I had no keep net, and so I lifted the landing net with the fish inside it into the area between the bank and the reeds. There was about a foot of water here in which to submerge the fish but still keep it contained.

'You stay here with it in the net, Harry, and for fuck's sake, don't drop it,' adding as an afterthought, 'please!'

'I won't, Baws, don't you worry,' promised Harry solemnly.

Needless to say, I was not totally convinced. I rushed off to where we had left Chris in the dark, but he was nowhere to be seen. He had certainly crept off more quietly than we had arrived. I hurried back to join Harry but slowed my pace as I became aware of voices coming from his direction.

As I approached I could see two figures dressed in white shirts and dark trousers, standing in front of Harry. I could hear Harry's voice.

'*Shufti kubrik!*' I heard Harry bark. '*Nicht verstehen. Polski. Zift!*'

Obviously confused by Harry's impromptu League of Nations address, the two men turned to confront me.

'Are you with this gentleman, Sir?' the first one asked, in finest police-speak.

Harry looked at me imploringly.

'*Sag' gar nichts, knabe!*' he hissed out of the corner of his mouth. ('Don't say anything, boy!')

That didn't seem like much of a plan to me. I could not just stand there and say nothing. If ever I was to rely on what Suzie apparently found attractive about me – that hint of Eastern European mystery – now was probably the time.

'This my uncle,' I volunteered in the best broken accent I could muster. 'I tell him only fish for sport, but he want make *gefillte* fish with nice carp like back home.'

'Well you can just tell him to release that fish right now,' said the man angrily. 'We are Police Officers, and you two are fishing out of season.'

He produced his warrant card. I knew it. Bugger. I didn't want things to escalate, what with knives and knuckle dusters in our pockets and all.

'*Los ihm gehen mensch,*' I motioned to Harry to let the fish go. I went over to help him and, with the two policemen watching our every move, I slipped the carp carefully back into the water.

'Where do you blokes come from then?' said Officer One. 'Where do you live?'

Harry readjusted his hat at an angle across his brow, and a far away expression came over him.

'*Rahat al-halkom,*' he voiced with a sigh. Far from being a country of origin, this was in fact an Arabic name for Turkish Delight. Recalling no doubt the taste of this, his favourite confection, he smiled. 'Is beautiful!'

'Well you can just clear off now, both of you. Don't let us catch you here again or you'll be nicked.'

'*Also, kommst du.*' I went over to Harry and took his arm. We gathered our belongings and walked slowly away. '*Schtum, H,*' I whispered, grateful that we had escaped and fearful that he would say something to ruin it.

We made our way slowly and silently round the lake. The brickworks were in full daytime production; lorries turned in the marshalling yards, forklift trucks scurried about, smoke rose from the kiln chimneys. We tramped across the yard, unchallenged. Eventually Harry spoke.

'Shame you couldn't get a picture of that carp, Tony. Fucking good fish wasn't it?'

Back on the road the taxi arrived at the appointed time. Thankfully it was not Mrs Tiny this time, but one of her drivers. He peered at us cautiously through a half-opened window, slightly disturbed by these two renegades who gave off a distinct smell of fish.

'Did you order a cab?' he asked disbelievingly.

'That's right,' said Harry, 'we're off to a wedding. Fairmead Avenue Westcliff please.'

Despite our brush with the law, we fished Star Lane for many years afterwards, chasing the magnificent rudd. Gleaming, brassy fish they were, often weighing in at two pounds, sometimes more. When the wind whipped up the water into choppy waves we fished directly into it with unleaded line, using the weight of a large chunk of bread flake to take the tackle out into eight or ten feet of water. Careful use of a plummet ensured that the float was cocked by the weight of the bait. There was no difficulty in registering a bite. First the float would lift, maybe lay flat. Then it would disappear, shooting down into the deep, green water.

Harry never caught any rudd at Star Lane, not a single one. He often reflected aloud on this mystery. He would catch the odd tench or jack pike, but never rudd. Perhaps of all the fish, those rudd took the greatest exception to the vestige of various cleansing and cosmetic preparations on Harry's fingers.

'I'm fishing in the next swim, Tone. Same bait, same size hook, same depth, same distance out.'

Another fine rudd would slide towards my landing net.

'You having any luck, Harry?' I would ask encouragingly.

'Fuck all, Baws!' would come the inevitable reply.

Then one season, on one particular day perhaps, the Star Lane rudd simply disappeared, and we never caught any again.

CHAPTER 6

Oh Danny Boy

'So he rode high and he rode low,
He rode through woods and copses-oh
Until he came to a wide open field
Where he espied his lady-oh'

TRADITIONAL *The Raggle Taggle Gypsies*

'Any more fares here?' The bus conductor swung along the upstairs aisle between the two rows of double seats.

We were on the last bus from Southend to Grays that Friday night. I offered up the money for Harry and me. 'Two to Corringham, please.'

I had fished Corringham Lake many times and remembered it with affection as the place where I learned the dubious art of the fisherman's lie. I rationalised these lies at the time as being of the white variety, to rank alongside feeble excuses for not being home straight from school or not doing my homework.

The plan was simple. Corringham was renowned for its stock of sizeable crucian carp. My friends and I would ask an adult fisherman nearby to give us a crucian carp from their net, on the basis that even their small fish were far bigger than any of the tiddler rudd or roach that we regularly caught ourselves. They rarely refused. We would put that fish in with our own catch and when we trudged home with our tins-on-a-string full of fish, to put in the ponds in our gardens, we would present the 'ringer' crucian as our own success. We took it in turns to report this fiction to our unquestioning and suitably impressed families. Now I was making my first trip to the lake since I was ten years old.

'Returns?'

'Please.'

The late journey was always a boisterous affair, with many a bleary drinker returning home after a raucous night out in Southend. There were shouts and whistles, fragments of popular songs and occasional personal remarks, but no real menace, not yet anyway. The bus carried a number of Gypsies, or people with a Gypsy background, who lived along this route. On the long ride home a few of them found it entertaining to make the odd comment at the expense of the *gorgio* passengers, none of whom was foolish enough to rise to the bait. Some of these Gypsies still lived in caravans, while others had settled into the small, detached, chalet homes so popular in this area. There were plenty of untilled fields for their horses to graze around Vange, Pitsea, Grays and Benfleet and there was no shortage of work for the self-employed. Their Gypsy ethos frowned upon the notion of being a wage-slave; in earning their livelihood and providing for their families they were answerable to no one but themselves.

The Gypsies were dressed in their finery for a night on the town, whereas we two were in our usual dishevelled state. I prayed that our appearance might protect us from their attention but I was concerned that it could backfire. Harry, with his feathered hat, bright kerchief and pencil slim moustache could easily be viewed as a blatant take-off of Gypsy Petulengro, a stereotypical (and probably fictitious) newspaper fortune-teller. Possibly the Gypsies might find this insulting. Or worse, he could be seen as a true Romany and engaged in a conversation. I had been pleased when his bizarre linguistic performance had got us out of trouble after we were challenged by the police at Star Lane, where the officers had not understood a word he said. I was less keen for him to dispense his doubtless meagre smattering of the Romany language to the present audience. They probably would understand what he was saying, and woe betide us if he insulted them by accident.

As a boy I was lucky to have counted a few of these people as friends. In Benfleet there was Paula, black-haired and beautiful, who worked for my mother in her dress shop. She lived with us for a while and often had charge of me when Mum was in London on buying trips. The pop group The Who wrote a famous song entitled 'Pictures of Lily', describing how a young man's sexual fantasy was based on an old photograph. I had Paula to weave my fantasies around and that was better than any photograph.

Paula had a boyfriend at the time, Danny. He was handsome in a swarthy, brooding way, of medium build with slick, black hair. He did have a light side, though, and he usually found time to lark about with me when he came to the house to pick up Paula.

Danny always arrived well dressed in shirt, jacket and trousers. He had a fine collection of garish ties, all bearing outrageous designs. I was fascinated by them. One in particular was very shiny, made of silk or even satin. On a dark blue background, it bore a magical design of bright yellow space-ships and rockets. I had never seen anything like it. One day he noticed me looking at it intently.

'Like the tie, boy?' he asked.

I was embarrassed, but I managed to say that I did, very much.

'I'll have to get you one then. Next time I'm round.'

Paula's sister, Queenie, as blonde as Paula was dark, lived in Pitsea in a chalet house with a small orchard full of old bikes, prams and laughing children. Paula sometimes took me there with her. One day, Danny called at Queenie's house while Paula and I were there. When he saw me, he straightway took off the tie he was wearing and offered it to me.

'There you are, Tony boy – a smart tie of your own.'

I was overjoyed. It was not the tie with the spaceships, the one that I really coveted, but it was handsome nonetheless, and I treasured it for many years.

A number of the Gypsies alighted from the bus at the Corringham stop. Still laughing and singing, they directed no comments at us. Breathing a sigh of relief, I held back with Harry to let them get ahead as we walked the short distance to the fishing spot in the still, warm night.

The entrance to the lake lay across a gravelled forecourt, with a breeze block building in the middle. Five old double-decker buses, in a range of liveries, were parked in front of this building. For as far back as I could remember there had been buses parked here, in various stages of dereliction, all unlikely to see active service again. The word among my friends was that these discarded juggernauts were destined to be dumped in the lake. Even landing upright at the bottom, their roofs would not have been seen above the water, so deep was it in the middle.

A path led off the forecourt and skirted the lake. Here, surrounded by high privet hedges, was the house where the fishery-owner lived. It was too late to knock but we would pay when he made his rounds in the morning.

'Where to, Baws?' asked Harry.

I shone my torch, sweeping the beam from left to right, over the bay where I used to fish as a boy.

'We'll go round to the right. Be careful, it gets quite steep.'

Torch lights pierced the night from various points around the lake, but we came across no one as we proceeded cautiously on the gravel alongside the house. The path became sandier as it climbed along the higher sides of the lake, which deadened the sound of our footfall.

'Let's stop and have a closer look here Harry,' I whispered, 'before we go on. Just stay right where you are.' I wanted to get my bearings without Harry crashing into me, as he had done at Star Lane.

On our fishing expeditions over these last few months I had, of necessity, taken on the role of *chef de mission* and quartermaster, since I recognised quite early that Harry was incapable of organising a piss-up in a brewery. Whatever role he had fulfilled in the war, the safety and wellbeing of himself and other men was unlikely to have depended upon his skill at making on-the-spot decisions. On the other hand, the equally valuable wartime traits of deviousness and skulduggery were very much his *forte*.

Acting as scout, guide and marshal of swims, I provided for all our needs; the rods and reels, the tackle and the bait. Billie still prepared the food. This left Harry nothing more to do than clothe himself appropriately, (or not, as the case may be). The single thing for which he insisted on taking sole responsibility was his torch.

I had come to an early decision about torches. I found I could rely on the superior construction, reliability, stability and luminosity of my Ever Ready 'Space-Beam' and I am not sure why Harry did not make the same choice. He had already experimented with a wide range of a lighting appliances, all of which failed miserably to live up to the job. He was about to test another.

'Hold on, Tone, I'll get my torch out as well,' he announced.

We set down our bags and our rods on the path. Harry reached into his duffle bag and pulled out this monster. Shaped like a motorcycle headlight, it was black, big and bulbous, with a brazed lug on each side securing it to a chrome, adjustable stand. This arrangement allowed the light to swivel up and down. There was a prominent on/off switch located on the top.

Harry turned it on, with something of a flourish. His new torch did indeed give out a fearsome beam as it shone skywards into the black night

'What do you think of that, Tony?' he enquired with pride in his voice. 'Smasher isn't it? You can see from here to Kent with the bastard!'

Illuminated by Harry's new pride and joy, we could make out the area around and below us. Although the path was safe, the bank on the side near the water had been piled and profiled to form fishable areas below. Access was by rough steps hewn out of the bank. There was some patchy reed cover and I could see no point in trudging on with our equipment in the dark. If there was a better spot, we could find it in the morning.

'Yes, great, Harry. Better turn it off now before you blind everyone. Let's try here but take it steady, it's very steep. Best we get everything down bit by bit and tackle up once we're there. It'll be safer that way. You hand the stuff to me. Rod bags first.'

I scrambled down the uneven steps, turned and reached up towards Harry.

'Okay, Harry, pass one down .'

Harry swung over my rod bag. As he did so, his new torch, still shining brightly, fell from his grasp.

'Fuck it!' cried Harry, followed by, 'Oh shit!' as he tried to catch the torch and lost his balance.

Falling headlong towards me, his momentum pushed me to one side and he slithered down the bank towards the lake. Frantically I twisted round and clutched at his legs. He managed to brace himself with his hands against the scaffold plank used to shore up the swim and came to a stop with his head inches from the water. His torch did not.

Like the *Titanic*, Harry's torch was doomed never to return from its maiden voyage. Down it rolled, over and over, the white beam giving a display in the dark sky, like a searchlight at the opening of a Twentieth Century Fox film, before splashing into the water. I still had my arms wrapped around Harry's legs as we lay there, gathering our breath, watching the torch descend to the depths of Corringham Lake.

'I can still see it,' said a dejected Harry as we glumly watched the eerie death throes of his new, but soon to be late, torch. The diminishing under-water glow triggered a further filmic memory, as it reminded me of the bow light of the *Nautilus*, the fantastic submarine in the Disney epic '20,000 Leagues Under The Sea'. This gripping story by Jules Verne had seen the vessel engulfed by a giant squid. It was impossible for such a monster to dwell in Corringham Lake, surely. On the other hand there were those submerged buses ...

Eventually the sunken light disappeared, the torch settled on the bottom and the weeds closed around it. Only then did we rise to our feet and take stock.

'You okay, Harry?'

'Yes I'm fine, Baws. Bloody shame about that torch. Look, you carry on, I'll just sit and watch,' he said balefully.

'No, it'll be fine. I'll fish free-line and you can borrow my torch. Let's just get set up.'

He took up his chair, a bank stick and his keep net and settled himself into a gap in the reeds ten yards to my left. I set about assembling the rods while Harry lit a cigarette.

'Blah! Christ, these are fuckin' rough!' he complained, coughing vigorously.

'What are you smoking now?'

'John Players 'Perfectos' they're called. 'Perfectos' bollocks! Nothing like Sullivan and Powell 'Perfectos Finos'.' He coughed again, somewhat theat-rically. 'I don't know why I bother to smoke Virginia cigarettes anyway – they all taste foul.'

I responded in an encouraging voice. I didn't want him any more depressed.

'Those new 'Woodbines Export' we tried the other day, they were all right. Why didn't you stick to those?'

'Bloody good cigarette for the price they were, Baws. Good as anything. Couldn't get hold of any though.'

Harry and I would try any new cigarette coming onto the market, in the forlorn hope that this time it would be of good quality. Wills's 'Three Castles' were currently high on our approved list, as was their short-lived premium product 'Woodbine Export', a full size and in all ways superior version of the diminutive 'Woodbine'.

'Anyway,' continued Harry, 'cigarettes aren't what they used to be. Those hand-made cigarettes you could get before the war – 'Chaliapin', 'Top Hat' – all gone. It's like biscuits nowadays – rubbish compared to a few years ago.'

'My uncle Mark used to smoke 'Top Hat',' I said. ''Rolled against a young lady's thigh like a Havana cigar' – that's what he told me. I can see the attraction in that. Never heard of 'Chaliapins', though.'

'Named after a Russian opera singer,' said Harry, 'Feodor Chaliapin. I suppose they wanted you to think their cigarettes were kind on the throat. They were quite smooth I suppose. Mind you, he died at 65.'

'What are the worst Virginia cigarettes you've ever smoked, Harry?'

'Capstan 'Full Strength',' came his instant reply.

'Even worse than those French things – 'Gitane' or 'Gauloise Untipped'?'

'Much worse. By the Jesus, Baws, Capstan 'Full Strength'? It's like swallowing bricks! If Chaliapin had smoked those bastards, he'd have died even sooner.'

Harry's real smoking delight was a Turkish cigarette. They offered him tactile satisfaction into the bargain as he held their oval shape gently between thumb and index finger, his little finger arched and extended. Turkish varieties manufactured by Abdullah or Sullivan and Powell supplemented by the occasional Egyptian import purchased at Harrods or Simmons in Burlington Arcade; these were his favourites.

'Yenidje leaf tobacco in Turkish cigarettes is the finest,' he continued. 'Won't make you cough. Shame the English can't make a decent Turkish cigarette. What were those oval things they brought out in a pink box? Had a grinning cavalier on the front?'

'Oh, you mean 'Passing Cloud'? I tried one once. Made me dizzy as a bugger.'

'Yes, that was them,' said Harry, 'should have been called 'Passing Out'!'

Harry smoked for pleasure and could limit his intake without undue distress. I, on the other hand, was a true addict. I had started when I was in the cubs at about eight or nine, smoking dog-ends collected from the gutter, before progressing to real cigarettes at grammar school.

I was never actively discouraged by my mother. She was a fastidious person in all respects, except when it came to her lifelong smoking habit. She would stub out and hide half-finished cigarettes; in empty jars, behind books, in her purse, even in her coat pockets. Disgusting as this behaviour was, it did mean that in times of financial hardship, which came round all too often, we could always find something to smoke.

Whenever Harry and I fished we smoked non-stop. By the time we released our catches from the nets, they were probably mildly kippered. I couldn't bear to leave a cigarette dangling from my mouth and so there was a lot of wastage whenever I had to set one down in order to free up my hands. Exclusively for fishing expeditions, (no one, surely, would smoke one solely for pleasure?), I had fixed upon 'Woodbines Tipped', a tiny squib of a cigarette that even when smoked in a leisurely manner, burnt away in about three minutes. I smoked or wasted about twenty a night, but they were cheap. There was one practical fishing application to mitigate all this smoking. I used the silver paper wrapper from cigarette packets as a bite indicator.

Free-lining was so simple. No lead shot or ledgers or floats, just the weight of the bait. After casting out, I pulled back enough slack line to make a 'V' shape between the reel and the first rod ring. Stripping away the thin paper backing, I folded the silver paper lengthwise until it was around half an inch wide. Clipped over the apex of the 'V' in the line, it showed up even in the poorest light. If a fish took the bait, it would tighten the line and pull straight the 'V', making the silver paper move towards the rod. Sometimes this movement was dramatic, at other times there would be a series of infuriating little twitches. Even if I could not see it, or was not looking , the rustle of the foil over a plastic sheet or the bare ground would alert me to what was happening. When a fish was hooked, the silver paper fell to the ground and did not get wound around the reel. Perfect. Lighting another 'Woodbine Tipped', I settled down to await events.

A gentle, misty dawn brought a couple of swans into our swims. They could be infuriating if they accidentally snagged the line, but it was always a delight to watch them glide by. Never hurried, seemingly unconcerned while alert to all possibilities, they fixed us with their beady eyes, challenging us to make them move on.

The night had brought no fish despite the fact that the weather had been fine and the water calm. This spot looked promising, but neither Harry's float nor my silver paper had shown so much as a twitch. We fished on, but the early morning brought no luck either.

There was a pleasant warmth in the rising sun after the chill of dawn, and I knew I would doze off unless I did something. I got up and walked over to Harry's swim where he too was on the nod

'I'm just going to have a look round, Harry. Okay?'

'Fine, Baws,' he replied sleepily, 'you take your time.'

I reeled in my line and watched the bread bait fall away as the hook reached the top ring of the rod. It was warm enough for me to remove my jacket. Folding it onto my bag and leaving the rod in its rest I clambered up the mud steps.

It was good to see that little had changed since my last visit some ten years previously. The trees seemed more lush, the banksides less severe, with a deep edging of reeds in most places. I began walking back the way we had come last night but had not got very far when I met someone coming towards me. He was about Harry's age; tall, well-built, with thinning hair and clear blue eyes. When he reached me, he spoke.

'How do?' he drawled. 'Would you be fishing or just wandering around?'

I was surprised to hear a pronounced American accent. 'Yes, just back there,' I replied, motioning in the direction I had come. 'Two of us. We've been here all night. Not much happening though.'

'Well, son, I'm the owner here and you need permits.'

He said this as if it would be amazing news to me.

'Fine. How much are they, please?'

He looked at me in a disinterested fashion. 'Let's see. Thirty shillings a rod for the day, and another pound each for the night fishing. Five pounds for the two of you.'

I can't say I took to him. He didn't say 'please' – he didn't strike me as the kind of man who would ever say 'please', come to that.

'My money's in my jacket. I left it back where we're fishing.'

He looked at me as though he didn't trust me, as though I was just making an excuse while all the time plotting my escape.

'I guess I'll just come round with you now and you can pay up.'

I walked back the way I had come, the owner keeping close behind. As we approached Harry, I could see that his head was slumped into his chest and I could hear him snoring.

'Shan't be a sec,' I reassured the owner, as I made my way carefully down the steps.

'Harry,' I said in a loud voice, 'are you awake?'

Harry stirred and looked at me blearily.

'Eh? What's up, Baws? Must have dozed off.'

'Man's here for his money. I'm just going to pay him.'

Harry yawned and stretched. He looked upwards at the owner. 'Smashing place you've got here,' he said cheerfully. 'Fishing's not so good at the moment though.'

'There are plenty of fish in here, Sir,' replied the owner, 'if you're smart enough to catch them.'

I felt like telling him what he could do with his fish, but bit my tongue. Instead I returned to my swim to find the money to pay him. I bent to pick up my jacket but in doing so I noticed a very strange thing. My rod was in the rod rest, exactly as I had left it some minutes ago, but the reel and line were missing.

'Harry!' I shouted, ignoring the owner who was still on the path above us. 'My fucking reel's gone!'

Harry came round from the next swim to see for himself. 'Can't have done, Tony,' he said disbelievingly, 'I've been here all the time.'

'Yes, but you probably dozed off. It's not your fault Harry. What puzzles me is, how in the hell has only the reel gone? The rod's still there. Some bastard must have cut the line, left the rod and stolen the reel. Why do that?'

I was absolutely raging, all the more since I could not understand the rationale behind this heinous crime. Harry was equally nonplussed. Then the owner spoke.

'That'll be those Gypsies from the site up there.' He pointed to indicate somewhere further along the path. 'We've had stacks of trouble with things going missing ever since they arrived.'

Annoyed as I was about my missing reel, I was not prepared to subscribe to his racist theory without any evidence, but it was Harry who spoke. 'Give a dog a bad name,' he said quietly, directing his words straight at the owner, 'and that *jucal* might bite you back.'

I searched around in my jacket pocket and eventually located a five pound note. Reaching up only so far, so that the owner had to bend down, I passed him the money. He took it without a word and went on his way.

'What's a Yank doing owning this place, I wonder?' I mused.

'He's not an American, Tony, he's Canadian.'

'How do you tell?'

'When he bent down, I recognised a badge in his lapel,' Harry told me. '1st Canadian Parachute Battalion. They were dropped in to soften up the beaches for the D-day landings in Normandy. Brave men those. All parachutists are brave bastards.'

I felt slightly guilty about the dislike I had taken to man. Harry rarely spoke about the active part of his own wartime service, and I seldom asked. He was always happy enough to talk about his training experiences though.

'Did you ever do a jump, Harry?'

'No fear. Going up a jump tower once at Cardington when I was on a wozbee evaluation course was bad enough. Standing there at the top, waiting to jump, even if I was attached to a line – fucking dreadful.'

'What's a wozbee?'

'WOSB – War Office Selection Board. They put you through tests to see if you should go on to an OCTU – Officer Cadet Training Unit.'

'So did you do that, officer training?'

'No bloody fear,' said Harry, seeming quite hurt by the suggestion. 'Not then at any rate. I wouldn't let anyone down, but I was no 'over-the-top-and-at-'em' hero. I just spent as much time as I could on selection courses over this side trying to avoid a nasty foreign posting.'

'Did it work?'

'For a time,' Harry said reflectively, 'for a time.'

I let the matter drop. 'Anyway,' I said, 'I didn't like the bloke, nor what he said about the Gypsies.'

'Me neither, Baws. You can be a hero and still be a pratt! Still, I respect what he and his countrymen did for us and I'll always be grateful. They paid a heavy price.' He was quiet for a moment, then he changed the subject.

' Bloody odd thing about your reel.'

'Bloody odd, Harry. I think I'll go up and have a scout round.'

'Want me to come with you?' he asked, 'just in case?'

'No thanks, H. I'm not going to do anything daft.'

I followed the path in the direction the owner had gone. He had apparently taken no further interest in my loss because by the time I came to a gap in the high hedge from where I could see the Gypsy encampment, he was nowhere to be seen.

In the field, close by where I stood, were three traditional bow-top caravans, all beautifully painted in bright colours. They were arranged in a rough circle, with several tethered horses grazing contentedly alongside. Further away I could see several more wagons, with cars and vans parked between them. I stepped forward into the gap to get a better view and was immediately grabbed by the shoulder.

'Can I help you, mister?'

I struggled to make words come, and at the same time to control my bowels. My voice acquired a higher register.

'I was just having a look at your beautiful caravans. Aren't they marvellous?'

I was anxious to appear friendly and non-threatening. Instead I sounded like the Lord Lieutenant's wife opening the local fête. My captor released his grip and stood back to look at me. He was middle-aged and stocky, swarthy with thick black hair. He wore a brown jacket, a white shirt and a dark blue tie, a tie with yellow spaceships and rockets vividly emblazoned upon it, a tie that I recognised immediately.

'Danny?' I asked nervously.

He looked me over carefully, and a broad grin spread across his face.

'Tony boy? What's you doin' 'ere?'

'Fishing,' I answered, pointing back towards the lake. This was amazing. 'How are you keeping, Danny? How long is it?'

'Must be ten years, boy. Got kids of me own now.'

I hesitated, but had to ask. 'Are you still with Paula?'

He looked away, into the distance. 'No, boy. She took off after a *gorgio*. Settled down somewhere I suppose. House and that.' He looked back at me. 'Come and have some tea, Tony boy, it's all brewed.'

I didn't want Harry worrying, but I could not turn down Danny's hospitality.

'Fine, Danny, that'll be nice.'

He led off to his caravan and ushered me onto one of the chairs arranged around a small table on the grass outside. Guarding the steps to the caravan door sat a lurcher.

'That's Toby,' said Danny, 'he won't hurt you. Be different if you was a rabbit though.' He ruffled the big dog's head. 'Move over, boy!'

Toby shuffled out of the way to let his master into the caravan. Soon Danny reappeared with a tray bearing two cups and saucers, a china teapot, two teaspoons, a bottle of milk and a bag of sugar. He laid these out carefully and poured the tea for us both.

'Me *monisha* Kathy's off shopping, otherwise she'd be doin' this. Everything okay?'

I could not express to him how very 'okay' everything was – to be here with an old friend, sipping strong, sweet tea. I just nodded. My appreciation of the moment was interrupted by the sound of a fishing reel ratchet. Approaching us was a boy, about seven or maybe eight years old, holding my reel in one small hand while turning the handle slowly with the other.

'Come and say hello to the gentleman, Danny,' said Danny to the boy. 'This is my oldest *chavo*,' he announced, with obvious pride. Then to his son, pointing at my reel, 'Where did you get that?'

'Down at the fish pond, Dad.'

I looked at the youngster, all grubby and pleased with himself. At his age I was only stealing loose sweets from shops and fruit from orchards. Danny Junior was obviously more ambitious.

'Danny,' said his father, 'how many times have I told you to leave that place alone. It's dangerous. You stay here with us. ' He looked at me and rolled his eyes, as if to say, 'Kids, what do you do with them?'

'I used to have a reel just like that one, Danny. I lost it though, just this morning.' I suppose I was addressing both Dannys, but only the older one spoke.

'He's like a magpie, my little Danny. If he sees something he wants, he takes it. He'll grow out of it.' Then he addressed his son, without raising his voice or showing anger. 'Now,' he said, 'give the gentleman back his reel.'

Little Danny handed me back the reel without a word. He was neither happy nor sad, and I thanked him. I wanted to know how he had managed to sever my four pound breaking strain line but I kept quiet – perhaps he just had strong teeth. The answer came soon enough, as, with his hands now free, young Danny reached into a pocket, pulled out a jack knife and began examining it carefully.

It was exactly the sort I had at his age. Black handles, incised in a diamond pattern for grip, a ring to attach it to your belt (no one ever did), several blades and, of course, a device for getting stones out of horses' hooves, which none of my contemporaries ever found a use for. Perhaps Danny would actually get to use his.

I stood up to leave. 'Best get back, Danny. I'm fishing with someone else and they'll start worrying. It's been good to see you.'

He shook my hand, his other one tousling little Danny's hair.

'Come over again next time, Tony boy,' he said, 'you can have some food with us.'

I started to turn the reel handle, enjoying the sound of the ratchet just as Danny Junior had done, as I began to slowly walk away. 'Yes,' I answered, 'I'd like that very much, Danny. See you then.'

We did not return to Corringham for some weeks afterwards. When we did eventually go back there, we found no Gypsy camp on the other side of the hedge. I never saw Danny and his son again.

Romany Gypsy language:
gorgio: a non-Gypsy [male]
jucal: dog
monisha: wife or lady partner
chavo: young man or boy

CHAPTER 7

Rods and Mockers

'If you grease the wheels, you can ride.'
SHOLEM ALEICHEM

The young man screwed up his face and his girlfriend turned up her nose as they squeezed past Harry and me. We were on the top deck of a bus, again, heading home after another all-night session fishing at Corringham.

'Cor, smells like bleedin' Billinsgate fish market up 'ere!' they grumbled, as Harry and I feigned sleep.

It was not the first time we had overheard that remark on our travels. Outward journeys at night were bad enough, when our Rameau-like appearance and the manoeuvring of rods and bulky equipment on the crowded late-night bus caused many adverse comments. The return journeys in the morning were far worse. In addition to the baggage and the way we looked, the bus was just as crowded and we were now comatose and reeking: a malodorous mixture of bait, cigarettes and fish.

We were travelling ever more frequently; buses to Greenacres and Corringham and by taxi to Star Lane. The Priory was becoming less attractive as rumours spread of sizeable catches, few of them true and certainly none of them involving Harry and me.

It was becoming too noisy to fish there in peace. As a public park, it was a popular venue for parents to bring their young boys, in the forlorn hope that they would become interested in fishing. Diligently and patiently, the reluctant fathers sought to impart the skills of angling to their equally reluctant offspring, whilst the attendant mothers, in charge of prams and babies, dispensed food and drink and offered occasional words of encouragement.

Naturally enough, the young fishermen soon got bored and formed into gangs, who would then run around the ponds, shouting and screaming.

Harry referred to these hordes as 'Sabus' after a famous Indian boy actor of the Forties and Fifties.

'Do you remember those awful black-and-white jungle films starring Sabu, Tony?' he asked, as another gang of children thundered past. 'Every single one had a scene where Sabu would trundle into a jungle clearing, seated on top of a huge, trumpeting elephant, and all these screaming kids would be running behind him, waving their arms about.'

If Harry and I only had independent transport we could spread our wings and fish in waters new. We would not have to struggle onto buses or into taxis. We would avoid the unflattering comments of the general travelling public. Since I could not yet afford the running costs of a car, I decided to buy a scooter.

The rise of 'Mod' culture at this time had made scooters extremely popular. Mods were fashion-conscious, wore sharply cut suits and listened to modern jazz, American Soul artists and British groups like The Small Faces. Large gatherings of Mods, dressed *de rigueur* in ex-Army parkas over their snappy suits, charged around on their beloved scooters, often seeking confrontation with their arch enemies, the motorcycle-riding, rock 'n' roll loving 'Rockers'.

I had absorbed my father's musical taste from his precious collection of 78 rpm records. He loved the popular American music, jazz and swing of the Thirties and early Forties; the Gershwin brothers, Cole Porter, Louis Armstrong, Cab Calloway, The Ink Spots, The Mills Brothers, The Andrew Sisters and The Boswell Sisters. All of these I loved dearly, adding to them in time my own favourites; American folk music and delta blues, (with a side helping of Buddy Holly rock-a-billy).

As to clothes, my style was of necessity hand-me-down – stuff given to my mother for me by her better-off friends and employers when their own sons tired of them. That was to change when I took a job as Saturday cashier in a menswear shop. I was poorly paid but by taking advantage of bargains and discounted ranges, I assembled a wardrobe with at least a hint of fashion. Now I could mingle with friends, and most importantly girls, without feeling I was literally second best.

I began to scour the pages of *Exchange & Mart* for a scooter, hoping to spot a bargain. Finding that the widest selection was advertised by a dealer in Streatham, South London, it was certainly one place I intended to explore.

Harry cautioned me strongly against the notion.

'You may get crooks and villains in the East End,' he said. 'but in South

London you run up against real gangsters.'

The distinction was lost on me.

'What's the difference, Harry?'

'They never look you in the eye, gangsters', he answered furtively 'They always look at a spot just above the eyes.' He strove to demonstrate. Shifting his gaze upwards from my eyes to my forehead, he looked earnestly at a spot on my forehead. I was left none the wiser by this performance.

'See what I mean?' he growled.

'You look to me as if you've forgotten something,' I said, 'or else you're suffering from a bad case of wind.'

'That's because you know me, Tony. You wait until it's someone you don't know. You just take it steady.'

'Okay, Harry. If someone looks me in the forehead I'll remember to be careful.'

Harry's warning was fresh in my mind as I set off by train to South London early one morning. In my pockets I carried a provisional motor-cycle licence, the ad. cut from the pages of the magazine and just enough money to pay my fare and put down a cash deposit.

Arriving at the premises, I was met by a vast display of scooters. Some were parked on the forecourt, others were arranged in parallel rows inside the building. I hadn't a clue where to start. Only two makes were available, Vespa and Lambretta. Apart from colour and accessories such as wing mirrors or a windscreen, all models seemed equally desirable to me as a novice. To make matters more confusing, they were all for sale at more or less the same price, the market in second-hand scooters being relatively new.

I walked up and down the rows of shiny machines, hoping to find inspiration. Passing a doorway I was pounced on by a salesman, at least I assumed he was a salesman. A huge man, he was attired in a camel hair coat belted at the waist. I particularly noticed that the top button of his shirt struggled to confine the bulging outline of his neck.

'Can I help you at all?' he growled, facing me and looking at a spot somewhere above my eyes.

My jaw became reluctant to work, but I managed to squeak. 'I'm looking for a scooter.'

'You've come to the right place my friend. See anything you fancy?'

'Er....'

'What about this one?' He pointed to a blue and grey Lambretta with a windscreen and an off-side mirror. 'Go on, try it out.'

He pushed the scooter forward off its stand.

'Steve Marriott from The Small Faces bought one just like this a couple of days ago,' he lied. 'Here we are.'

He invited me to take control, removing one huge hand from the handle-bars and leaning the scooter towards to me.

I had never handled a scooter in my life. Having passed my car driving test and able to ride a pushbike, I was not unduly bothered. How difficult could it be? I awkwardly gripped the handlebars and pathetically tried to push the scooter forward. It refused to budge.

'You've got it in gear my son. Pull the clutch and twist the handle – no, the other one. That's it.'

Embarrassed and starting to perspire, I depressed the clutch and after twisting the handle this way and that, eventually managed to put the thing in neutral. With much effort, I rolled the surprisingly heavy machine over the kerb and into the road.

'Here,' said the salesman, 'let me start it for you. They can be a bit tricky when they're cold.' He reached down below the seat and twiddled with something. With his huge right foot, he smartly depressed the kick-start lever while twisting the throttle with a ham-like fist. The scooter sprang into life. He revved it up a few times before turning to me. 'What do you think?'

I had rehearsed a list of searching questions which I would put to the dealer, to enable me to make a wise and balanced decision. In that scenario, I would certainly not be rushed into a rash purchase and if I was not totally convinced, or didn't see anything I liked, I would be prepared to return home scooter-less, with my hard-earned savings intact.

Instead I heard myself say feebly, 'Er – yes, seems fine.'

He must have been used to innocent novitiates like me buying their first machine and he launched into an obviously rehearsed *spiel*.

'Dead easy to drive these are. Throttle and brake, lights 'n 'ooter on the right, gears and clutch on the left. Back for first, through neutral for the other three, footbrake on the floor, choke between yer legs, fuel cap under the seat, steering lock behind the 'eadlight. That's all there is to it. It's the dog's bollocks! You'll be wanting HP? Let's go and do the paperwork.'

Like a lamb to the slaughter, he led me into the rudimentary office at the back of the showroom. In what might have passed for a scene from a Raymond Chandler movie sat three men playing cards on an upturned tea chest on a bare, wooden floor. In the middle of the chest was a small pile of grubby notes and coins, and in front of each player was a smaller mound of money.

Above the tea chest hung a naked light bulb. The air was heavy with cigar smoke, (which I loathe in inverse proportion to how smokers enjoy it). I stifled a cough. The three men turned to look at me briefly, focusing on a spot just above my eyes. No one said a word. They turned back to look at their cards. The salesman made an announcement.

'This young man has just made an investment. What's your name, son?'

'Tony,' I mumbled.

'Can I trouble one of you to make sure everything is kosher for Tony? After the next hand of course. Here's the log book.'

Then he turned to me, looking at a spot just above my eyes.

'Where're you from Tony?'

'Essex, Leigh-on-Sea,' I croaked, 'just outside Southend.'

A lizard-like smirk played across his lips.

'Lovely place Southend. The 'Kursaal', the Pier; cockles, whelks, jellied eels.'

Was he really being wistful? Surely such a character could not be wistful? He soon snapped out of it.

'Well, Tony', he continued, 'any problems, just bring the bike back here and we'll do our best to sort you out. You done well son. One of the chaps'll take care of you.'

And off he went, leaving me standing to contemplate the three gentlemen playing cards, and to reflect on the import of his promises to 'sort me out' and for 'one of the chaps' to 'take care of me.'

One of the card players, a small man, with dark greasy hair and the face of a ferret motioned me wordlessly to join him at the kneehole desk, the only other item of furniture in the room. He lifted an agreement from one of the desk drawers and began to write on it vigorously, occasionally barking out staccato questions: 'Name? Address? Occupation?' I could only manage hoarsely whispered replies, such was my apprehension.

Raising his eyes from the paper, he looked at a spot just above my eyes, offered me a pen and said, 'Sign here,' indicating with a stubby finger the precise place where this should be. I took the pen and signed, a trembling, scratchy signature bearing little resemblance to my normal one.

'Deposit?' he enquired.

'How much do you want?' I cringed as I heard myself speak. No 'please'? Had I been too blunt, too forceful, confrontational even? To my great relief, my rudeness had passed unnoticed.

'Third deposit, 'L' plates, insurance, tank o' gas – that'll be a ton exactly.'

Greatly relieved and perspiring profusely I counted out the exact one hundred pounds, which he checked and put in his trouser pocket. Then he reached into the drawer again.

'You'll need these,' he said, handing over two new 'L' plates. 'There's plenty of juice in the tank to get you home. Two stroke, remember?' Finally he detached a copy of the HP agreement and handed it to me with the customary valediction, 'Be lucky.'

Thus I took possession of my smart Lambretta scooter. I had intended to ride it back all the way to Southend but by the time I reached the City, a few miles into the fifty mile journey, I was trembling with tiredness from the strain of driving a strange machine, coupled with the nervous exhaustion I still felt from my dealings with the 'chaps'. I made it as far as Fenchurch Street Station, where I used the goods lift to get my weary self and the scooter up onto the platform. Luckily, a train was ready to depart. Stowing the scooter in the guards' van, I slept soundly all the way to Leigh-on-Sea.

Gaining my full licence a month later gave me the right to carry a pillion passenger. Suzie was stick-thin, quite *à la mode* for the fashion-conscious Sixties, and I hardly noticed her weight on the back seat. Harry, at 16 stones and over six feet, would be a different matter.

Our first scooter outing was also to be our first expedition as members of a bona fide angling club (albeit one with an apparently limitless membership). Simply by paying the requisite subscription at an angling shop in Southend, we had acquired membership cards, badges and a map of club waters in the Chelmsford area.

So on a bright morning in late October we prepared to head out to Little Baddow on the Chelmer and Blackwater Navigation, the canal in mid-Essex which connects the rivers Chelmer and Blackwater. Harry chose this precise moment to pass on some unwelcome information.

'I've always been bloody hopeless with anything on wheels, Baws.'

Oh joy! Hang on though …'What about that open top sports car then, Harry? The one you always talk about?'

'The little Singer Le Mans you mean?' said Harry. 'I had that for a while when I was at the War Office – used to think it was fast as buggery! Probably only did about 60 flat out. Modern cars would probably piss straight past it. Still,' he said, with a wicked smile and a twinkle in his eye, 'the ladies liked it. It went well with the Sam Brown belt and the swagger stick.'

Yes indeed. My very own mother was apparently one of those ladies. After being introduced to Harry for the first time (or so I thought), she took me to one side and gave me some rather disquieting news.

'Do you know,' she said, 'I swear I was once picked up in an open top sports car in Hadleigh by that man. I remember him distinctly. Thin moustache, hair parted in the middle, army uniform. He hooted to me from his car and waved at me with some sort of stick. I was walking along the London Road down towards Thames Drive. There were no buses, so I was grateful for a lift.'

I had been enormously relieved when she assured me that there was no more to the story than that. I attempted to shut the event from my mind as I pressed Harry about his driving skills.

'You must have passed your test, surely?'

'Not needed. Remember, I was at the War Office after the fighting stopped. You could get hold of all sorts of useful bits of paper there.'

'So you never passed a driving test? But you could drive?'

'I'd picked up a bit during the war. I was fine going forward. I could never quite get the hang of reverse. They did ask me to take a test some time later on, when I was working in Bath. Full of hills, Bath. I lost control reversing on a steep hill. Managed to back the firm's car into a lamp post. Never drove again.'

Harry decided that his woollen army hat pulled well down was just the thing for pillion riding, but after considering the risk posed to feathers in a high, face-on wind he wisely dispensed with them. Naturally he had on his water-boots. Over his clothes he wore a camel-hair coloured British Warm, the standard British Army officers' out-and-about overcoat. I was trying out a new raincoat; a particularly cheap, plastic affair, with rubber buttons. The printed design was intended to imitate tree bark and the inside was gold coloured. The Mods certainly had nothing to fear from us in the fashion department.

'Right,' I said between clenched teeth, 'all you have to remember, Harry, is to lean over with the bike. Don't try to stay upright or you'll have us off.' I sincerely prayed that his usual physical incompetence would not be a dangerous factor once we were on the move. Our bags and keep nets were

carried on a rack over the rear wheel and the rods were held alongside the seats by elastic straps. It was up to Harry to keep these firmly in position between his legs.

I kicked the motor over and pushed the scooter off its stand. I made myself comfortable and put a steadying foot to the ground.

'On you get, Harry, and just sit still please.'

'Ready when you are, Baws' he said jovially, settling onto his seat behind me.

'You can put your arms around me if you like,' I told him, 'or you can hold onto your seat.'

Harry put his arms lightly either side of my waist. I slipped the engine into first gear and we were away. Remarkably, Harry proved to be a natural pillion passenger. In a short time we were cruising along steadily, the scooter perfectly stable and wobble-free, negotiating the roundabout at Rayleigh Weir as though we had been riding two-up for years.

Just outside Chelmsford we hit a snag. I could see brake lights ahead and slowed right down.

'What's up?' asked Harry.

'Don't quite know. Seems like some sort of tailback. They look like army trucks.'

There was often a military presence in and around Chelmsford due to the long-established army barracks at Colchester, not very far away. Maybe these troops were on manoeuvres? There was no civilian traffic ahead of me and I edged the scooter slowly forward. A soldier in full battledress, but armed only with a clipboard, approached us and held up his hand, signalling me to stop.

'Sorry sir, you can't go any further. You'll have to turn round and go back.'

'Bugger,' I said, turning to Harry so that the soldier did not hear. 'There isn't another way to Little Baddow without going all the way round the houses.'

The soldier walked towards us, as if to re-enforce his instructions, until he stood alongside the scooter, at a point midway between Harry and me, looking at us intently.

Harry said not a word, and I was not aware that he had moved or made any gesture, but a then a curious thing happened. The soldier looked at Harry, took a step back, and saluted!

'I'll clear the way for you up ahead, Sir' said the soldier, directing his speech to Harry.

'What the …?' I hissed to Harry, but he whispered in my ear, '*Schtum*, Baws, *schtum*!'

I eased the scooter forward, following the walking soldier. When we got to the first truck, he leaned inside and reached for a field telephone. We could not make out what he said, but we could see him looking this way and that, ahead and behind us. Eventually he spoke to us:

'You can go through now, Sir. I've told them to expect you.' With this he saluted again.

Off we went, past a column of trucks bearing rows of stern-faced, seated, armed soldiers, past assorted field artillery and command vehicles, past huge transporters bearing tracked vehicles, half-tracks and tanks. After about half a mile, we were carefully directed around the front of a truck that had slewed across the main road, coming to rest with its rear wheels embedded in a roadside ditch. Another brisk salute for Harry and we were clear.

We travelled in silence for the rest of the journey. Arriving at Little Baddow, we parked the scooter in a small copse beside the canal and unloaded our things. I questioned Harry again about the strange engagement with the soldiers, but he was not forthcoming.

'Maybe they mistook me for someone else,' was all he would say. I was sure there was more to it than that. The few snippets he had let fall concerning his time in the army, the various comings and goings of his active service and his career at the War Office after his eventual release from prisoner-of-war camp, only served to make the whole episode even more mysterious.

Any further thoughts I had on the matter would have to wait as a small man on a noisy motorbike pulled up and parked beside us. On his back was a haversack and through the straps protruded a canvas rod bag.

'Good morning,' said the new arrival. 'Just coming or just going?'

'Oh we're just about to start,' I said. 'It's our first time here. I'm Tony, this is Harry.'

'I'm Aintree Forbes. Pleased to meet you.' We all shook hands. 'My father loved horse racing in case you wondered about the odd name,' he said. 'If it's your first time you can come along with me and I'll show you the ropes.'

We trotted in line along the bank for some fifty yards, where Aintree set down his rod and haversack.

'I'm going to go just here,' said Aintree. 'You two can shuffle along a bit further. What bait are you using?'

I told him I had brought along maggots and bread, the usual.

'I find hemp quite good here, Tony. Needs patience though.'

'We'll try maggot first and see how we go,' I answered cautiously, 'thanks for your help.'

Hemp? Wasn't that a drug? I thought most fisheries banned it.

'Did he say hemp, Tone?' asked Harry when we were safely out of earshot. 'Smoked a bit of that in North Africa. Gave you weird dreams and made you go a bit funny.'

'I think it's just the seed they use for fishing, Harry. They stew it first.'

We set up a short way downstream from Aintree. Both of us looked forward to the new experience of fishing in moving water, even if the flow on the canal at this point was modest.

Willow, alder and poplar trees lined both banks, moorhens and coots busied themselves in the bulrushes, a water vole splashed into the water by my feet. The day could not have passed by more pleasantly, except for the noticeable absence of fish.

After about an hour I walked round to where Harry had set up. 'Any good, H.?'

'Not a thing, Tone,' answered Harry somewhat dejectedly. 'It would help if the bloody float would stay still. Talk about hemp, I'm getting slightly dizzy again now.'

'Come on, have a break,' I suggested. 'Let's go along and see what that chap Aintree is up to, then we'll have a spot of lunch.'

As we came up to Aintree's swim we could see he had hooked a fish – quite a decent one judging from the acute bend in his unusual, two-piece rod which consisted of a lower section of split cane and a top section of natural, seasoned willow, so fine at the tip that it could be bent round in a circle. To this thin tip of the rod he fixed a yard of what modellers called aeroplane elastic, an eighth of an inch square, and to that a length of nylon. Float, shot and hook were attached as normal; there was no reel.

As blank a day as Harry and I were having, so Aintree in contrast enjoyed consistent sport, catching sizeable roach one after the other, all on hemp.

'Here we are boys,' he said, chuckling as he dipped his hand twice into his bag of boiled hemp seed and offered a handful each to Harry and me. 'Try some of this. Chuck a few bits in round the float first to get them interested.'

Harry and I walked rather furtively and carefully back to our swims, with our gifts of hemp seed cupped in our hands, as though we really were in possession of some banned substance.

I did as Aintree suggested and almost immediately had a bite, but it was lightning quick and I missed it. The same thing happened on the next trot down, and the next, but on the fourth cast I hooked a plump, shiny roach. Several more followed, and then things went quiet again.

I went round to check how Harry was doing with this 'magic' bait, only to be hit full in the face by a flying gudgeon!

'Blast it, take the ruddy thing....'

There was a bit of a time delay here, since Harry was still addressing the fish he thought he had failed to hook, while in fact the tiny object of his annoyance was now flapping wetly inside my collar, projected there by Harry's desperate strike.

'Oh, you can get bites with that hemp all right, Baws,' he fumed, 'but you can't fucking connect. Drives you mad. I've changed back to maggot.'

That would account no doubt for the small fish inside my shirt. No self-respecting gudgeon can resist a juicy maggot.

Harry continued to catch gudgeon and I landed the odd roach until late afternoon when the weather took a turn for the worse, changing from bright and mild to cold and overcast quite quickly. Rather than push things on the first scooter outing, I suggested to Harry that we start packing up.

'Relief, Baws! Relief!' he cried at my suggestion, lifting his rod immediately from the water. Apparently the entertainment value of catching gudgeon had passed.

We said our farewells to Aintree, who was also on the point of packing up. Thanking him for his help and expressing our hope that we would all meet up again, we set off back towards Southend.

The sky continued to darken. A flash of lightning preceded a clap of thunder and the rain began to lash down. The windscreen afforded some protection from the driving rain, for which I was grateful – the only pity was I could no longer see the road ahead through it. I slowed right down to a crawl and put on my lights. Harry began to sing in a loud voice to lift our spirits:

> *'I am not the pheasant plucker, I'm the pheasant plucker's son,*
> *And I'm only plucking pheasant till the pheasant plucker comes.*
> *But while I'm plucking pheasant, here in the pleasant sun –*
> *I think that pheasant plucking, is pleasant plucking fun!'*

I am not sure who of us fared the best in the downpour and cold. Harry was wet, but his British Warm kept him – well, warm. My odd, brown and green camouflage plastic raincoat had become quite stiff. Not only did I resemble a tree in colour and pattern, but now also in rigidity. Nevertheless I was dry. Cold, but dry. The restrictions on personal comfort while travelling on a scooter were fast becoming apparent.

Worse was to come. Approaching a forked junction outside Bicknacre, in the fading light and driving rain I lost my bearings. I should have gone left, and if that failed, at least I should have veered to the right. Unfortunately I did neither, but instead took the central route, ploughing straight across the tiny village green which separated the two roads. The front wheel skidded on the wet grass, the back wheel slewed around and Harry and I parted company with the scooter.

We landed in a ditch ten yards apart. The scooter engine screamed, the throttle jammed wide open.

'You all right, Harry?' I yelled.

Back came the reply. 'Yes, fine, Baws. It's quite comfortable down here really. Bit wet though!'

I scrambled to my feet and righted the scooter. Harry appeared out of the gloom, flicking away mud and debris from his coat.

'Smoke, Tony?'

He opened a crumpled packet and offered me a bent cigarette. We stood there for a while saying nothing, amazed to have escaped without a scratch, smoking our cigarettes behind cupped hands to shield them from the rain. Our contemplative mood was disturbed by the sound of a motor cycle approaching through the gloom. It was Aintree.

'You blokes all right?' he asked, pulling up to us and cutting his engine.

'Never better,' answered Harry before I could say a word. 'Just stopped for a smoke,' he continued. 'Bastard rain. God, I hate this fucking British climate!'

Aintree pursed his lips and his head moved slowly from side to side.

'Does he always swear like that, Tony?

'Oh no,' I answered, 'that's pretty mild for Harry. He must be feeling a bit under the weather.'

CHAPTER EIGHT

The Big Green Ford

"I was born one mornin' when the sun didn't shine
I picked up my shovel and I walked to the mine
I loaded sixteen tons of number nine coal
And the straw boss said 'Well, a-bless my soul'.'

TENNESSEE ERNIE FORD *Sixteen Tons*

Undeterred by our tumble off the scooter at Bicknacre, we were attracted to the canal and returned regularly. Over time we explored its length from Chelmsford to Heybridge, learning which were the best places to fish. A few barges still came through the locks and we noticed that fishing improved immediately in the wake and turbulence of these passing vessels. Their propellers raked vegetation from the canal bottom, releasing organic material and providing free ground bait. For a small waterway, the canal had great charm. On slow or fishless days it was, as Harry put it, 'no hardship' to simply sit and enjoy the surroundings.

Aintree often accompanied us on these outings – a knowledgeable guide but an unlikely companion. In contrast to ours, Aintree's speech was prim and reserved. He winced whenever Harry launched into a bout of what Aintree called 'cussing and swearing'. A diminutive man who regularly dressed in a blue anorak and a flat cap, he never spoke of his work nor his home life. Though we never did so to his face, Harry and I could not resist taking Aintree's name in vain and cracking the odd horsey joke, such as ' he was under the whip' or 'his wife has been saddled with him.'

Travelling by scooter was fun, but it became less and less comfortable. Although I had replaced the plastic tree-design raincoat with an ankle-length, black leather 'Buckmaster' motorcycle coat, (and as a result now regularly sported a look much favoured by the Gestapo), we were always at the mercy of the weather. The amount of equipment we carried grew ever more burdensome as I greedily acquired this or that new design of tackle or accessory as soon as it came onto the market. By finishing my five year period of articled servitude, my salary had shot up to the princely sum of £10 per week. It was time to think about buying a car.

I could see Harry through the partly opened kitchen door. He stood on a towel in his vest and pants, performing his ablutions. His black, wet hair hung lankly down over his eyes, which were narrowed in fierce concentration. For a second, despite the moustache being not quite right, I fancied that he bore a vague resemblance to Hitler. Hitler in his underpants.

'Morning, Harry.'

'Tony!'

There followed a series of slapping sounds as Harry applied assorted cosmetic concoctions to his face and body. I waited for a pause before I continued.

'We've just got back from synagogue.'

Suzie had almost finished her instruction as a proselyte and we had both been conscripted into the synagogue choir. Calls for us to perform were irregular, but on this particular Saturday morning there had been a *bat mitzvah* (a *bar mitzvah* for girls) and our tuneless contributions and feeble Hebrew pronunciation had been pressed into service.

'You have?' queried Harry.

He had this infuriating habit of absent-mindedly questioning my every statement, if his attention was focused on something else.

'Yes,' I answered, keeping my irritation in check. 'I was wondering if you wanted to come and look at cars.'

'You were, Baws?'

There was a further sound of slapping, followed by humming.

'How long are you going to be, Harry?'

'Nearly ready. There's some sherry there if you want some.'

'No – bit early for me thanks. Suzie's gone to have her hair done. I'll go home, get the scooter and pop back for you.'

'You will?' said Harry.

Billy Rook ran a scrap yard in Prittlewell. Some cars destined for breakage he sold straight on, runners too good as yet to consign to the acetylene cutter.

Physically he resembled his avian namesake. A small man, black of hair and pointy-beaked, he had a bird-like gait, strutting purposefully around the yard with his hands thrust firmly into the pockets of his dungarees.

'What can I do for you gents?'

'We're looking for a run-around to take us fishing,' I told him, feigning a degree of self-confidence which had been sadly lacking on my scooter purchasing adventure. 'Big enough to take all the gear, but not too pricy.'

'There's an SS Jag over there,' he announced, 'that black one. Eighty quid. Or was you lookin' for something cheaper?'

'What do you recommend, Flight?' asked Harry.

Mr Rook visibly puffed out his chest at Harry's acknowledgement of his rank. Harry pulled this trick on more than one occasion, recognising intuitively the build and set of a former RAF Flight Sergeant.

'Well sir,' beamed Billy, 'if it's cheap you're after, there's that London Taxi at seven-parn-ten. Or I got a nice Austin Seven convertible for a tenner.'

Neither was really what I wanted. The taxi tempted me and it was certainly big enough, but the layout meant I would have to carry Harry as a passenger in the back, separated by a glass screen. Thinking of Harry in his more loquacious spells, the idea had some appeal, but comradeship prevailed.

The Austin was tiny by comparison, but very pretty. It appeared to be in excellent condition. The coachwork was handsomely painted, maroon and black. The roof was likewise black, made from some canvas-like material. As for the interior, this was lined top and sides with beige felt. With seats of well-worn maroon leather, and a discreet, isinglass window at the back, the overall design and style put one in mind of a motorised Regency carriage. Despite the obvious drawback of size, I felt tempted.

'Could we take the Austin for a run please?' I asked.

''Course,' said Billy jovially, ''old on.'

He shuffled off to the caravan that served as his office and returned with the keys. The car started with his first swing of the starting handle.

'I'll 'ave to drive,' he announced. 'you ain't insured.'

'That's fine,' I replied, pondering that the condition of most of the vehicles in Billy's possession made it unlikely that any claim would inconvenience the insurers, even if his entire stock went up in flames.

Harry and I squeezed into the back of the car, jammed together like sardines. The Regency carriage-like characteristics of the car obviously appealed to Harry. As the car pulled out of the yard he raised his right arm to wave, in a regal manner, at a gaggle of pedestrians who had been forced to stop and make way for us.

'It would seem the peasants know their manners!' exclaimed Harry. 'You may proceed, coachman. To the house of Mr Nash, post haste!'

I turned my head away and peered desperately out of the window. Billy Rook either did not hear, or chose to ignore Harry's outburst. The little car pottered merrily along and after a short round trip, we headed back into the scrap yard. Pulling on the handbrake and switching off the engine, Billy asked our opinion of the vehicle. Before I could say a word, Harry drew attention to the roof.

'Seems a bit thin in places,' he said.

'Where?' asked Billy Rook.

Harry struggled to lift his left arm from where it was pinned against my body, in order to indicate an apparently defective spot above his head. Liberated suddenly, his arm shot up, his hand hit the weak canvas – and went straight through it.

'There,' said Harry.

I opened the door on my side and pushed the passenger seat forward, tugging at Harry's coat sleeve, urging him to follow. Soon the three of us stood surveying the damaged roof.

Holding his obvious anger in check, Billy spoke.

'That's nothing. Won't take me a second to fix that.'

'It's a nice car,' I said, wanting now to get as far away from it as possible. 'but it really is too small. Have you anything larger?'

'Only the Jag or the taxi,' answered Billy, his eyes displaying the annoyance which he could not voice, as his salesman persona gained the upper hand. 'That's it at the moment. Mind you, we get stuff in all the time. Come back next week and I'll 'ave somethin' for you.'

Looking directly at Harry I moved my eyes rapidly, indicating that we should perhaps be going. That 'somethin' for you' brought to mind the *double entendre* offers of the scooter salesman to 'sort me out' or to 'take care of me'. Billy Rook might just think that the extra ventilation Harry had put in the Austin could be offset by similar work on me.

Our scooter route home took us past the Priory. On such a fine spring day, the opportunity to stop off and have a look at the lakes was too good to miss. As always, the next best thing to fishing was watching someone else at it. It just so happened that the someone else that day turned out to be none other than our good friend Chris.

'Hi Harry, hi Tony. How you doin'?' Chris welcomed us with his usual friendly greeting. He was fishing from the footpath, just beyond the bridge that takes Prittle Brook round the lakes in a sharp S-bend. We said hello, and in the next instant watched transfixed, as Chris's float keeled over and disappeared.

Chris struck firmly. It was as though he had hooked a boulder. He said nothing, his face an equal mix of elation and anxiety.

'Looks like you've got something decent there, Chris,' observed Harry encouragingly.

As Chris's rod curved over and the line stripped off the reel, I too volunteered the obvious.

'That's no roach Chris! What breaking strain are you using?'

'The usual,' replied Chris, between grunts of concentration, 'two pounds. This is going to be a hard one.'

So it proved. A small crowd gathered over the next half hour as Chris fought his Leviathan to a standstill. But how to land it? Chris had come armed to catch roach, not this mighty beast. A call to arms was raised. 'Anyone got a landing net big enough for this?'

A large man with a full beard stepped forward from the crowd.

'If you can bring it into the corner here, I reckon I can get it out.'

Gingerly, Chris walked the huge carp along the footpath to the corner of the lake, where an overflow gulley into the brook had silted up. The depth of water here was only a few inches, although the silt was about a foot deep. The bearded man removed his shoes and socks, rolled up his trousers and waded in.

Slowly the exhausted fish was drawn into the shallows, rolling onto its side to reveal a smooth, ochre flank, practically devoid of scales – a leather carp. As the fish pouted we could see the hook, maintaining only a fragile hold inside the upper lip.

'Grab it, for Christ's sake!' yelled the normally mild-mannered Chris.

The crowd edged forward for a better view. The bearded man extended his thick arms under the fish and with one scoop, grasped it to his chest. Turning, he displayed it to the onlookers, who broke into relieved applause.

Laying down his rod, Chris gently removed the hook and gave the monster fish an amiable pat on the flank. Thanking the man for his help, he appealed for anyone with scales, in order to weigh his catch, but no one came forward.

'What we gonna do?' asked Chris, turning to Harry and me.

'I caught one at Star Lane that I couldn't weigh,' I said, 'and I tell people that one was about ten pounds. Yours is twice as big – must be a twenty pounder at least.'

Chris looked at the fish thoughtfully.

'No,' he said, shaking his head. 'If I'm gonna tell people I caught a twenty pounder, I want it done proper – weighed, photographed, all of that. Let's settle for eighteen, eh?'

So saying, Chris turned to the bearded man.

'Put it back now mate, please.'

There was a moment of anxiety as the fish lay motionless, gills hardly moving. Then, with an imperious swish of its tail, the great carp glided off into the deep water, taking with it the secret of its true weight.

I carefully read the advertisement pinned to the notice board in the café in Priory Park:

> For sale – 1937 Ford 10
> Bargain at £5
> Bodywork sound but engine needs attention hence price
> Mr Jameson, 26 Garrison Way, Shoebury

We were finishing a welcome cup of tea and some sandwiches after the excitement of the morning and Chris's monster catch.

'Garrison Way, Shoebury. Fancy a run out, Harry?'

'Worth a try. Can't be worse than that tin can from the scrap yard.'

'I thought you liked it?' I ribbed him, 'Regency dandy and all that.'

'The Regency gentry were all right,' opined Harry, sitting back in his chair and stretching. 'Stacks of booze and scoff – I'd have liked that,' he grinned. 'Do you know, Prinny drank half a pint of gin at a time. Half a pint, Baws! Can you imagine? On top of all the bottles of wine he used to put away? And cherry brandy – he used to swog that down as well. Must have been pissed all the time. And he was fond of laudanum too! To think they let him run the fucking country!'

I allowed Harry's rant and his ambivalence towards his favourite period of English history to pass.

'Drink up. We'll go and have a look at this car.'

Not being entirely sure of where the place was, I drove too far and ended up at the military command post and barrier guarding Shoebury garrison itself. The soldier in the sentry box took one look at Harry – and presented arms. I briskly turned the scooter through 180 degrees and headed back the way we had come.

'How do you DO that Harry?'

Harry said nothing by way of explanation, but instead launched loudly into a song from his bawdy repertoire, of which he was inordinately proud:

'Arsehole, arsehole, a soldier I shall be,
Too pissed, too pissed, two pistols at my knee.
To fight for the old cunt, fight for the old cunt, fight for the old countreeee – '
(a pause before the climax)
'Fuck you! Fuck you!, For curiosity!'

After our military detour, we eventually arrived at the house. An ancient, green Ford was parked in the front garden. We knocked on the front door and were greeted by the owner.

'Have a good look round,' he said, leading us to the car and opening the driver's door. 'Take your time.'

The body work and tyres were fine, the leather seats were comfortable. Strap handles hung at each door and roomy glove compartments provided ample stowage space. Mounted on the simple dashboard were switches for ignition, choke and lights. Above the dash, a small silver handle served to wind open the windscreen. Illuminated orange semaphore arms saluted left or right at the flick of a chrome lever in the steering wheel; the steering boss concealed a button to sound the robust horn.

The vendor seemed honest enough. 'It overheats a bit,' he said, 'Could be a blocked rad. Or hoses. It doesn't have a water pump, so it can't be that. Mind you, I haven't run it for a while, so the battery's probably flat. Still, it's got a starter handle, so you can always use that. Do you want me to show you how to do it?'

There followed my first and only lesson in the correct use of a detachable starter handle. Locating the engaging slots in the engine block with the two lugs on the end of the handle required much fiddling and poking about, but having achieved that, (and ensuring that the gearbox was in neutral), the trick was to push half a turn down, then to complete the revolution by pulling the handle smartly up towards you in one, smooth movement.

A short trip in the car, with no sign of steam coming from the engine compartment, persuaded me that this would be a very acceptable purchase. Here was four-door luxury, ideal for stowing fishing equipment. One look at Harry's smiling face as he sprawled contentedly across the back seats confirmed that he too approved of this new mode of transport. Handing over the money, I arranged to pick up the vehicle the following week. Despite the drawbacks, for an outlay of a mere five pounds, I figured I was not taking an undue financial risk.

Unfortunately, the overheating problem did become more apparent a short while after I took possession and it proved to be more serious than merely a leaking hose. We were soon returning, cap in hand, to Billy Rook's scrap metal emporium, seeking this time not a whole car, but an engine transplant. Flight Sergeant Rook (ret.) happily supplied and fitted a replacement engine and all the trimmings for £20 (twice the sum he had intended to charge us for an entire Austin Seven.)

I still felt that I had got a bargain. The old Ford had great character and a willingness to please. She deserved a name, and despite her green colour, we decided to call her Rosie.

CHAPTER NINE

The Res

'Blow, winds, and crack your cheeks! rage! blow!
And thou, all-shaking thunder,
Strike flat the thick rotundity o' the world!'

SHAKESPEARE *King Lear*

We had come across the Res purely by chance. Rochford reservoir, situated at the side of the tracks, originally supplied both the railway company and the local fire brigade with water for their respective engines. When these uses had ceased some years ago, a group of railway employees had formed an angling club and stocked the water with fish.

I was now travelling regularly up and down the line from Southend to my new workplace in London. One evening I sat facing two men dressed in railway uniform; not the functional work clothes of the footplate but the blue serge and gold trimming of station staff. Eavesdropping on their conversation, I soon gathered that they were talking about fishing at Rochford. I began to listen intently.

'If that by-pass plan goes ahead, I reckon that'll be Rochford Angling Club buggered,' said the older of the two.'

'Come on Dad,' replied the other, 'they've been talking about it for years and nothing ever gets done.'

'Still,' said Dad, 'it would be good to get our hands on Doggetts in case the worst comes to the worst, as a failsafe.'

'Yes, and we've been talking about that for as many years as the Council have been talking up the by-pass. The club doesn't have the money for the rent he's asking. We can't add to the membership because of the damned rules and it's always a bloody struggle to raise the fees. Plus, no one wants to agree to the issue of day tickets. It'll be the same at the AGM next week. You'll still be Chairman, I'll still be Secretary; no one else will come forward to stand for the committee and things will just carry on. You'll see.'

'Trouble is,' said his father, 'a lot of the members are getting on a bit now, like me. We need to attract some fresh blood.'

They were still reviewing this grave state of affairs, and whether the club should be opened to public membership, when I introduced myself. On learning of my enthusiasm for fishing, they cordially invited me along to a members' meeting, 'just as a spectator you understand.' I managed to wangle an observer's seat for Harry too.

It transpired that in addition to being father and son and Chairman and Secretary of the Rochford Railway Angling Club, they were, moreover, the Stationmaster and the Deputy Stationmaster of Rochford railway station.

There was an ancient club rule which insisted that all members had to be railway employees, past or present. As former employees aged and the present British Rail policy of swingeing staff reductions nationwide began to bite, this founders' rule was having a detrimental effect both on club finances and on the number of able-bodied participants available for work parties.

Somewhat surprisingly, at the AGM the club rules were changed 'on a temporary basis' to expand the membership and save the club from extinction. Harry and I were among others invited to become members, an offer we accepted with relish. For the first time in our angling adventures, we felt legitimate. It was not simply a matter of handing over some money in a shop, (which was all that was required to fish the Chelmer and Blackwater). Now we had actually been proposed, seconded and voted in; we were bona fide members of a fishing club. Our poaching days were almost over.

Rosie the Big Green Ford was officially christened as our fishing wagon on a sultry evening in late August. Armed with our pristine Rochford membership cards and rod licenses, we felt like new boys on our first day at school.

At the entrance to Rochford station I swung Rosie off the main road. She climbed the steep ascent to the top of the railway embankment in fine style. A gravelled cul-de-sac ran for several hundred yards along the top of the embankment parallel to the railway track until it ended abruptly at a gated fence. Turning the car completely around, I parked alongside two earlier arrivals. Harry and I clambered out, rather pleased with ourselves.

'Jolly comfy the new car, isn't it, Tone?' said Harry jovially, stretching his arms above his head and taking a deep breath. 'You could get a good fug up in there.'

He leaned on the fence and peered over. Steep steps led down to the one-and-a-half acre lake. At the bottom we had a choice of walking straight ahead or turning right across a small wooden bridge. Beneath the bridge ran the nascent river Roach, not much more than a brook at this point, skirting the reservoir before entering the river Crouch on its way to the sea. These local Essex rivers were murky affairs and soon became tidal. It seemed sad that a river which had given its name to a village at the place where it was forded, and which bore the name of the most common freshwater fish in England, was actually so uninspiring. There were rumours of fish being caught in the Roach but we never met anyone who had actually done so.

Just downstream of the bridge, a manually-operated sluice allowed the little river Roach to enter the reservoir. At the far end of the reservoir, a concrete overflow channel set into the bank allowed excess water back into the river. The question of whether or not to let the river water (and any pollutants it might contain) into the reservoir at any particular time proved to be a topic of endless, unresolved, and often acrimonious debate among club members.

'Looks smashing doesn't it?' said Harry enthusiastically. 'Can't wait to get in the water.'

I walked over and joined him to survey the scene.

'Those swims just across the bridge look fine. Fancy giving them a try? We can always do a full recce in the morning.'

'Whatever you say, Baws' replied Harry, all grins and enthusiasm.

We busied ourselves unloading the car. Our baggage was becoming increasingly heavy as more and more equipment was acquired. Most recently, I had bought two fishing umbrellas. Their simple design consisted of a pointed, threaded, aluminium ground pole which could slide up and down inside a shaft to provide height adjustment. The pole was locked into place by a plastic wedge, operated by a plastic lever. The green cotton umbrella canopies were some four feet in diameter, providing adequate shelter.

Rosie had brought a welcome dowry hidden in her small boot; a leather covered, fully sprung car seat. Soon this became my luxurious and comfortable fishing seat, but it was heavy and unwieldy and an absolute brute to carry very far. Harry, on the other hand, had recently insisted on using a lightweight, collapsible stool; the type used by landscape artists in the field. In fact it belonged to Suzie and it was fine for her slim build, but it looked desperately unsafe with Harry on board, his bulky frame perched perilously on the edge.

The sky had darkened noticeably in the short time since our arrival.

'Getting a bit breezy, Harry. Reckon we could be in for a bit of weather.'

Preparing for the worst, I decided to pull on another of my recent acquisitions – thigh-waders. Harry was wearing his water boots as usual. For the time being we eschewed donning our last line of storm defence – the Buckmaster motorcycle coat for me and for Harry a full length, semi-transparent, grey plastic 'Pac-a-Mac'. Hoisting our bags onto our shoulders, we struggled through the baffle gate at the end of the path and staggered down the wooden stairs.

The reservoir was earth-sided and almost rectangular, with a small island in the middle which could only be reached by boat. Mature trees lined the banks and they proved a source of both cover and frustration. Many a fish escaped into the tangle of twigs and broken branches shed by these trees and now littering the lake bed. Many a maggot bait wriggled and burrowed and disappeared into the thick leaf layer which had built up over time, dragging the hook with it. There it lay undiscovered by any fish, leading to many a biteless hiatus.

Our chosen swims backing onto the track at least were free of trees, these having been zealously cleared by the railway company, on the grounds that they were a safety hazard. There still existed plenty of cover in the form of the reed beds, which reached out into the lake until the water became too deep to support them. On a flat area of grass between the embankment and the water we deposited our equipment and set up our rods.

All in all it was a cosy spot, especially when viewed from the considerable comfort of my new fishing chair. I plumbed the depth, attached a decent-sized piece of bread flake and cast in. My float settled nicely on the edge of the reed bed. Lighting a cigarette, I settled back as the daylight faded.

Steam trains ran throughout the night and fearsome engines worked away above our heads. A red glow, a clank of iron and steel, a billow of smoke and hissing steam revealed the great, black beasts as they shunted goods wagons back and forth in the siding yard. It felt comforting to have the company of Harry, settled in the next swim. He was in fine voice:

'Oh Danny boy,' he sang, 'the pipes – the fucking pipes – are fucking c-a-a-lling. From glen to fucking glen – and down the fucking mountain fucking side!'

It was a novel version of the old Irish song, one I had not heard before. He sang it slowly and deliberately, with a pause between each phrase, placing stress on the first syllable of 'fucking'.

A sudden lightning flash lit up the sky, followed shortly by a roll of thunder.

'Boom!' shouted Harry, as if he could challenge the deities at their own game. 'Come and get me, you bearded bastard!'

I checked my watch. Almost midnight. Another intense flash illuminated the trees and the lake. It began to pour.

My float bobbed down and up at the precise moment the rain started. Suspecting a direct hit from a large raindrop, I lifted the rod tentatively. A solid resistance, then the pulse-raising, high-pitched noise of the fixed-spool reel ratchet, whining as the fish headed off. Heart pounding, I stood, prepared to fight. But the line went slack. Frantically I wound hard. I tried to make out the profile of the rod top against the sky, but it was pitch black. My eyes had not adjusted from the lightning and the torch beam – all I could see in the blackness were rainbow colours.

'Have you got something, Tone?'

'Yes, I think so. Can you get round here. I can't see a bloody thing.'

'Coming, Tony.' A brief silence. 'Bollocks!'

Thump. Slither. Thump. Harry's torch beam strafed the sky as he slipped.

'You okay, H?'

'Coming, Baws.'

I was excited because I had hooked the fish, but now I was apprehensive at the prospect of losing it. This overload of adrenalin made me unfeasibly irritable.

'Just shine the torch out there, Harry. For fuck's sake, I can't see what's going on.'

Harry appeared in a frozen moment, silhouetted by the lightning. Almost at my feet, the fish thrashed in the water. It had turned in towards the reeds and was now in the shallows.

'Down there, Harry, right down there. The landing net – here! Fucking hell!'

Harry flashed around with his torch and made a pass at the fish but missed.

'Jesus H, Harry. Just grab it!

'Got it! ' He scooped up the fish and placed the landing net on the grass. A wild carp of about five pounds. 'Lovely fish, Baws. What a beauty!' He said not a word about me swearing and cursing at him. All was forgotten in the deep joy of landing that fish. With shaking fingers, I unhooked it and placed it in the keep net. The rain began falling harder.

'I'm going to get our coats, Harry. Best break out the brollies as well.'

When I arrived back after the short trip to the car I found Harry on his knees in the rain, grumbling and cursing.

'How do these bloody things work? Complicated bastards!'

He had helpfully removed the umbrellas from the rod bags and opened them, showing admirable initiative, but then he had loosened the plastic locking mechanisms and pulled the extendable inner poles completely out. Now the two opened canopies lay on the ground like giant, upturned mushrooms, collecting rainwater as opposed to deflecting it. Negotiating round them in the dark was difficult. The inner poles were nowhere to be seen.

'Harry. Look, tip the water out of this one,' I said, handing him one still-opened umbrella, 'and hold it over your head while I try and find the poles.'

He stood there in the pouring rain like a naughty schoolboy, both hands gripping the shaft of his umbrella. Meanwhile I folded the other one and shone the light around on the ground. Eventually I located the poles.

'Here you are. Here's your coat. Give me the brolly and I'll set it up for you.'

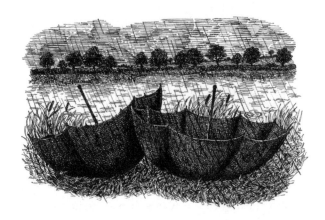

While Harry struggled to pull the tight-fitting Pac-a-Mac over his already sodden clothes, I re-assembled the two umbrellas. One I put just behind my ground sheet. Picking up Harry's torch, I went to put the other umbrella in the spot where he had been fishing. Flashing the light around I could see his rod rest, but no rod. The rain continued to hammer down.

'Where's your rod, Harry?' I shouted to him.

'It must be there, Tony. I haven't moved it.'

I swept the torch beam over the reed bed. There, some few feet out, was Harry's rod. He must have kicked it when he fell over in his rush to get to me when I hooked the carp.

'I see it. Can you keep an eye on my float?'

'Okay.'

I stepped cautiously onto the reed bed, where my foot sank immediately. A stench of rotting vegetation filled the air.

'Lovely, Baws' said Harry, sniffing hard. 'Do it again.'

I took another step forward, trusting my waders to do their job, and managed to grab the rod with my left hand. As I lifted it up, so the rod tip bucked downwards. There was a bloody fish on the end!

'You've hooked something, H!'

I retreated slowly, rod and attached fish in one hand, torch in the other. Harry, excited by my news, had left my swim and rushed forward with the landing net to help, which was a mistake. We collided at the water's edge, collapsing in a sodden heap. A flash of lightning exposed for a brief moment this sorry tableau. An enormous crash of thunder followed.

Harry raised himself up, laughing and cursing.

'Come on you bearded bastard!' he ranted, shaking his fist at the sky. 'By the blessed saints and the twelve apostles!' he yelled. 'Boom!'

We staggered to our feet.

'Do you want to land this fish, Harry?'

'No, you do it, Baws. Too much excitement for one night.'

In the driving rain, I steered the fish towards land. It hadn't put up too much of a fight and had probably become bored, swimming around with no one taking any notice of it. Harry slid the landing net under it, rather competently it has to be said. Another wild carp, smaller than mine, but in fine condition. I carefully took it back round to my swim and popped it in the keep net.

It was proving an eventful night. Two more carp followed, small mirror carp this time, but rewarding and fun to catch. Then the storm subsided, and with it the sport. I settled back into my seat, listening to the hypnotic sound of raindrops landing on the umbrella. Soon I was drifting in and out of a light sleep.

I was startled by the splash of a moorhen as it scurried into the water from the reed bed, swam a few yards, panicked and dashed back towards cover.

'Have you got something?' yelled Harry.

'No, Harry' I replied sleepily, 'it's just a moorhen.'

'Ah, a Jesus bird, eh Tone?' That's what he called them – moorhens and coots – because they give the impression of walking on water.

'No. I think this one's Jewish – a Red Sea pedestrian maybe.'

'Oh very droll, Baws.' He paused for a moment. I could sense the thoughts whirring about in his head as he strove for a repost.

'All right, Tony. What's the difference between a water bird and a mandrake?'

He chuckled at his own cleverness as he considered the answer to his impromptu Spoonerism.

'I don't know, Harry, what is the difference?'

'One's a cunning root,' he prompted, 'and the other's a.....'

' A running coot,' I replied.

'Or,' suggested Harry, now beside himself with laughter, 'a rooting cunt!'

'What a coarse fellow you are,' I observed, which only served to make him laugh even harder.

The wood pigeons had stopped calling. The dawn chorus of birdsong, muted by the pouring rain, was coming to an end. All the action had come in the early part of the night, during the height of the thunderstorm. Harry had a few bites when it became light but failed to connect. I had none.

Even now, at eight o'clock in the morning, it was barely light. The rain had fallen with increasing venom for the past hour. Peering across the lake, I watched glumly as volley upon volley of raindrops hit the water. Concentric circles and splashes merged on the seething surface. Glancing down at my rod I could see droplets of water hanging below the rings and water running off the cork handle. My plastic groundsheet, stiffened by the early morning chill, held pockets of rainwater containing the debris of the night: ground bait, breadcrumbs, cigarette ash, a few disconsolate maggots and a lone worm beyond revival. The captive carp remained quiet in the keep net.

It had been a busy night and I felt drained. Slowly I eased myself up from the confines of the car seat and half rose, raising the rod butt and swinging the tackle in towards me. In my zombie-like state, I failed to allow enough room to complete this manoeuvre successfully. As a result, the fishing rod jarred against the edge of the umbrella and the line whiplashed back towards the lake, only prevented from further progress by the hook, which now snagged my jacket under the left elbow.

That was it! Enough! With my right hand I grabbed the line and bit through it, cursing between clenched teeth.

'Are you packing up?' yelled Harry.

'Yup.'

'Go on – give it a bit longer, Baws. Be a man!' he chuckled. He was incorrigible.

'No more. That's it. *Genug.*'

'*Genooo!*' mocked Harry, '*ich habe genooo!*'

My homespun Yiddish, coupled with Harry's halting German acquired during his time as a prisoner-of-war, had worked its way into our fishing parlance. It certainly came in useful at Star Lane and on similar occasions; caught red-handed, fishing where, or perhaps when, we were not meant to be. By this subterfuge we had managed on more than one occasion to convince wardens, water bailiffs and other upholders of the law that we understood little English and had strayed from the path of piscatorial probity purely by accident. Over time *ganz genug*, (both German and Yiddish for 'that's quite enough of that'), had become elongated into *genoo*.

I detached the hook from my elbow with some difficulty, wound the line back onto the reel, dried the rod and the landing net handle and packed the gear away. I could hear Harry humming cheerfully to himself as he busied about a similar task. Finally there came a 'pop, pop' sound, as he pulled apart the sections of his rod.

'Relief, Baws, relief!' he shouted. He began singing in the style of an old time music hall artiste, nasally intoning the tune of an old French song:

'*Pechez pas le reservoir encore*… Don't fish the reservoir any more, oh….'

What was it that took hold of us, turned us into crazed zealots, impelled us to fish to the point of exhaustion, not daring to call '*genoo*'? What was it about fishing that was so addictive? Maybe it was the attainment of exactly this feeling: a metabolic, chemical change, a post-coital moment when the fishing high, maintained over many hours, was at last allowed to subside, to be replaced by a warm feeling of satisfaction.

'Do you want to see the fish before I put them back, Harry?'

'Please.'

I reached down and gently raised the closed end of the keep net until it was practically parallel to the water.

'Fine fish, Tony.'

'That one's yours,' I said, pointing.

'Not mine, Tony. You caught it.'

'Yes, but you hooked it.'

We paused, hands on knees, looking down at the fish. Then I lowered the keep net into the water and we watched as, effortlessly, the carp swam away.

Shouldering our rod bags, we gathered our belongings and tramped back to the bridge, stopping to gaze at the rushing brook. Swollen by storm water, it had begun to lap over the sluice and spill into the reservoir.

'Wonder if there's any fish in that brook,' mused Harry. 'You'd probably get something with a hand line if you tackled up again.'

I was too exhausted to rise to the bait. We made our weary way back to the car. I changed out of my coat and waders and helped Harry lever off his wellington boots. For a while we sat in the car, smoking and drinking coffee, watching the condensation form on the windows, what Harry called 'getting a good fug up'. After a while he spoke.

'Would you…?' he began.

I groaned. I knew what was coming next. It was always the same game, a good-natured tease.

'Would you, Tony,' he repeated, 'tackle up again right now for five pounds?'

'Would I fuck!'

'One question at a time please,' quipped H. 'For twenty pounds then?'

'No bloody chance!'

'What about for fifty pounds?'

Harry looked at me with a wicked grin. It was a lot of money. I mulled it over. I hesitated long enough for him to change tack. Bugger the money…

'Not even if you could catch a 20lb carp?'

That was the point of this auction. The offer of the glittering prize, the Holy Grail, the acme of fishing achievement which would make all of the suffering worthwhile. The prospect of catching such a fish would surely outweigh the misery: the cold and the wet, the starvation, the stinging nettles, the assault of various wild beasts, insects and vermin, to say nothing of the wrath of spouses whose patience was already stretched. So what if the record stood at 44lbs! A 20lb carp – a 20-pounder – a mighty fish indeed. A fish of such renown that at the Priory not long ago, Chris had been prepared to forego his claim to it, rather than be seen as a braggart. A mighty fish.

'A mighty fish, a mighty fish, a mighty, mighty fish!' sang Harry, beating out the rhythm on the dashboard.

'A mighty fish, a mighty fish, a mighty, mighty fish!' We drummed on the dashboard together and swayed back and forth in our seats. The additional fug generated by our enthusiasm increased the condensation. I wound down the window to see out and draw breath.

'It's bloody stopped raining, H. Would you Adam and Eve it?'

'That's good,' said Harry. 'Want to tackle up again?'

Surely he knew the answer to his question. I would always tackle up again. Not right now perhaps, but whenever I did it would not be for money and it would not be for the guarantee of a 20lb carp. It would be for the huge and simple pleasure of fishing with Harry.

CHAPTER 10

The Wager

'Stewball was a good horse, he bore a high head,
And the mane on his foretop, was as fine as silk thread.
I rode him in England, I rode him in Spain,
And I never did lose boys, I always did gain.'

TRADITIONAL arr. Joan Baez

I pressed my face to the window, seeking a last glimpse of the Res as the train pulled out of Rochford station on its way to London. I always became excited whenever I saw a lake or pond, a river or stream, that could possibly be fishable. Now here was one to torment me each working day. I could see a car parked on the reservoir embankment. Even at 7.30 on a wet Wednesday morning in September, someone was already down there fishing, the lucky blighter.

Although the odd steam engine was still clanking around in the sidings, diesel was taking over in the goods yards, and the passenger services were already electrified. These new units were clean, bright and fast. The train gathered speed and the lake disappeared from view.

The accountancy office where I was employed was but a stone's throw from Liverpool Street station. I worked with two Jewish boys of about my own age, Ray and Mick, whose major hobbies seemed to be betting on horses or dogs, or indeed anything that moved. While Ray was tall and lean with sleek dark hair, all darting movement, Mick was more easy-going, his hair curly and blond. He wore Buddy Holly glasses, identical to mine. Apart from the hair colour, we might have passed for brothers.

One morning Mick arrived in the office and launched into a monologue concerning a dream he had the previous night. As his tale unfolded, I was amazed to find that I recognised some of the *dramatis personae*. When he gave a very accurate description of my aunt Fanny and her husband Jack,

89

and then called them by name, I was utterly bewildered.

'What the fuck...?

Mick roared with laughter, and then explained that we were actually second cousins! He himself had only discovered the connection the previous night when these mutual relatives had paid a rare visit to his parents. We laughed and shook hands and celebrated with a cup of coffee all round.

Each morning Ray and Mick pored over the Racing Times and the Sporting Life, discussing the merits of this or that 'nag' or 'pooch' until lunchtime, when we all made a swift exit in the direction of Spitalfields, they to the betting shop and I to Alf's Café, a few doors down in the same street . Bets placed, they would join me in the café where they eschewed food but instead whiled away the lunch break standing in the corner, playing a pin-ball machine.

The object of the game, simple but addictive, was to compile a line of three, four or five consecutive numbers. Success yielded a cash prize of one, two or five pounds respectively. On those rare occasions when a line of five was achieved, the five pound winnings were handed over by the surly proprietor with a grimace of intense pain, as though all his teeth were being extracted one by one without anaesthetic.

On leaving Alf's Café, the boys would pop down to the betting shop to check on results. Wins were met with jubilation, losses with admirable stoicism. Mick in particular believed in a philosophy of logical positivism, (or as he would say, 'stating the bleedin' obvious'), as demonstrated by his oft repeated catchphrases, such as, 'Find a penny, pick it up, all day long, you'll have – a penny', and, 'He who laughs last laughs last!'

Although I played the pin-ball machine with enthusiasm, I had no real interest in racing or betting, being what the gambling fraternity refer to as a 'mug punter'. These losers surface periodically, to bet on the classic races: the Derby, the Grand National, the Oaks, the Dog Derby and so on, putting their money on a horse or a dog simply because they like the name, (such technical niceties as 'form' and 'going' being totally lost on them). Most will certainly not know personally, nor second nor even third hand, any owners or trainers or jockeys – those contacts in the racing world essential to long-term gambling success.

I did, however, once have a bet on two greyhounds running at Walthamstow. Standing in the doorway of the tiny betting shop, waiting for the other two, I happened to glance at the board where the bookies chalked up the list of runners. There I spotted my mug punter's dream; two dogs whose names beckoned me like blazing beacons. The first went by the name of Lady Jane and the other was called Seymour Suzie. Jane is Suzie's third name. Irresistible!

I ventured cautiously in and, guided by Ray and Mick, I placed a dual-forecast bet on the namesakes of my beloved. In order for me to win, the dogs would have to finish in the first two places, in either order. The odds were so long on these unfancied canines that when they did miraculously both come in ahead of the field, I received over seventeen pounds for my four shilling outlay. Mick and Ray were dumbfounded, but pleased for me. It was quickly dismissed as beginners' luck. I agreed and thought it best to quit while I was still ahead.

Back at the office, between the preparation of accounts, Mick and Ray again studied the racing papers, this time for the evening action – horses in summer and dogs throughout the year. Happily both were expert at their work. Figures simply flew from their pens onto the accounts analysis schedules so there was no discernible loss of output. Our daily workload was not arduous, unlike in some slave-driving, 'No Talking' accountancy offices where I have worked. On the contrary, there was ample time for idle chatter.

Ray, Mick and I shared a love of Beatles music and of football, but otherwise I was very much the country cousin in the company of these East London city dwellers. Angling was as alien to them as flying to the moon. I tried hard to explain my addiction but I might just as well have been speaking a foreign language. Yet it was their obsession with gambling that led to an unexpected fishing outing.

One day, as I was attempting yet again to inspire the pair with tales of my fishy exploits, Ray posed a question.

'Do you reckon you could ever catch a fish, Mick?' he asked casually of his best friend.

''Course,' said Mick looking towards me, with a broad grin on his face. 'Must be dead simple if Tony can do it.'

'Bet you couldn't,' Ray continued, drawing his victim in.

'Yeah? How much?'

'Bet you a tenner.'

'What do you think, coz?' asked Mick. 'Would you take me with you sometime so I can prove this smug bastard wrong?'

'Sure,' I replied, 'it would be a pleasure. What about coming down this Saturday?'

Mick pursed his lips, mulling the matter over, weighing the odds.

'Okay Ray,' he chuckled, 'cover my train fares as well and you're on!'

'Where were you thinking of taking him?' asked Harry when I announced the plan that evening.

'Over the Res, I suppose. Or maybe that place the club talks about acquiring – Doggetts. We could give that a try.'

Doggetts Farm in Rochford – here indeed was a venue fit for a gambling man. In 1921 Lord Louth, scion of the noble Plunkett family of Ireland, had approached the owners to create a racecourse on the land. After endless negotiations and disputes, and in the face of hostility from God-fearing locals, the course was eventually constructed in 1928. It operated successfully for three years, until the prize money ran out. Now, after a period as a gravel pit, the lake at Doggetts was notionally a public fishing spot.

Unlike Star Lane, which was still an active site, the gravel working at Doggetts had ceased many years ago. The machinery stood gaunt and rusted, its iron girders twisted to the sky. Old steel cables lay on the ground, or squirmed in death-throe coils from the mounds of abandoned gravel spoil. Youths on scrambler bikes sped up and down the sand hills left by the excavations, pausing to catch their breath in the flat area beneath the cascade and the hopper, where lorries had once waited to be filled.

'Bit gin clear, people say. Lots of weed too. I've heard it holds nothing but pissers,' said Harry balefully.

'You can't believe all you hear, Harry. Anyway, he's only got to catch one fish. Doesn't matter what size it is. Maybe the rain will have coloured it up a bit. The Res has been a bit slow lately.'

'Well you know me, Tony, I'm game for anything. Let's give 'em both a go. We've got nothing to lose.'

Harry was fond of this expression, 'nothing to lose', but his use of 'we' in this context was highly inaccurate. He might well have nothing to lose at the prospect of being ferried about between the two lakes with Mick, and the two of them having to tackle up twice. Personally I felt I could have something to lose – my sanity.

On a dull Saturday morning, we stood at Rochford waiting for Mick's train to arrive. The autumn chill had seen Harry press into service a voluminous, ankle-length, ex-army greatcoat, of a colour best described as horse manure brown. Black wellingtons poked out from beneath its swathes. On his head was perched a black astrakhan hat, into which Harry had impaled several pigeon feathers. Garbed in my 'Wiznewski' jacket I was restrained by comparison. Staff and passengers at the station were used to sartorial oddities. That part of Essex was home to many Irish traveller and Romany Gypsy families. Nevertheless, as a pair, we drew worried looks – and at that point we were still relatively clean and mud-free.

I had not thought it necessary to instruct Mick as to clothing suitability.

It was nice to see his cheery wave as he stepped from the train but slightly disconcerting to note that he was dressed in a well-cut, three-button, blue mohair suit, a white shirt and a dark tie. On his feet were shiny black brogues.

Nor, I now remembered, had I spoken to him about fishing equipment. I had fully intended to supply his needs from our own ever-increasing stock of rods and reels. In the event, he bore in one hand the two separate sections of a sturdy, ancient cane sea rod. Lord knows where he had acquired it at such short notice. This monstrous instrument, I mused, if wielded with sufficient strength and skill, might well have subdued the white whale Moby Dick in a straight fight. From the other hand swung a two-tone brown, plastic shopping bag.

'Hullo Tony!'

'Hullo Mick. Good journey?'

'Yeah, thanks. Weather looks a bit murky though. I didn't think to bring a raincoat.' (If he had, I felt sure it would have been a smart Burberry or an Aquascutum.)

'It was raining a bit earlier,' I said, 'but it should be okay. This is Harry.'

I could not remember ever describing Harry to Mick in detail. Not that it would have made any difference. Nothing prepared strangers for the sight of Harry in full fishing fig.

'Hullo boy,' said Harry, reaching out a hand, (forcing Mick to smartly drop his bag on the ground in order to reciprocate). 'Tony says you need to catch a fish. You don't want to take any notice of me then. Baws is the man to teach you. If he can't catch anything, then they're not there to be caught.'

Mick grinned at Harry's sales pitch. I was flattered but not too confident. We all piled into Rosie for the short trip to Doggetts.

There was a steel barrier across the road leading to the farm and the lake, so we had to leave the car and travel the last quarter mile on foot. Mick and Harry chatted amiably as we walked, while I went over in my mind how best to equip Mick for success.

A centre pin reel would work well with his antique sea rod. Fortunately, we had such a reel, although it was a fly reel loaded with a shooting-head floating line and a sinking cast. Harry had been given it by a friend, together with an assortment of flyfishing paraphernalia, none of which we could use. A permanent fixture at the bottom of Harry's bag, the reel travelled around with him on the remote chance that it would come in useful some day. That day had now arrived. A heavy float with plenty of shot would further aid

Mick's neophyte casting. Small perch, watch out!

There were swims right by the entrance from the road, but they were occupied. We were also aware of some lads on scrambler bikes. revving up their machines in the clearing by the old cascade.

'We'll carry on round,' I suggested. 'I think there's more cover further on.'

'Whatever you say, Baws,' said Harry cheerfully.

'You all right Mick?' I asked. 'You seem kind of quiet.'

Mick grinned. 'No, I'm fine. Just trying to look where I'm going. It's a bit slippery.'

I looked down at Mick's shoes. They were no longer in the pristine condition they had been when he arrived, and we had only advanced a few yards. His trouser turn-ups too showed signs of muddy encroachment.

Swims were few and far between on this side and we came eventually to the far end of the main lake. The choice was to retrace our steps or to negotiate a narrow path lined with blackthorn, a swampy area, where willow boles rose darkly from the manky water. I decided to forge ahead.

'Watch where you're going, you two,' I said back over my shoulder. 'It's a bit tricky.' My warning came a bit late.

'Fuck!' It was Mick's voice. I turned to see him tugging at his jacket, trapped by thorns.

'Bollocks!' cried Mick again as his foot sank up to mid-calf in the stagnant water. More cussing followed as, trying to free one leg, Mick's other leg slipped into the swamp. The stench of rotted vegetation filled the air.

'Have you farted, Mick?' chuckled Harry, bringing up the rear (so to speak).

'Very funny,' replied Mick, with laudable East End resilience. 'If I had, you wouldn't be laughing.'

We emerged from this overgrown area onto a bare bank and Mick flopped down for a breather. This was a mistake as the wet sandy soil made more marks on Mick's increasingly vulnerable attire. Frustratingly, this area also failed to offer much by way of piscatorial encouragement, the sand bank merely a backdrop to an uninspiring curve of reed-free, featureless water.

'Come on chaps, let's move on,' I exhorted my party.

Mick rose to his feet somewhat reluctantly. But he did manage a grin as he asked the question uppermost in his mind.

'Do you reckon my tenner's safe?'

'No question,' I answered, although I was beginning to doubt that we would ever start fishing, let alone catch anything. We were heading back towards the road where we had come in. Now there was a choice of two paths, one at water level with the quarry wall at our backs, the other rising above us to skirt the neighbouring field. Keeping to the lower path, scanning anxiously ahead for somewhere to fish, we were almost back to the road when we came to a level stretch with no obstructions or reeds. While it would be cheek-by-jowl, and more exposed than I would like, it did mean that I could keep a close eye on both Mick and Harry – a distinct advantage if mayhem were to be avoided.

'This'll do fine,' I announced, setting down my stuff. 'Let's get tackled up.'

I had already decided to be the non-playing captain of this little team. All we needed for honour to be satisfied was that Mick should hook and land a fish. Leaving Harry to his own devices for a moment, I set to assembling Mick's tackle. After a few practice swings, he was able to send the float out underarm more or less in a straight line. Now for the bait.

'I'm not touching them,' said Mick, as I showed him the maggots wriggling in their container. 'You'll have to put them on for me.'

'We could try a worm then,' I suggested, opening the box of brandlings and pulling one out for his inspection.

'They look just as horrible,' moaned Mick.

Harry offered his support. 'In France, Mick, the pole fishermen on the Seine put maggots in their cheeks to keep them warm and lively. The maggots that is. You ought to try it.'

Mick's face wrinkled in disgust.

'Come on, Mick,' I said, 'I'll put some maggots on for you. Then we'll have some food.'

I attached three maggots and bent down to wash my hands in the lake, more to reassure Mick than anything, since I am sure that many a maggot had found its way into my stomach by now, and I was normally the most squeamish of souls. Maybe I was immune to them. The lake water probably posed as many gastro-enteric threats as any maggot.

Mick swung the baited line out with some confidence, set down the rod and reached into his plastic bag.

'Anyone want a bit of pork pie?' he asked.

Harry feigned shock. 'A pork pie? What sort of food is that for a nice Jewish boy?'

'It's okay, it's a kosher pie,' replied Mick.

'Oh, that's all right then,' said Harry. 'I hope you catch a *gefillte* fish to go with it.'

I looked at Mick, who was gazing fixedly with rapt attention at his float as he ate. It surprised and gratified me to see him so engrossed and obviously enjoying himself. It surprised me, and Harry even more, when Mick began to sing, to the tune of 'Dixie':

'Oh I put my finger in a woodpecker's hole
And the woodpecker said, 'well bless my soul,
Take it out, take it out, take it out, reeee-move it!'

We had not figured Mick for a coarse fellow like ourselves, but Harry joined in enthusiastically, offering a second verse:

'Oh I put my finger in a woodpecker's hole
And the woodpecker said, 'well bless my soul,
Turn it round, turn it round, turn it round, reeeee-volve it.'

At that moment it began to rain.

We had left our umbrellas in the car, thinking to travel light for this short mission. The rain made it especially difficult for Mick and myself, both being of the Buddy Holly persuasion. Peering through smeary lenses at the water ahead of us, I for one could see very little. I certainly could not see Mick's float.

'Strike, Mick!' I shouted, 'I think you might have something.'

'Strike what?' asked Mick.

'Lift your rod.'

Mick stood, tried his best to balance for a moment as his shoes failed to gain a purchase on the slippery ground then staggered backwards, where his fall was partly broken by the quarry wall - the very wet, very muddy wall. With one hand he sought to break his fall, but with the other he clung tenaciously to the rod. He looked up.

'Have I caught something?'

For a moment, through the drizzle, I could see his heavy float, bobbing along in that run-and-dip, 'I'm a little perch' fashion.

'I do believe you have. Steady now. Reel it in.'

Mick rose unsteadily onto one knee, facing the water. In this position he held the rod steady and turned the centre-pin reel slowly as I had shown him. There was a splash as the perch surfaced and sought to escape. It was a small fish, but just to be safe I reached out with the landing net.

'Let's have a look,' gasped an excited Mick, oblivious to the wet and his own discomfort. Harry came over to see and we stared at this perch as it flapped in the net. 'Must take a picture for Ray,' said Mick, 'otherwise he'll never believe me and he won't pay up.' Reaching into his plastic bag, Mick took out a battered old Kodak Brownie box camera which, judging by its age and appearance, came from the same source as his sea rod.

'Can you take it while I hold the fish?' he asked.

'Of course,' I replied, 'but leave it in the net. You don't want to risk losing it now. And those little spines on its back can give you a nasty scratch.'

With the photograph safely taken, I detached the little perch and released it. Harry had had no bites at all on worm or maggot. Fishing continued for another half-hour, but there was no more action and it began to rain harder. Harry was receiving no response at all to his urgent and repeated requests to God to 'turn it up for fuck's sake!' A decision needed to be made.

'Do you want to fish on Mick?' I asked. 'It's up to you. You've come all this way, but I don't think the weather's going to get better any time soon.'

'What do you think, Harry?' asked Mick

Harry was always ready to fish on, but this time he had a guest to consider.

'I'll carry on if you want, but like Tony says, I think the weather's buggered it. Shame. Still, you caught your fish. That's the main thing.'

We packed up the rods and slowly made our way back to the fork in the path. Here we climbed above the lake, to be greeted by the roar of scrambler bikes as they appeared out of nowhere. We just had time to step back down the path as they passed us flat out, their rear wheels throwing up mud, much of it landing on us. We cursed and swore and shook our fists at them but they had no intention of stopping, their shouts and laughter following them as they disappeared onto the road and were gone.

Rather than leave Mick in the rain on the unroofed platform at Rochford station, we drove him to the terminus at Southend. I had asked if he wanted to come back with us to get cleaned up, but he preferred to go straight home. From his plastic bag he took a soggy copy of the Racing Times to read on the journey. He shook our hands and thanked us for such a good time.

''Bye cousin, see you at work on Monday,' he said, and walked away down the platform, tired but happy.

We looked on with some dismay at the retreating figure; wet, bedraggled and caked in mud. The carriage seat would certainly take some cleaning at the other end.

Harry had the last word on the outing.

'We really shouldn't have let him go home in that state, Baws. He looks like a fucking unwashed King Edward potato!'

CHAPTER 11

Walking on Water

'Look out! Look out!
Jack Frost is about!
He's after our fingers and toes;
And, all through the night,
The gay little sprite
Is working where nobody knows.'

CECILY E. PIKE

In late autumn and into the winter, the Res came into its own, its stock of fine roach out-shining even the great fun of the summer carp. These roach were fast and alert, often taking a lightly presented, slowly descending chrysalis or single gentle as it made its way down through the coloured water. Although the autumn leaves could be a nuisance once they sank, they provided cover and camouflage while still floating on the surface.

Most of the roach were half-pounders or so, and good fighters. I already had a few in the net. But in the particular place I was fishing, the 'pump swim', (so-called after an abandoned appliance from the reservoir's fire service days) lurked a monster. Many members, Harry and myself included, had hooked it here more than once but no one had landed it. Estimates of size put it anywhere between two and three pounds, or even more.

It was cunning, this fish. Rarely was there an indication of a bite. Only when line was retrieved for re-baiting was an uncommon resistance felt, a moving weight. Now it happened to me again.

'Bloody hell!' I hissed through clenched teeth, as the rod bent over. No line was free to let me play out against the strain; I had tightened the reel tension down, thinking to deal only with the shoal roach. Frantically I tried to loosen it. Too late! For an instant I saw the huge, forked red tail as the roach surfaced, turned, detached itself from my hook and was gone, leaving a whirlpool eddy in its wake. Dejected, I put the rod in the rest and went round to where Harry was fishing. He was singing happily to himself:

> 'Little boy kneels at the foot of the stairs,
> Gazing with joy at his new pubic hairs.
> Hush, hush, clinkety-clank,
> Christopher Robin is having a...'

He broke off as I approached.

'Had any bites, Tony?'

'I just hooked that bastard roach again.'

'Did you get it?'

God, he could be infuriating. 'No, of course I didn't bloody get it. I wouldn't be round here moaning to you if I'd got it.'

'Hmmm,' said Harry, by way of noncommittal comment.

I calmed down. 'What about you?'

'Bugger all, Baws. Stacks of bites but I can't connect. Getting a bit clawry now isn't it? You carrying on?'

The morning had been bright and shown promise of good sport, despite the early frost on the ground, but now it was late afternoon and growing colder by the minute. The wan December sun was sinking and a thin film of ice began to spread on the open water of the reservoir.

'No, I think we'll pack up now. Missing that roach again ... I don't know how. Maybe we can give it another go on Boxing Day. Freddie Frobisher says they make quite an event of it over here – mince pies, mulled wine, that sort of thing.'

'Sounds a good idea. Be nice to get out for a bit over Christmas.' As we started to pack up, Harry began singing to himself again:

> 'Hush, hush, lickety-spit,
> Christopher Robin is having a ....'

It was bitterly cold as I set off to walk to Suzie's place for Christmas Day dinner with my prospective in-laws. My Mum never had made much of Christmas Day itself – in view of our Jewish heritage I suppose this was not surprising. Nonetheless, as a child in a predominantly Christian environment I was never made to feel left out and always received magnificent presents on Christmas Day morning. Mum's gifts were usually second-hand, due to her straitened circumstances, but what she did give to me always made up in bulk and quality what it might lack by way of original packaging: one year a cardboard box full of Hornby clockwork trains and track, the next a box of Bayko building pieces, another year a box of Meccano and Dinky toys. These delights did not share the fate of many toys, discarded along with the wrapping by Boxing Day, but remained with me as rewarding hobbies and playthings for many years.

This would be my third Christmas dinner with Harry and it ran true to form. Arriving at 1 o'clock I was greeted with a welcoming sherry.

'That enough for you, Baws?' an already inebriated Harry enquired, as the glass overflowed and the contents poured onto the carpet. 'Say when.' Then, turning to face the tiny, hot kitchen where his wife was slaving away over the food preparation, he addressed her, his features an unconvincing blend of piety, solemnity and insincerity.

'Do you want a hand, Bill?' He always put this question safe in the knowledge that it would be refused, since Harry never so much as boiled an egg. Neither was his redundant offer born of innate courtesy, but rather because his wife's irritated responses amused him. He was like a naughty schoolboy being rude to teacher but he would go only so far in this goading of Billie in company, ever mindful of his need to weigh in the balance the inherited and deep-rooted protocol calling for gentlemanly behaviour towards one's spouse against the wicked pleasure he derived from teasing her.

Gradually the meal was assembled. Each vegetable, sauce and garnish was carried carefully from the kitchen to the living room table in its original saucepan or baking tray, there to be transferred onto serving dishes and thence to pre-heated plates. Billie herself served everyone individually from these dishes, enquiring as she went around the table as to who wanted what and if the portions were sufficient.

This procedure could take a considerable time, interspersed as it was with Harry, fuelled with sherry and Marsala wine, continuing to goad the long-suffering cook, (who was herself virtually teetotal, limiting her intake to just one small glass of sherry each year).

'Have you plucked the pheasant, Bill?'

'Don't be such a silly arse,' Billie replied, 'we're not having pheasant.'

'I only wanted to know if we had a pheasant plucker, you know...'

Silence, except for the rattle of pots and pans.

'Bill – are we having fish?'

'What are you talking about? Of course we're not having fish!'

'Oh, I was just thinking. Are soles flat fish?'

'Harry!' snapped Billie.

Suzie and I rolled our eyes to the heavens but could not resist a giggle.

'Tony says it's freezing outside, Bill.'

'They say it's going to snow, Harry, so I'm not surprised,' came the impatient response from the kitchen.

'Would you like me to recite a poem about the Arctic then?' he offered. Without waiting for her to reply, he launched with relish into a sanitised version of 'The Ballad of Eskimo Nell', substituting a hum for words which might offend Billie's sensibilities:-

> *'When a man grows old and his hmmms grows cold*
> *And the end of his hmmm turns blue – '*

'You listening Bill?' No answer came. Harry continued.

> *'When it's bent in the middle like a one-string fiddle*
> *He can tell a tale or two.*
> *So don't look at me that way barman,*
> *I didn't hmmm on the seat.*
> *I come from the northern hemisphere*
> *And my hmmms are covered in sleet.'*

'These you have loved,' grinned Harry, turning to Suzie and me. 'Another drink you two?' he asked, filling our glasses over our muffled protests. He took down a small, decorative stein from the mantelpiece, part of a collection of Teutonic memorabilia inherited from Billie's German ancestors. This he filled to the brim with sherry. 'No point in buggering about,' he said, taking a lengthy swig. 'Cheers!'

The festive fowl was eventually ushered in, some two hours after I arrived, to be greeted by murmurs of appreciation and, in my case, a not totally stifled sigh of relief that we might soon be on the point of commencing the meal.

Thankfully Harry was denied the traditional male role of carver, although he could not resist the temptation to brandish the carving knife above the beautifully roasted capon, crying, 'Have at you Sir Percy!' before Billie persuaded him to be quiet and sit down.

When engaged in the actual business of eating, Harry was a model of decorum, although it was perhaps his state of inebriation that caused his head to wobble slowly from side to side, like a hunting heron, as he attempted to focus on the plate. He habitually wore a white handkerchief up the sleeve of his jacket, or in this case, jumper, a foppish accessory which, like a waving flag, drew attention to the almost sensual manner in which he wielded a knife and fork, raised at a just-so angle, engaging the food and persuading it to enter his mouth. He seemed to be a very slow eater and yet he always managed to clear his plate first, despite pausing frequently to reply, 'Fine, thanks Bill,' to his wife's nervous and oft-repeated questioning as to the quality and quantity of his gargantuan helping.

To bring the meal to an end, all the lights were turned off as Billie lit the heated brandy on the pudding, to the sound of 'oohs' and 'aahs' from Suzie and me, and gentle snores from Harry, who had retired to an easy chair after the main course and fallen soundly asleep.

He stayed that way until Suzie and I left at about seven to spend some time at my home. He stirred briefly as we left.

'You off, Baws? See you tomorrow then. I expect to see you catch that monster roach from the pump swim.'

But we were not to fish that Boxing Day as heavy snowfalls overnight had carpeted the land. Fierce blizzards raged for days and the snow built up in places to a depth of several feet. With the snow came freezing fog. There was no thaw in sight. The Great Freeze had begun.

For a while, people continued to drive their cars, but as fast as the snow was melted to slush by the moving traffic so it froze again, to be covered by fresh falls. Snow ploughs fought to keep major roads clear, with snow piled high onto the pavements. Within a few weeks, deep, frozen ruts became permanent hazards. The side roads were gradually ignored and became impassable. It hardly mattered because with less and less use, most car batteries died and the cars would not start in any case. Of the few that did, many succumbed to the ruts, their exhaust system pierced and broken by the solid ice.

Rosie – dear Rosie – was able to sail through this mayhem with great aplomb. She had a high wheelbase to traverse the ruts, and, most importantly, she was equipped with a starter handle. Bugger batteries! Rather than trudge through knee-deep snow on the pavement, I took Rosie out regularly for my visits to Suzie's flat without any problems. Once or twice we even drove as far as Southend to the cinema.

The car did have one or two drawbacks: there was no heater and the windscreen wipers were operated by diverted exhaust pressure, so that they practically stopped when she was moving slowly or uphill, when the engine was under strain. On the plus side, the entire windscreen could be wound up and forward by winding a chrome handle on the dashboard. By hunching slightly at the wheel, I could see clearly ahead. And, in the absence of a heater, it was the only way to see the road when the windscreen iced up. Of course, since the wind and snow could then get in, the interior of the car became bitingly cold, thus the technique was of limited application if it was actually snowing.

There had been no question of going fishing during those dark, freezing first weeks of the winter snow storms, although Harry and I often spoke about the lakes. Had they frozen over? Were the fish okay? Now, in early February, the days were still exceedingly cold but sunny, and although ice and snow lay everywhere, the evenings were noticeably drawing out. Nothing could depress the delicious feeling of approaching Spring. That meant that the fishing season would soon be over. It was time to be bold and venture forth.

Wrapped in several layers of clothing, we set off for Rochford early one fine morning. There was no point in taking too much equipment with us until we knew for certain that we could fish. A rod and reel each, landing net, tackle box and some bread was all we needed. And two Thermos flasks full of hot coffee, fortified with a shot of brandy.

It was a battle to keep the windscreen from icing up inside, and soon I had to resort to the winding handle.

'Christ, Baws,' said Harry, peering out of the slit at the bottom of the windscreen and dashboard, screwing up his eyes against the blast of cold air entering the car. 'It's like being in a fucking mobile pill box.'

By the time we reached the Res my face was rigid with the cold and my hands were locked onto the steering wheel like a buzzard's claws, despite wearing woollen gloves inside leather ones.

The steep slope up to the railway embankment was impassable, so I parked alongside the now-frozen brook outlet, by the tree-lined River Roach end of the lake. We stepped out of the car, stomped our feet on the hard ground and wrapped our arms around ourselves, slapping at our bodies to get warm. Our quickening breath condensed immediately in the freezing air.

The previous May, which now seemed a lifetime away, the club had erected a handsome wooden hut at the railway end of the reservoir and christened it 'The Bobbing Float'. Furnishings were basic: a small table and several battered chairs, a notice board, a supply of paper and a pencil to record notable catches and comments. The hut was also where the club kept the various tools for work-party days: saws, axes, spades and forks, rakes, rope and so on. Not only did this haven provide shelter from the elements but it even boasted a tapped keg of beer for the needy. For the honest, there was a tin in which to place a modest payment for ale consumed. More than once during summer night manoeuvres, overcome by fatigue and cold, Harry and I had crept into the hut, snuggled into our coats and lay down on the bare and dusty floor to catch a few hour's sleep.

'We'll go over to the hut first, Harry – see if anyone else has been here. Let's leave the rods in the car for the moment.' I took my waders from the car boot and sat in the front passenger seat, heaving and straining to remove the work boots I had worn for driving and pull the boots on over two pairs of thick socks. Harry stood by, peering around with hands on hips, his wellingtons already in place as usual. By the time I was ready, I felt as warm as toast from the physical exertion.

Taking only our flasks, we set off down the fenced path which ran between the houses to the lake. Here the snow had been compacted, but as we reached the end of the path and could see the lake clearly for the first time, we were greeted by a scene from a tinselled Christmas card. The hazy sun shone down on a frozen lake surface of pure white, broken only by withered brown reeds poking up through the ice covering the shallows. The leafless trees surrounding the lake edge stood in gaunt silhouette, their branches bedecked in crystalline snow. There was no open water and not a footprint to be seen.

We made our way down to the far end of the lake and entered The Bobbing Float. The club notice board bore a red and green wreath, wishing members 'Happy Christmas', but the daily log bore no entries beyond Christmas Eve.

'Fancy a beer?' asked Harry, glancing at the keg.

'You're joking, Harry. It's bloody freezing! The last thing I want is a beer.'

'Go on,' he urged, 'a nice pint of thin, cold, flat bitter beer. Lovely! Then sit out on the ice without a jacket or trousers. Would you? For five pounds?'

I ignored his game for a moment and concentrated instead on examining the tools at our disposal, because if we were going to fish, we would surely need to break the ice. The most useful pieces of equipment I could see were a 14lb hexagonal digging bar, a felling axe and a long-handled rake.

'Ten pounds, then?' he said, upping the ante.

I gestured to the tools stacked along the wall of the hut.

'Here, Harry. You take the axe and I'll grab the bar and rake. We'll come back for a couple of those folding chairs later, rather than *schlep* our stuff round from the car.'

He was still bidding while he stood by as I padlocked the hut.

'Twenty pounds, Baws. Go on, be a man!'

The Bobbing Float was only a matter of yards from the swims where we had caught the carp in the summer thunderstorm. Here the water was made shallow by reed beds beneath. This would be a safe place to start (if any venture onto a frozen lake could be described as 'safe'). We deposited the tools on the ground and paused to survey the scene. Time for a coffee and cigarette break.

Harry took a deep draw and exhaled the smoke slowly. 'Ever see the film 'Alexander Nevsky'?' he asked, looking pointedly at the frozen lake ahead of us.

As it happened, I had. It was one of the few foreign language films I had found entertaining, out of the dozens that Suzie had dragged me to see at her cinema club. Who could forget Eisenstein's dramatic masterpiece? The awesome sight of the medieval Teutonic knights, their emblazoned armour and shields, their fearsome, crested steel helmets, as they galloped across the frozen wastes of Russia, leaving a trail of death and destruction in their wake, only to be repulsed by the good people of Novgorod in a tumultuous final battle and sent crashing through the ice at Lake Peipus.

'I see no knights,' I replied, trying to clear my mind of the imagery, 'but keep alert, and tell me if you hear approaching hoofbeats.' I stubbed out my cigarette and screwed the top back on my flask. Then, holding one end of the five-foot digging bar in both hands, tapping and sweeping the other end ahead of me like a blind man, I gingerly advanced onto the ice.

The first few feet were the most terrifying; a void, a no-man's land between dry land and water. I fought hard to control the upheaval in my stomach and ignore a tightening feeling in my scrotum. Thankfully, the response to my tapping was a solid 'thunk', no vestige of cracking or breaking ice. Ten feet from the bank I paused and turned to address Harry.

'Come on in – the water's lovely.'

It was a scary but exhilarating feeling; to stand on the ice and be able to see both banks of the lake, from a perspective normally reserved for wildfowl. Ahead lay the island, while below our feet was a spot where in times not long past we had cast our lines and hooked good fish. I imagined it to be around four to five feet deep at the point where Harry and I now stood together. Had our combined weight caused the ice to break, we would have been in serious trouble. Waders and wellingtons full of water, no one around to hear our cries – it didn't bear thinking about. Instead I set to work, making a hole big enough to fish through.

The digging bar didn't make much impression at first, chipping away only small amounts of ice.

'Let's try with the axe, Harry.'

I swung the axe onto the small depression I had made so far. This was better. Soon I had cleared an area 18-inches square, down to a depth of a foot or so. Harry helped by raking up the broken ice and skimming it away across the lake, like a rudimentary game of curling.

Picking up the digging bar once more, I broke through the ice into open water.

'Are you really going to fish, Tony?' asked Harry, positing a rhetorical question, since he continued, without waiting for me to reply. 'Might as well, we've got nothing to lose.'

'What about our lives?' should have been my sharp, witty, ironic, paranoid response, but I said nothing. Instead, I headed back to the car to collect some equipment, so that all our efforts to clear a space to fish would not have been in vain. In the short time it took me to collect my rod and tackle and return to where Harry was waiting on the frozen lake, the hole we had made was completely covered in a thin film of ice.

I laid the rod on the ice so that only the top joint protruded over the hole. There was no point in using a float, since I was continually having to clear the ice as it formed around the sunken line. Any bite should register quite clearly at the rod tip, braced against the ice. I had to use two BB shot to ensure that the bread sank, but otherwise it was my usual free-line rig, fished Eskimo-style.

To exhort and encourage me, and the fish, Harry launched into his version of the finale of Eskimo Nell. Since Billie was not present, there was no need for the humming self-censorship he had employed on Christmas Day, (which said, the last few verses are, in truth, remarkably free from swearing or profanity):

'Oh I'm going back to the frozen North, to the land where spunk is spunk,
Not a trickling stream of lukewarm cream, but a solid, frozen chunk!
Back to the land where they understand what it means to fornicate,
Where even the dead sleep two to a bed and the corpses copulate,
They tell this tale on the Arctic trail where the nights are sixty below,
Where it's so damned cold, French letters are sold wrapped up in a ball of snow.
In the valley of death, with bated breath, it's here our song floats free,'

'Floats, we're not using floats,' I observed.

'Please don't interrupt the artiste,' said Harry solemnly, before finishing:

'As the skeletons rattle in sexual battle; their final, fucking spree!'

There was no response to my fishing efforts nor to Harry's incantation. After an hour of inactivity, the cold began to eat into our clothes and our brains. It was time to pack up.

'Give it a bit longer, Baws. Be a man!'

'Any longer and we'll both be frozen solid,' I said. 'The rod's stuck already.'

'Suddenly my float shot under!' mused Harry ironically, as I prised the rod from the ice. That immediate and joyful expression of exultation, that peak of piscatorial pleasure, was not to be voiced at Rochford on this day, nor for many months to come.

A thaw began in March, just in time to herald the closed season and the commencement of club work party details. Our priority was to clear the lake of fish carcasses, revealed in their hundreds, entombed in the ice. It was not the cold that killed them, but the lack of oxygen. Perhaps if Harry and I, and more like us, had thought to dig holes in the ice sooner...

None of the splendid carp we had caught in that summer thunderstorm survived.

CHAPTER 12

Walking on Air

'He yaf nat of that text a pulled hen,
That seith, that hunters been nat holy men,
Ne that a monk, whan he is cloisterlees,
Is likned til a fish that is waterlees.'

CHAUCER: Prologue to *The Canterbury Tales*

The scale of fish deaths at the Res during the Great Freeze led to much heated debate, recrimination and soul-searching among the club members when it emerged that not all angling venues had suffered losses of the same magnitude. A meeting was called to discuss the tragedy and what should be done.

Many members supported the theory that the huge build-up of rotting leaves, branches and twigs which had been allowed to accumulate on the bottom of the tree-lined reservoir had generated methane, which in turn had contributed to the fatal oxygen depletion as the water temperature dropped and thick ice covered the lake. There were renewed calls from some quarters for a draconian thinning of the trees. The long-running debate concerning the brook inlet, and its concomitant threat of pollution, intensified.

One thing was certain – we would have to restock. It was common knowledge locally that Greenacres was up for sale and that Ken was already running the place down. A committee member was deputed to approach him and ask what he intended to do with his fish. Someone else knew of a pond in Little Wakering 'which holds good fish' and which the farmer wanted cleared so that it could be filled in.

To allow time for the clean-up and restocking, it was suggested that we forego the legal opening day of the season on 16 June for this year; others thought we should continue to fish to the seasons as normal. I, as a reformed sinner with some previous experience, chanced my arm by proposing the heresy of actually fishing during the close season, 'in order to gauge just how many fish are still alive', but my suggestion fell on stony ground. After the usual childish squabbling, it was eventually agreed that fishing would not start again at the Res until 1st October.

Perfect. That would allow me to get married to Suzie on the 1st September as planned, enjoy our honeymoon and be back in plenty of time for opening day!

It would be hard to describe my pre-wedding bachelor celebration as a 'stag night' – more of an early evening 'Bambi'. The 'crowd' gathered at The Woodman pub in Eastwood to give me a good send-off consisted of Malcolm (the husband of one of Suzie's friends) as driver, my best friend/ best man Bernie, Harry and me.

On arrival, Harry strode straight up to the bar, patting his breast pocket as usual to signify the availability of limitless funds. I knew that this was not the case, that Billie would have given him a modest allowance for the event (as she always did) which he would grandiosely rampage through in no time if left unchecked, much to his own and our joint potential embarrassment.

'What're you having, Baws?'

'Oh, I don't know, Harry. A half?'

'A half?' he repeated scornfully. 'You're getting married tomorrow. Double Scotch please landlord. What about you Bernie – Scotch? Gin? Rum?'

Bernie was even more of a lightweight than me, but gamely ordered a Scotch and ginger ale, which Harry of course converted into a double. With a drink for Malcolm and a pint for himself, I could see Harry's allowance evaporating quite soon.

'Cheers!' said Harry, and by way of a toast, 'everything you wish yourself, boy.'

By careful stewardship, we three managed to nurse our drinks and at the same time buy another three pints for Harry. He returned unsteadily from a visit to the gents, chuckling to himself.

'What's so funny, Harry?' I asked.

'There's a bloke in there doing a bit of a wobbly goblin,' he chortled.

I was none the wiser. 'What's a wobbly goblin?'

Repeating the phrase only made Harry laugh more.

'It's,' he spluttered, between hoots of laughter, 'it's like a gobbly wobbling. You should have seen it. The bloke with him kept asking, 'Are you all right,

Bert?' 'Fine,' says Bert, starting all over again. All over his shoes, everywhere. I had to jump out the way.'

Harry and I saw this event from entirely opposite perspectives – one man's entertainment being another man's emetophobia.

Eventually Harry calmed down when he saw that his enthusiasm for third-party vomiting was falling on deaf ears. Bernie and Malcolm each bought another round of drinks, the mood mellowed and soon we were in a pleasant state of inebriation.

'I love this man,' said Bernie, putting his arm round me.

'So do I,' said Harry, not to be outdone.

Malcolm probably would have loved me as well, but had only known me for a short time.

The wedding car arrived suitably late. Suzie looked stunning in a full-length, cream satin dress, her long black hair framed by a drawn-back veil and coronet. Harry was resplendent in bowler hat and regimental tie as he helped Suzie from the wedding car. As Suzie took his arm and their faces were contrasted in the bright sunlight, there was a moment when I suspected that Harry was wearing rather more make-up than the bride.

Among the waiting crowd, Lily and Billie bore the smug expressions that proud mothers summon up at such events. Relatives and friends seemed relaxed. For myself, I have only the wedding photographs to go by. I looked like a geek.

At the synagogue door, my uncle Ben, also dapper in a bowler hat, took over from Harry to accompany Suzie down the aisle, while everyone filed in behind to take their seats. Approaching the *chuppah*, Suzie stopped and smiled and waited for me to veil her. We turned to face the Rabbi.

In that theatre of ceremony, hearts beating, we listened to and gave our responses to the Hebrew blessings.

We made our solemn vows and drank wine from silver cups.

'*L'Chayim!*'

A given ring, a glass broken underfoot.

'*Yasher Koach!*'

The first kiss as wife and husband.

'*Mazel Tov!*'

A day of joy to last the whole of our lives. We were married, 'according to the usages of the Jews'.

Our wedding feast was a modest, self-catered affair. Neither of our families had much money and various aunts from both families had busied themselves with preparations of food right up until the last minute. We had ordered the sparkling wine on a sale-or-return basis, which was the only way we could afford to do it, but this fact was assiduously ignored by Bernie, who saw the popping of corks as a way of entertaining the youngsters. I tried to ignore it, but as a good auditor I began to mentally count the pops and recalculate our dwindling rebate.

I glued my face to the window as the plane banked steeply to the left on take-off from Southend Airport at Rochford.

I was slightly disappointed that our honeymoon aircraft was not the appositely named turbo-prop 'Accountant', of which exactly one model was built, at Southend in 1957, from where it flew on its maiden voyage. Lack of commercial interest led to its retirement in 1958 and it was scrapped in 1960. (Maybe the name alone failed to inspire potential customers). Instead we were flying British United Air Ferries to Bruges via a rail-air link at Ostend.

'Try to relax,' said Suzie in a soothing voice, squeezing my arm. She knew how anxious flying made me. Normally I sat rigid in my seat, staring straight ahead. Transfixed, sedated with travel pills, I would check my watch every twenty minutes against the estimated time of landing, praying there would be no delay or diversion.

Fortunately it was a clear, windless day and the take-off was smooth. Besides, my attention was diverted and my fears temporarily allayed by the possibility of glimpsing the Res far below us. I thought I could just see water through a clump of trees – that must be it. There were other small areas of water visible as we flew over, but I could not pinpoint where they might be. I wondered if they held fish? It could be worth checking when I got back. I might be on honeymoon, but my priorities were unwavering.

We arrived hot and tired at our canal-side hotel in Bruges. Friends had warned us that in summer the smell there could be as bad as Venice. Now in the cooler weather of early autumn, there was just the faintest whiff of methane in the air. I for one found it strangely welcoming, certainly no worse than when Mick stepped into the mud at Doggetts. Suzie was rather less impressed.

Our attempts at school-level French, aided only by a pocket English/ French dictionary, made little impact on the large, dour woman with a bun who met us at reception. Having carefully checked our reservations and passports, she stomped purposefully up two flights of stairs, beckoning us to follow with our luggage.

'*Voilà!*' she announced brusquely, ushering us into a medieval-looking room with dark oak panelling. Against the walls stood one cupboard, a wash stand and two beds.

Suzie and I looked at the beds, then at each other, then at the Madame.

'*M'sieu?*' she questioned, no doubt anticipating a complaint from 'those never-satisfied English'.

Lost for words, I grabbed Suzie's hand and pointed to her wedding ring, while making what I hoped was a despairing-glance-to-the-heavens-rolling-eyes face. The centime dropped.

'*Ah, nouveau mariés. Je comprend. Un instant, s'il vous plait.*'

Briskly she moved the beds together, stripped the bedding and replaced it with double sheet and blankets from the cupboard.

'*Voilà, Madame, M'sieu,*' announced the lady whom we soon began to refer to as Madame Defarge. '*Le petit dejeuner commence à huite heure du matin. Bon chance, et bon nuit.*'

We were alone at last. But not for long.

After taking a surprisingly effective and refreshing shower in the antiquated bathroom down the corridor, we sat side by side on the beds, glowing and eager as we watched the sunset over the canal. Suzie's perfume and freshness made me dizzy and very, very aroused.

'*Ah, nouveau mariés!*' I took Suzie's hand and repeated the phrase uttered earlier by Madame Defarge, but in simpering tones, as I strove clumsily to unlock the key to early wedding-night romance. Suzie was unimpressed.

'Should we go out and have something to eat first?' she suggested, 'I'm starving.'

'Fine,' I said through clenched teeth. 'Let's do that.'

Leaving the room, we paid little attention to the strange, window-size wooden frames propped up against the wall. Painted green they were, with perforated zinc in place of glass.

'*BIER KELLER – BIER/ BIERE – MOULES FRITES*' read the sign, the umpteenth we had observed conveying a similar message, as we trekked around Bruges in search of the perfect restaurant, unable to make a decision. We were happy, but exhausted. Now I was hungry too.

'Come on, let's try this one,' I suggested, with just a hint of desperation. 'It's getting late.'

Descending the first few stairs to the basement, we were greeted by a buxom waitress with blonde plaits, holding four one-litre steins of beer, two in each hand. She paused to greet us in the act of swaying expertly around one table in order to serve people at another.

'Sit where like,' she said cheerfully, 'I be with you moment.'

We took our seats in a banquette snug. The atmosphere was convivial, bustling with conversation but mercifully without any Tyrolean 'oompah' music and from a quick peek at what others were eating, the food looked wholesome enough. When the waitress returned, swaying towards our table on her way to replenish the four empty steins in her hands, we avoided the tyranny of a mainly incomprehensible foreign menu and ordered mussels and chips.

'And for drink?'

I hastened to caution Sue, pointing my finger at the steins in the waitresses hands. 'You might have seen Harry drink sherry out of one of those at Christmas but you take it steady. Foreign beer's much stronger than we get at home.'

The visual memento of that night, captured by a local 'smudger', confirms that Suzie was oblivious to my best advice, as indeed was I. Giggling our way up the hotel stairs to our room, after an enjoyable meal and a splendid night out, we were as relaxed as a newly-wed couple could be when facing their first night together as husband and wife.

I removed my jacket and Suzie her cardigan.

'It's bloody hot in here, isn't it Sue?' I suggested, crassly hoping that my unsubtle signal would accelerate our honeymoon disrobing.

Her reply was a sort of happy grunt from where she lay, spreadeagled and grinning, flat out on the bed.

'I'll open the windows,' I offered, cleverly keeping to the same line but swiftly changing tack. Now the plan was to revive her from her comatose state as quickly as possible. Throwing the windows wide, I took an extravagant breath. 'There, that's better.'

'You would say that,' moaned Suzie, giving out an exaggerated cough as the smell from the canal entered the room, 'you're used to it.'

I lay down beside her and moved to put a consoling arm around her and kiss her, but she flapped it away, striking me on the forearm.

'Bugger!' she yelled, sitting bolt upright.

'That's not fair,' I replied, 'I only want to be friendly.'

'I've just been bitten,' she complained. 'Ouch – and again! Vicious little sods!'

'I'll turn the light off and shut the windows again,' I suggested, more in desperation than hope. 'That might help.'

It was even worse in the dark. As soon as we lay down, the drone of strafing mosquitoes filled the air. Thus we spent most of our wedding night rushing around the room and bouncing on the bed; not in the throes of passion, nor overcome by methane gas, but attempting to swat mosquitoes with rolled-up newspapers. They had arrived in droves, delighted to find some idiot who had left his windows open alongside the canal without the obligatory zinc-mesh covered, protective screens.

By dawn we were exhausted through effort and lack of sleep. Suzie suffered badly from the bites. I brought a cold, wet flannel from the bathroom to bathe and soothe her body. Soon our wedding morning turned into something magnificent, (even if Suzie did have to stop to scratch every so often).

With the window grills firmly in place, the mosquito problem in the bedroom was more or less solved. There were always one or two determined individuals who, Houdini-like, would squeeze through the smallest aperture and snuggle under the sheets until bedtime. Suzie bore the brunt of these attacks – she obviously tasted much sweeter than me.

Otherwise we spent a very pleasant week as tourists in Bruges. We did the round of galleries and museums, cafes and restaurants. We enjoyed visiting churches although trips up their bell towers were a masochistic affair. Suzie suffers from vertigo and I from claustrophobia. We would race up a tower, so that I could reach the top and get into the open air again as quickly as possible, only for Suzie to sink to the floor and cower under the parapet brickwork on seeing the view and becoming aware of how high up she was.

Then of course there were the canals to attract young lovers. Arm in arm, like us, they ambled along or sat on the wooden benches, cuddling and kissing, gazing at each other and whispering sweet nothings. Only a short walk out of the city, we found ourselves in charming country-side. The towpath, the long, lock-free pounds and the occasional passing barges reminded me of the Chelmer. Sometimes when Suzie was staring lovingly into my eyes, I returned her gaze slightly off centre, looking over her shoulder to see if any of the omnipresent fishermen lining the banks of the canal had managed to get a bite.

At one spot we came across a curious sight. It appeared to be a fishing competition for monks. Some two dozen, tonsured, brown-robed Franciscan friars lined the bank, spaced five yards apart, their long rods extending into the water. Walking carefully round behind them, we elicited only the briefest '*M'sieu 'dame,*' as they glanced at us before returning their earnest attention to their floats.

'Let's stop and watch them for a minute,' I urged Suzie, as we overtook the last monk in the line. I had never witnessed pole fishing before. Our friend Aintree's willow rod hardly counted, although he did use that without a reel and with a length of elastic secured between rod and line, just as these fishermen were doing.

The monks were using very long fibre-glass rods, which reached almost across the canal. I saw that to affix the bait, they pulled the rod inwards towards them, parallel to the water, and detached the butt section in one swift movement, so that the hook and line were swung in to hand using the top section only. Having re-baited, the butt section was reattached for the next cast.

The nearest monk to where we had stopped noticed my interest. He smiled, beckoning us to come closer.

'*Anglais?*'

'*Oui.*'

'*Vous aimez la pêche?*' he asked with a gentle smile. Without waiting for a reply, he continued. '*Peut-être vous voudriez tenir la ligne un instant? Je vais bavarder avec mes frères.*'

He nodded towards the row of monks and I gathered that he wished to talk to them. Then he indicated two small boxes on the bank just behind the rod butt.

'*Voici l'amorce,*' he said, pointing to a bait box, full of very lively maggots, '*et voici les articles,*' pointing to box two.

(Tackle? Wait till I tell Harry that I've been put in charge of a monk's tackle!)

'*Vingt minutes, maximum.*' Twenty minutes. '*Merci beaucoup. Bon chance!*'

With that he put the pole in my hands and off he trotted.

On another day I would welcome the sight of a still float on mill-pond calm water such as this, and wait expectantly to see it disappear beneath the surface, heralding the hooking of a fine fish. Now, with the responsibility of a stranger's rod, and a monk's rod at that, I hoped that nothing whatever would happen until he returned.

I looked along the line of friars. None appeared to be exactly in the Tuck mould, and I was reminded of Harry's comments one time when the fishing was slow at Prittlewell Priory. 'Those monks,' he had observed, 'they must have been thin bastards!'

Gripping the rod tightly, I stared at the static float. 'You okay for a while, Sue?'

'Oh yes,' said Suzie, in a flat tone, 'I think this is a great way to spend the last day of our honeymoon.' Then she relented. 'No, I'm fine, you just carry on.'

'He shouldn't be long,' I remarked. At that precise moment the float shot under and I felt a decisive pull at the business end of the rod.

'Christ!' I shouted. Several tonsured heads turned towards me.

'*Pardon, messieurs,*' I apologised, as I grappled with the unwieldy pole, seeking to gain control of the fish, which seemed to have some weight to it. I realised that the absence of a reel called for a deft touch, which was sadly beyond my skills. With a twist and a turn, the fish was free.

'Bugger!'

That particular English swearword was fortunately lost on the brethren. I had watched attentively when the friar had detached the rod sections in order to re-bait. Now I followed the same procedure. As the float swung in towards me, I reached for the hook. But there was no hook attached to the line. The cunning fish, which I assumed was a roach, had snapped me.

'Sod it!'

'Something wrong, love?' asked Suzie with false solicitude.

'I've lost that bloke's hook. He'll be back in a minute. I hope I've got time to put another one on.'

I opened the tackle box and rooted around among the lead shot, spare floats and obligatory chrysalis. On locating the compartment with the hooks, my heart sank. They were all spade-ended and I had no idea how to tie a spade-ended hook.

'Bollocks!'

'Another problem?' asked Suzie, as footsteps announced the monk's return.

'*Ça va?*' he enquired jovially. '*Vous avez attrapé quelque chose?*'

Time for confession. What was the French for hook? I suddenly remembered the cod-French phrase concocted by a good chum in my class at school, the carrot-headed 'Caggie' Carter. He would repeat it endlessly, it amused him so much. It was his version of the English phrase 'sling yer hook' and he translated it (incorrectly of course) thus: '*Jettez votre hameçon!*' It was worth a try.

'*Je suis désolé Monsieur.*' So far so good. '*J'ai perdu votre hameçon.*'

I dropped my shoulders to signify my guilt at the crime of losing the hook, and the possible murder of the French language. Although not of the faith, I felt that a good helping of Christian guilt might assist at this stage. It must have worked, as the good friar sought to put me immediately at my ease with some secular, not to say fruity language:

'*Pas de problème,*' chuckled the monk. '*Ils sont une espèce de salaud, les poissons d'ici!*'*

116

I was immensely relieved when the plane touched down at Rochford. Low cloud covered the Channel and the North Sea and the trip back had been quite bumpy. Having taken the precaution of a large brandy to bed down the travel pills, I was still quite woozy by the time we paid off the taxi and staggered down the Undercliff with our baggage to begin married life in our 1930s flat overlooking the sea and the railway platform.

Looking out at the yachts in the estuary, drinking tea on the balcony, I reflected on my good fortune: a beautiful wife, a lovely little flat, a great big ginger cat who had adopted us, work going well. Of course, it would not last.

★ 'The fish around here are real bastards!'

CHAPTER 13

Old Friends

'I shall be before, beside, and behind thee.
When a little bird hops, jumps, or flies before and above thee in thy travels,
that will be my Spirit.
When there is a little wind moving the leaves near to you,
when there is no wind elsewhere,
it shall be my breath making that wind.

And when sleep comes to thine eyes,
it shall be the bridge by which I shall cross
from the Land-of-the-Spirits to the Land-of-Dreams
to talk with thee.'

YVONNE ROY: *My husband Namba Roy*

Two weekends spent in the gruesome business of retrieving and burying dead fish was not exactly the start to wedded life that I had in mind but the grimmest part of the clear-up after the Great Freeze was thankfully behind us.

Now Harry and I were at the lakeside again for the final work-party before restocking could begin. The schedule this time was to prune some particularly annoying overhanging branches whose nuisance factor as a hazard to casting overhead outweighed the little benefit that they offered by way of cover.

'Anything I can do to help?' shouted Harry, shielding his eyes as he looked skywards towards me in the bright, late autumn sunshine. 'The others have gone off to fix something at the sluice.'

I stood on a thick branch, twelve feet up. I had climbed the tree with the end of a good length of rope tied around my waist and had attached a bow saw to the trailing end left on the ground.

The idea was that I would untie the rope at my waist and run it over an adjacent higher branch, to act as a static pulley, then attach the end of the rope to the branch I was to cut. After that I would hoist and untie the bow saw ready for use. Lastly I would drop the loose end of the rope back down for someone on the ground to grab, so that when I sawed through the branch, they could take the strain. The man on the ground would lower the cut branch gently down to the water, hook the slack rope with a boathook readied for the purpose and retrieve and untie the cut branch. Simple.

There was now an unexpected flaw in this otherwise ingenious plan. The only man left on the ground, in charge of the rope, was Harry.

'Right, Harry. I'm going to pull the saw up now. Just stand back and let it come.'

'There you go, Baws. I'm not touching anything.' Harry lifted both hands high in the air to show me that he was true to his word.

I detached the bow saw and dropped the free end of the rope back down to the ground across the pulley branch, having already secured the other end around the branch I was about to saw through. So far so good.

'Okay, H., I'm going to cut now. When the branch is nearly sawn through, you take the strain. It shouldn't be too heavy – you can see from there.'

'Fine, Tony, you go ahead. I've got it.'

I made an undercut and excised a two-inch wedge, then began to saw carefully through the top of the eight-inch branch where it extended out over the water.

'Don't let the rope go slack,' I called down. I could hear Harry chuckling to himself. 'What's so funny?' I asked.

'Do you know, Tony,' he said, laughing now, 'there was an Egyptian god called Munt?'

I chuckled myself at this unlikely name, although what relevance it had to the job in hand was a mystery.

'War god he was,' Harry continued, 'head shaped like a falcon.'

'I thought that Bast and Anubis were your favourites.' The cat-goddess and the jackal-god of the ancient Egyptians.

Harry, just like the Egyptians, loved and worshipped cats. He would call out 'Bast' when he saw a black cat run by. Cats of other colouration he referred to as 'fusks', (as opposed to dogs, which he called 'fuskos'). He would never explain the etymology of these odd words, but simply smiled and turned his head on one side when asked.

As to Anubis, there was certainly something of the jackal about Harry's demeanour and he was happy to promote the comparison. He of course firmly believed, and frequently averred, that cleanliness, together with the application of assorted preparations, served to extend one's lifespan. Sometimes when observing the results that Harry obtained with his own extravagant cosmetic processes, it seemed highly relevant that Anubis was, to the ancient Egyptians, the patron-god of embalmers.

'Anyway, Harry, what made you suddenly think of Egypt?'

'Oh, you know, slaves in Egypt, that sort of thing.'

'Come on, we're not exactly building the Great Pyramid of Cheops. We're just pruning a tree.'

'Still,' said Harry, 'it is manual labour.' He laughed again. 'Makes me feel a bit of a Munt!'

I began giggling again at the mention of the name, but continued to wield the saw as best I could.

'Hold on, Harry,' I shouted down, 'it's nearly through. Don't pull, just take the strain.'

My words of caution floated away on the wind, as the branch snapped and Harry gave the rope an almighty tug. I had the presence of mind to brace myself and hang on to the tree trunk as the severed branch slammed against the pulley branch and twisted around towards me. In the process, a particularly whippy and leafy growth reared up and smacked against the side of my face, deftly removing my glasses and depositing them with a plop into the lake.

This episode was still fresh in our minds two weeks later as we made our way to Greenacres Farm for the 'Great Fish Rescue'. Unable to see well enough to drive without glasses, I resorted temporarily to using the pair I wore each Sunday morning, playing football for the Jewish Youth Club.

Some time in my teens my eyesight had deteriorated rapidly, to the point where I could no longer see a rugby ball or a football clearly. From playing rugby at scrum-half for the school, I slid down the rankings and gave up the game until much later.

To solve the football problem, I acquired a National Health Service wire frame, complete with sprung side-pieces. These stayed firmly in place, regardless of physical mayhem. Fitted with unbreakable plastic lenses, they enabled me to play in my favourite position. without fear of injury.

At first, some opposition forwards were wary of attacking the ball too hard when a glasses-wearing goal-keeper came out to dive at their feet, but after one or two matches no one held back. Fine as these glasses might be for football, as a fashion statement they were before their time (though I looked more like Lenin than Lennon).

'Those glasses are very smart,' remarked Harry. 'Pity you weren't wearing them up that tree.'

What could I say? He was right, sod it. The name of that Egyptian bird-god came to mind, but I clenched my teeth and said nothing as we arrived at the farm entrance.

Little remained of the charming Greenacres where we had fished not long ago. I sensed that a part of my childhood memory had been brutally obliterated. The farmhouse had been reduced to rubble. Only the chimney stacks still stood, gaunt against the skyline, like so many blackened stumps in a mouthful of decayed teeth.

'Jesus,' said Harry, surveying the scene for the first time. 'Fuck me!'

I could not have put it better myself.

'Monte Cassino,' he muttered sombrely, 'without the flak flying around.' He stood, silent for a while, biting his lower lip, moving his head slowly from side to side in disbelief.

The sties where I had scratched the pigs' backs then stolen their apples had disappeared. During the Battle of Monte Cassino, Harry had dived for cover at the height of the shelling, when the artillery barrage came too close for comfort. He landed face-down in a pigsty on a run-down Italian farm in the foothills of Cassino, where he was captured. Before being transported to a PoW camp, he witnessed the dreadful annihilation of the monastery, and with it the appalling loss of life. At least he would no longer have those sties to remind him

The barn had gone too, the place where I had slept in the straw on that first magical but itchy night. As for the pond itself, little more than a puddle remained. Here and there, stems of rushes rose above the shallow water, white fluffy seeds contrasting against the split, velvety brown pods.

The reed beds were dying off with the onset of autumn, but there would be no rebirth for them come the following spring. Now, in place of the rhythm of natural regeneration, a sign announced the imminent arrival of 'an exclusive development of desirable executive homes'. Debris and detritus from the demolition littered the water's edge.

About a dozen club members in an assortment of vehicles had assembled by the pond for the rescue operation. They were led by a fireman from Hadleigh, who was responsible for the low water level, courtesy of a brigade

pump. Harry and I went over to chat to them and see how the work party was to be organised.

Two open-topped water bowsers, borrowed from the Corporation parks department, were hooked up to flatbed trucks. People had brought along a variety of drums, cans and buckets. Where there was no room in a car boot for large, upright water containers, (as in Rosie's case), sacks were provided to transport the larger fish .

A staking net, once used to trap eels in the creeks that criss-crossed the marshes of Leigh and Benfleet, had been retrieved from an attic somewhere, still bearing traces of fishbones, crustaceans and starfish. The idea was for a number of us to wade forward in the shallow water with the weighted net stretched between us, driving the fish ahead and corralling them into a small area where they could be caught in landing nets by the rest of the party.

Not everyone present had fished at Greenacres with rod and line, so there was a *frisson* of excitement as to what fish might appear from the now murky water. My own thoughts centred on what best to do with Harry, who had for the moment disappeared. Should I leave him to thrash about with a landing net at the far end, or should I have him alongside me holding the trawl net, where at least I could keep an eye on him? In the event, the decision was made for me as Harry reappeared, bearing aloft a landing net with a fish in it.

'Look, Tony,' he shouted, a huge grin on his face. 'It's Quasimodo!'

This loveable little crucian carp weighed about a pound-and-a-half. It had been apprehended many times, perhaps too many, which possibly accounted for its deformed mouth. That, plus a distinctive humped back, made it instantly recognisable. It was my turn to catch it one night at Greenacres when Harry, peering at its ugly face and mis-shapen body, had come up with the nickname. Now he had found it marooned in the shallows.

'I'll put him in one of the bowsers,' he said gleefully. 'We want to make sure he arrives safely. You never know, we might catch him again.'

The rescue expedition went well and very few fish were injured or left behind. Don, the fireman on the pump, slowly reduced the water level to reveal more and more fish. The smaller ones were taken first, leaving the bigger fish to be rescued one by one. Of these, the biggest was probably no more than ten pounds – Greenacres was noted more for its surroundings and sport than its specimen fish.

Harry was enjoying success in his role with a landing net, scooping up a fair number of fish. I hoped this newly-honed skill would serve us well in angling, when he would have to land only one fish at a time.

For myself, I was given custody of three larger carp. These I wrapped carefully in wet grass and sacking before placing them in Rosie's boot. Harry came over to the car and gave each fish a sympathetic pat, as though to reassure them before the journey. His face expressed obvious concern for their well-being.

'I wonder what they're thinking, Baws,' he said. 'Talk about chauffeur-driven luxury.'

There were surprisingly few losses on the rescue transport and the Greenacres fish provided a welcome boost to the reservoir's depleted stock.

A subsequent expedition was mounted to the small farm pond in Little Wakering. Here we took the fish in the orthodox manner, on rod and line. Some twenty of us lined the banks, 'shoulder to shoulder, flogging the water,' as Harry disdainfully put it, pulling out small roach and rudd in considerable numbers. These too were transported back to Rochford and released into the wide waters of the Res.

By the following Spring, when our truncated season ended, there was a renewed feeling of optimism at the club, despite the fact that the fishing between October and March had been, as Harry put it so well, 'piss-poor' This was despite the large number of fish introduced from Greenacres and Little Wakering. There had been few actual fish casualties reported, so most agreed with the club Chairman that 'they had to be given time to settle in'.

There was always work to do in the closed season. Although most of the accessible pruning had been completed, there were still many unreachable overhanging branches which continued to shed leaves, twigs and smaller branches into the water. We would have to do what we could each season to reduce the debris on the lake bottom, at least near to the banks where we fished.

Thus on a fine day in early May, a work party assembled for one such clearing operation. I had brought along a tool of my own devising. It consisted of two long-tined, metal rake heads, lashed together with fencing wire so that they presented prongs on two faces back-to-back, attached to a length of rope.

'That's a wicked looking implement,' remarked Harry, a note of covetous praise in his voice. 'Just the kind of thing Richard the Lionheart would have liked to have with him on the Crusades.'

He was obviously impressed by the potential of my unique design as a weapon of war. I was more interested in whether it would actually be effective in retrieving sunken twigs and branches.

'Stand back, H, I'm going in.'

I decided that an underarm approach was probably safest although a round-the-head twirl-and-release might attain greater distance and there certainly were precedents for that technique; the bolas of the South America gaucho, the sling-shot used by David to slay Goliath. However, the likelihood was that I, as a novice, would release the device precipitously somewhere around its 360 degree arc, allowing it to fly off and hit someone on the head instead of finding its intended trajectory towards the water.

I managed to lob the double-headed rake a fair distance on its maiden flight and I was extremely pleased with the amount of material it cleared on a single trawl. After about half an hour, we had collected an impressive haul of potential hazards from the lake floor.

Harry's job was to gather the spoil as I dragged it to the side, marshalling it into a pile on the bank where it could be left to dry before burning. Although he was wearing gloves, he carried out this task with an air of extreme disgust, picking through the blackened twigs at arms length with index finger and thumb, as though sifting the putrefying remains of a dead animal. Suddenly he gave a yell:

'Tony!' he shouted, 'come and look at this.'

'What is it Harry? Saxon treasure?'

'There,' he said, pointing to the still-dripping pile. 'Look!'

I stared in disbelief. Balanced atop a small branch, still in perfect condition, were the glasses I had lost in the lake the previous autumn.

After all their hard work, the club members deservedly looked to the coming season with eager anticipation. In our case such joy was tempered by my mother Lily's ill-health. The onset seemed sudden to us, but in fact she had been unwell for some time, only now she was unable to keep her illness a secret.

As I wheeled her down the long, eerily deserted corridors of Rochford Hospital, grasping her admission papers, I resolutely refused to acknowledge either to myself or to her that she was seriously ill, shrugging aside her frequent assertion that she 'would not make old bones'.

She still grieved for my young father whom she had loved so deeply and lost so soon. Subsequent liaisons had never assuaged that loss. Such relationships were undertaken cold-bloodedly in the main, to provide funds for my education. She endured nagging pain from a brittle spine, made worse by the years of being on her feet hour after hour as a sales assistant in this or that dress shop. Despite everything, she strove to find fun and joy and beauty in each day.

Brought up in the squalid surroundings of the East London tenements, Lily loved the countryside with a passion. She instilled this love in me and, what is more, allowed me the freedom to enjoy it to the full. Through her I discovered the wonders of fields and ponds, of newts and slow worms, grass snakes and fishes. Many times we foraged together for berries and mushrooms in fields of horses and cattle, laughing – always laughing. She had shared the best with me. We were joined at the heart.

Now it was payback time for all the effort Lily had put into my upbringing. I could do that and build a life for Suzie and me, no problem. The Yiddish word *naches*, broadly translated, means 'unbridled joy'. For a parent, *naches* is derived predominantly from one's children or grandchildren. Lily surely had *naches* to come.

Shortly before she died, Mum wrote me the briefest of shopping lists:

'A bottle of PLJ lemon juice, a box of Newberry Fruit Jellies, and a new arsehole!'

Bizarrely, the Mexican slang use of their word *naches* is apparently 'arse-cheeks'. It was a complication following ulcerative colitis that killed her, at the age of 51, on 6 June.

After the funeral and the seven mourning days (*shiva*) spent at my cousin Evelyn's house in North London, we returned home. Numbed by my mother's swift descent from vibrant life to painful death in just six weeks, it was hard to know what to do. My bosses generously gave me two weeks off. Suzie, however, worked for an international advertising agency. Unsurprisingly, their current campaign on behalf of the makers of 'Scoffalot' or 'Whoopsybix' or 'Eau de Badger – 'the fragrance for the woman you are", or whatever the product of the moment was called, meant more to them than the grieving of a junior employee. Now she had to return to work, leaving me to fill my time as best I could until she came home.

Harry had also very thoughtfully taken some holiday time to keep me company and offer support. He always had a great respect for my mother, probably founded on his admiration for her colourful use of the English language, at which she had shown herself to be his equal. We sat on the balcony drinking tea.

'Come on, Tony,' suggested Harry, 'let's go fishing. It'll take your mind off things. First day of the season tomorrow.'

For the first time that I could remember in ages, the approach of 16 June had almost been overlooked.

I could not face the particular bonhomie of opening day morning at the Res; the fried breakfast in The Bobbing Float with the usual crew, the ribbing, the good-humoured chatter. But late afternoon found Harry and me fishing those same swims where we had caught carp in a thunderstorm. It seemed like an age ago.

From my seat I could glimpse through the trees on the far bank the giant chimney of Rochford Hospital, where Lily had died less than two weeks previously. I began to wish we had chosen a more sensitive spot, or indeed a different venue. I was shaken from my dark thoughts by a cry from the next swim.

'Got 'im!' shouted Harry.

I could see his rod bend over. 'Good one?' I yelled. Without waiting for an answer I put down my own rod, picked up my landing net and hurried round to where Harry stood, his face furrowed in concentration as he battled with the fish. Gradually he recovered line until the fish surfaced about six feet from the bank.

Recognition was instant, a poignant reminder that life must go on.

'Well I'll be buggered!' spluttered Harry, 'It's bloody Quasimodo!'

CHAPTER 14

False Dawns and New Horizons

'Up over the rocks and ruts of the hills; down through the sand and mud
of the valleys; veering around corners, spurting ahead –
Pleasure, satisfaction, a feeling of security – can only come with reliance
on good axles and bearings.'

CAR ADVERTISEMENT

Numbers were drawn at 8.45am and we competitors shuffled off dutifully
to our mandated swims. At precisely 9.30 a whistle blew, the signal to
commence fishing. The water hissed and rippled as though hit by a volley
of grapeshot as, to a man and in unison, the massed ranks of eager anglers
cast in.

Neither Harry nor I had entered a fishing match before, politely avoiding
the few arranged at the Res. Competitive fishing was to us a denial of all
that we held sacred. 'Flogging the water, pulling out stacks of pissers, just to
win a bottle of cheap Scotch or a box of mouldy chocolates. Not my idea of
fun, Tony,' summed up Harry's feelings.

Many local clubs ran an annual 'Fur and Feather' match each Christmas,
a carnivore-friendly affair where the prizes might include a brace of pheasant
or an unplucked chicken and an unskinned rabbit. There was an unsavoury
link between this latter prize and our present venue, a strangely unattrac-
tive farm pond known as Purdey's, situated just off the Southend Road in
Rochford, about half a mile east of the Res. Purdey's Farm, as we were to
learn much later, provided rabbits for medical research.

The fishing rights belonged to South Essex Angling Club. Harry and
I had been persuaded by fellow members at the Res to enter this 'open'
match, much against our better judgement, solely on the basis that if we
liked the venue and the feel of things, we could apply for membership of

this second club and our applications would go through 'on the nod'.

Despite the pleasure of reacquainting ourselves with Quasimodo the Crucian Carp and the satisfaction of seeing the lake reasonably stocked once more, the familiar surroundings of the Res were temporarily tainted by their close proximity to the hospital where my mother had spent her final days. Greenacres was gone and both the Priory and Star Lane had recently been taken over by different clubs. Our immediate choices seemed limited.

There was also a problem with Rosie. She could not see in the dark due to her almost complete lack of candle-power. Our fishing torches cast better beams than Rosie's tarnished headlights. Like cosseted children, we were allowed out during daylight hours but had to be home by dark.

It was unusual to find Harry and I more than one swim apart on any of our fishing expeditions, but this being a match, the swims were allocated by lot. I found myself on one side of the pond, with Harry on the other. We peered at each other across the featureless expanse of Purdey's Pond,

Purdey's resembled Star Lane in the way the wind whipped off the water into my face. I settled on the tactic which had served me well when fishing for rudd into the wind: sinking flake and minimum shot. Almost immediately I was into a fish, a rudd indeed, of around eight ounces. Sadly it proved to be my only bite of the session.

Three hours of acute boredom followed. Match fishing did not allow for the camaraderie of the waterside which Harry and I found so enjoyable on our fishing adventures and was indeed the reason we went fishing at all. Here people did not venture far from their allotted swim and talk was kept to a minimum. Faces rigid with concentration, all fell prey to the competitive spirit, not daring to relax until the whistle blew again to announce the end of the match.

I released my solitary fish before making my way past the queue of competitors waiting to have their catches weighed and recorded. I met a grim-faced Harry coming towards me.

'Did you get anything?' I asked.

'Absolutely fuck all. Not a bite, not even a knock. Might as well have been fishing up my arse!'

I briefly visualised the painful outcome of Harry's colourful phrase, but swiftly dismissed it and pressed on.

'Did anyone near you catch anything decent then?'

'I think the bloke next to me got a tadpole or a newt,' said Harry, straight-faced. 'He seemed delighted.'

'So what do you think about trying to join the club?' I asked, as we trudged back to the car.

'Well, it's somewhere to fish,' he replied, with a distinct lack of his customary enthusiasm.

In the event, it did not remain 'somewhere to fish' for very long. Within a short time of that miserable experience of our one and only match, Purdey's Farm was redeveloped into an industrial estate. The pond was filled in.

In the immediate aftermath of Lily's death, my obsession with fishing continued unabated; if anything it increased in intensity, since fishing offered both a balm and a diversion. Harry, having suffered loss and grief in his own life, sensitively acknowledged those times when I needed to be silent, even though he had to abandon temporarily, and no doubt with some difficulty, his habitual and nagging need to know where I was and what I was thinking at any given moment. Like some lovesick swain, he would frequently call out to me at the lakeside or persist in following me around indoors, the better to check on my innermost thoughts and my minute-to-minute location. 'What are you doing, Baws?' he would ask, or 'What are you thinking, Tony?' or 'Baws, where are you?'

We racked our brains to come up with venues we had not tried before. Harry insisted that there was a good water behind the Paul Pry pub in Rayleigh, but no one we asked seemed to know exactly where it was. Several other suggestions were made by people Harry knew. None of them sounded exactly like Redmire, but then Redmire itself was just any other pond before it became famous for yielding the record Carp – the forty-four pound beauty called 'Clarissa'.

'You never know,' said Harry, as we made our way along the footpath which ran parallel to the chain-link perimeter fence of Rochford Airport. 'There might be huge fish in it.'

'It' was a pond that had been recommended to Harry by a neighbour who vaguely remembered fishing the place as a boy. For all we knew, it no longer even existed.

'About half a mile from the road, he said,' Harry continued optimistically.

But distances are deceptive and after walking alongside bramble and scrub at a stout pace for a good twenty minutes with no pond in sight, we were grateful that we had pared down the equipment to a minimum for this reconnoitring mission. We walked on, not voicing our doubts but becoming increasingly anxious. Eventually we came to a clump of small trees away to our right.

'Ah, this looks promising Harry.'

Using our rod bags as weapons to beat a path through the surrounding thicket of thorn, we looked onto a small, dark, rectangular pond, overhung with leaf-laden tree branches and seemingly impossible to fish with rod and line.

Harry was silent for a moment. We were here on his recommendation and, after all, *noblesse oblige*. 'We could try a hand line,' he suggested.

He really liked the idea of hand lines. With the introduction of a hand-line, anywhere became instantly fishable in his mind; the smallest of ponds, the most meagre of streams. I had only once fished with a hand line, when I was about ten years old and we were visiting relatives in Bristol. On a day trip to Cliftonville, from a tiny tributary of the mighty River Avon, I actually hooked a roach on a hand line intended for catching crabs at the seaside. So maybe Harry had a point.

'No. I tell you what though – we'll fish without the reels and the bottom sections. We'll just tie the line to the top, like in pole fishing. I'll do yours for you. Let me get set up first.

'Anything you say Baws.'

I broke out the tackle, tied the short lengths of line and attached the hooks. Small floats cocked with a single BB shot seemed ideal. 'This should be all right Harry,' I said, carefully passing him his rod, ' I don't think there are any monsters in here.' I did not want to be dismissive of his welcome recommendation, but I could not prevent a hint of sarcasm creeping into my voice.

Somehow Harry and I manoeuvred ourselves into position about six feet apart and cast in with our truncated rods. Bread flake, our stalwart standby, was to be the bait.

It measured barely twelve feet from one side of this tiny pond to the other. The plummet, (after allowing for the years of tree debris accumulated on the bottom), indicated a depth of about four feet. Our floats settled, but not for long.

'Yes!' exclaimed a startled Harry as he swung an equally startled roach towards his outreached hand. 'Not a bad little fish, Tone.'

My mouth was still agape with surprise when my float too shot under. Another roach, slightly bigger I thought. With much laughter we re-baited.

'Got 'im!' yelled Harry as his float disappeared again. 'This feels better.' Indeed it was – a fine roach approaching half a pound. 'You wouldn't credit it, would you, a tiny place like this? Baws? You okay?'

I sat transfixed, staring at my float as it swung slowly back and forth in mid-air, minus the hook. 'It snapped me Harry, the bastard snapped me. Four pound breaking strain and the bastard snapped me.'

Whatever the monster was, it kept its identity a secret. The bites stopped as suddenly as they had begun. Reluctantly, we packed up and made our way home, determined to give the 'The Airport Pond' as we christened it, another go - and soon.

Sadly that was not to be. Shortly after our first and only visit, this charming little pond fell victim to the building boom as had Purdey's. No one we knew could tell us what happened to the fish.

There followed a succession of keenly-anticipated outings to various locations, enthusiastically recommended by this friend or that neighbour. None was destined to change the course of angling history, to be 'the next Redmire'.

At Ballard's Gore we were advised to 'fish heavy' since the place 'held some large carp'. At the time of our visit it also held some invasive variety of weed, so dense that fishing was well-nigh impossible. There were rumours that fish were taken regularly on floating crust, cast into the few holes not covered by weed. Harry and I took one look and decided it was not worth wetting our lines, heavy or not.

Fortunately Ballard's Gore avoided the curse of the industrial estate construction boom. Instead, the pond suffered an equally depressing demise. After being drastically reduced in size, it was incorporated into a private golf course, as a hazard.

Next up was a tiny woodland pond at the top of Bread and Cheese Hill in Thundersley. This contained a single variety; stunted, hybrid fish I found impossible to identify. Small and chubby, they bore a greenish-red, patinated hue, similar to the colour of bronze disease on old metal ware. We caught about fifty of these little creatures, most no longer than three inches, before we became bored.

'They shouldn't just give prizes and records for big fish,' moaned Harry, repeating a favourite mantra as he landed yet another tiddler. 'Think of the skill it takes to catch things this size.'

No such identification problem arose at the pond in nearby Thundersley Glen, an area open to the public, since we caught not a single fish. I did however manage to identify a Labrador, a Dalmatian and a German Shepherd as their owners threw them sticks to retrieve from the water, ignoring the fact that we were fishing there.

Behind derelict greenhouses at the foot of Crown Hill in Rayleigh, former owners had built a small, concrete-sided reservoir to store and supply water when their fruit and vegetable farm was in full production.

Now it lay abandoned and neglected. Being assured by yet another well-meaning fishing contact that 'this water holds good fish' we arrived early one morning to give it a try.

Tench have a deserved reputation as being, pound for pound, one of the best still-water fighters. What I caught was definitely a tench, but a tench as seen through the wrong end of a telescope. Perfectly formed, with a wondrous green sheen and little red eyes, it was all of five inches long. Inch for inch, it certainly put up a titanic struggle. It was all we caught in five hours of fishing.

'Might as well pack up, Harry. This is a waste of time.'

'How do you think these shithouse rumours get around?' asked Harry as we packed up our things. 'Oh, you want to try 'Bollocks Farm',' he mocked. 'Old Biggins caught a monster there and he didn't even have any bait on his hook. Took seven men to land it!' He chuckled as he continued his impersonation of the universal know-it-all. 'My eight-year-old Tommy and his friends caught thirty roach in half an hour just last week from this little place up the road, and it's only about six inches deep.' He took a breath. ' I don't know,' he sighed, 'monsters be buggered. Any fish would be good.'

Our search for new waters was not proving very fruitful, but there was still one place to try; Eastwood Rise, located at the end of a long, unmade road in Eastwood, about three miles from where we were.

'We could have a quick look on the way back, Harry,' I suggested, putting Rosie into first gear and joining the main road. 'Bugger!'

'What's the matter?'

'She won't go into second.' I de-clutched and tried again, but the gearbox was jammed solid. Fearful that it might fail completely, I remained resolutely in first as we made our way slowly and painfully back up Crown Hill, with a small convoy of irritated motorists accumulating in our wake.

Motoring all the way back to Southend stuck in first gear proved to be Rosie's sad and undignified swansong. Billy Rook came one day with a pickup and crane, lifted her by the front end and towed her away. With a lump in my throat, I stupidly waved after her, hoping that perhaps she would see service with a new owner somewhere. But I never saw her around town again.

I did not expect any immediate motoring problems with Rosie's replacement. It was August Bank Holiday and Suzie and I were off to visit my Uncle Sid and Aunt Sandie in Brighton.

Sid was my late father David's brother, younger by some three years.

Older sisters, my aunts Fay and Bessie, completed the family. Surviving photographs which transcend the cheesy grin and the 'smile for the camera' poses give the impression that these four siblings were a happy and riotous bunch. Their mother, my grandmother Rachel, came from a distinguished Sephardic family in Amsterdam who could trace their Spanish-Portuguese ancestry in the city to the 17th century. Some genealogists go further, with family connections to the Zacuto family of 1265. This line continues to the illustrious 17th century Rabbi Mozes ben Mordechai Zacuto – 'the Remez'. Thus I trace my descent from illustrious rabbinical stock, a sobering thought.

I was very fond of Uncle Sid, and not only because he was my uncle. I learnt little from Sid of his relationship with my father, except he once told me, 'your Dad could be a bit of a bugger,' which I took to be a compliment. After Mum died, he and Sandie were generous with their sympathy and hospitality.

I had passed my driving test at the second attempt in a Ford Anglia, a very basic car but capable of endless modification. It had soon been latched onto by the erupting 'boy racer' crowd, who were especially numerous in Essex and particularly in Southend. But it was the innovative Mini, powered by a transverse engine and front-wheel drive, that was the most popular with the stylish youth of the swinging sixties.

My own considerations in choosing a vehicle were prosaic by comparison: what could we afford, and what was the fishing gear carrying capacity? I settled for the staid 'older brother' version of the Mini – a second-hand Morris 1100. Not fast, but spacious and solidly built. It was pure coincidence that it happened to be shiny red.

Like Harry, Uncle Sid had served in the Second World War, and like Harry, he was reluctant to talk of his wartime experiences.

There were other similarities. Both were fastidious in their appearance. Sid was so smartly turned out when he joined the RAF that he was selected as part of the honour guard outside Buckingham Palace for the coronation parade of King George VI. On the fall of Singapore, Sid had to be whisked away to safety as the spotlight fell on his possible role in intelligence operations. Both remained in the services after hostilities ended. Both Harry and Sid retained their well-trimmed, military moustaches. There was, however, one matter in which Sid was the complete opposite to Harry: he was extremely competent in all things manual.

The two men never met. It would have been interesting to see Sid's response had Harry pulled his trick of addressing him as 'Flight', (which was indeed his rank). I doubt that there would have been any of the self-preening à la Billy Rook the scrap car dealer, Fl/Sgt Retd., in Sid's case.

A love of electrics, flying and travel had encouraged Sid to join the Royal Air Force in 1936 at the age of nineteen. During war service in Coastal Command, flying Catalina and Sunderland flying boats, he had seen his share of action, one time crash-landing on the Andaman Islands in the Indian Ocean. Here he and his crew survived on a plentiful supply of fish caught with a hand line, which would have pleased Harry no end.

After the war, Sid and Sandie and their young son Michael emigrated to the newly-established State of Israel. There, leading a team of reservists on a night-manoeuvre exercise, Sid captured Mount Carmel 'from the wrong side'.

'People seeing it from the seaward, coming into Haifa, think it only has one side,' he joked, 'like a Cecil B DeMille film set – held up with scaffolding and made from plywood!'

My uncle's given name was Simon, but everyone in the family had nicknames and his was Sid. In the ironmongery and DIY shop in Brighton where he worked, he was known to all as Pete – 'after 'Simon called Peter''. He had renovated, re-plumbed and re-wired his solidly-built, terraced house in Brighton. An intriguing innovation was the speaker system he had installed throughout, balanced so that he and Sandie could listen to their favourite radio programmes without interruption no matter where they might be in the house. There were even speakers in the toilets, including the outside secondary toilet on the garden terrace.

His own car, a Vauxhall, was immaculately maintained, so when the Morris 1100 arrived in Brighton that Saturday morning, making an horrendous noise and blowing smoke, you could not have wished for a better man to solve the problem than Uncle Sid. The diagnosis was swift.

'Your exhaust's gone,' announced Uncle Sid.

While my aunt welcomed Suzie and me, my uncle disappeared, only to reappear shortly, clad in a blue boiler suit. Setting to work immediately, he parked the car with the two nearside wheels up on the pavement, placed a brick behind the rear wheel to combat the hill and then jacked it up on the road-ward side. A brief inspection underneath revealed the extent of the problem.

'Quite a hole in the silencer. Not worth patching I'm afraid, it's all rusted away. You'll need a new exhaust, or at least a new box and rear section. There's a parts shop just opened down the road. Let's go and see what they've got.'

The new shop was a petrol-head's delight, stocking every spare part and conceivable modification for Minis and Anglias. Since the 1100 series shared many of the Mini's features, that marque too was catered for in the huge display of machined black camshafts, gaskets, leather wheels, wooden gear stick knobs and chromium plated exhausts.

I was smitten, like Toad in 'The Wind in the Willows' when he sees his very first car. Glazed of eye and almost speechless with admiration and envy, he can only utter, 'Poop, poop!' That was all I too could think to say in this wonderland of motoring magic. 'Poop, poop!'

We returned from the shop with a basic baffle box and rear exhaust section. I was quite sanguine when, after much huffing and puffing, Uncle Sid announced that the new parts did not fit. I welcomed the chance to go back to Aladdin's cave.

We came away the second time with a much grander piece of equipment; a straight-through, twin-outlet, large-bore exhaust pipe, painted an attractive gold. Unfortunately, this too failed to fit when Sid offered it up for connection to the manifold.

A third visit to the shop solved the problem – a matching, copper-brazed, water-heated, cross-flow manifold. By now we were becoming quite friendly with the staff.

Our fourth and final visit was not made through mechanical necessity, but because I had fallen in love with the notion, cunningly sold to me by the eager young salesman, that the new manifold, the overall performance of the car, indeed my own life and personal happiness, would be incomplete without a chromium plated, one-and-a-half inch, Cooper carburettor and air filter.

'Right,' said Sid, stripping off his boiler suit after installing this last component. 'Let's give it a try.'

A dab on the throttle produced a mighty roar. 'Blimey,' I said, easing back and selecting first gear. The front-wheel drive and 'Hydrolastic ©' suspension kept the nose down and the cornering tight as we sped away on an exhilarating test drive, up the hill and across the top of the Downs to Devil's Dyke.

'Seems fine, Anthony,' said Sid, pleased with a job well done.

With no external signs of modification, the little 1100 was a she-wolf in sheep's clothing and I could not resist putting her through her paces. Coming through London on our way back to Southend, I excessively negotiated Trafalgar Square not once but twice, so impressed was I with her acceleration and road holding. A white-faced Suzie remained underwhelmed.

Unlike Toad, I did not immediately discard one hobby for another. 'Mandy the Modified Morris' was merely intended to be a workhorse for fishing trips. Nevertheless, she demanded jewels and finery, like many a young lady suddenly come up in the world. Her fashion magazine of choice was *Motor Sport* and I now awaited its appearance at my local newsagent almost as impatiently and eagerly as the arrival of the *Angling Times*.

CHAPTER 15

Halcyon Days

'There's cold chicken inside it,' replied the rat briefly;
'coldtonguecoldhamcoldbeefpickledgherkinsaladfrenchrollscresssandwiches
pottedmeatgingerbeerlemonadesodawater....'

KENNETH GRAHAM *The Wind in the Willows*

I was doing my best to concentrate on the twists and turns of the Maldon Road. We were on our way to Kelvedon and beyond, to fish the River Blackwater at Coggeshall.

The morning mist had cleared, heralding a fine, brisk, autumn day. Occasionally we spotted a pheasant wandering along the hedgerow. Unconcerned by approaching traffic, they would wait until the last moment before disappearing into a convenient gap in the hedge, seemingly reluctant to fly over it. As a fine cock pheasant eventually took to the air ahead of us, Harry began to reprise his song from our first outing to the Chelmer:

*'I am not the pheasant plucker, I'm the pheasant plucker's son,
And I'm only plucking pheasant till the pheasant plucker comes.'*

I could not resist joining in:

*'And while I'm plucking pheasant, out in the pleasant sun,
I think that pheasant plucking can be pleasant fucking fun!'*

Harry nodded approvingly, pleased with the increasingly confident use of bad language shown by his erstwhile *protégé*. 'The old ones are the best, Baws,' he observed, peering out of the window at the road ahead. 'Have we come to Schwantz Stores yet?'

This general store, a converted Nissen hut, was actually called 'Wantz'. It might have been the owner's name, or maybe a clumsy play on the word 'wants'. With Harry's minor adjustment in pronunciation however, it became the German slang word for 'prick'.

'Should be coming up any time soon,' I replied, as we entered a rare straight stretch of road.

'Schwantz Stores!' announced Harry delightedly, spotting the shop sign ahead. 'Means we must be near that bend.'

The bend that Harry anticipated with such glee was a merciless, ninety degree deviation in the road, not far beyond the shop. It lay in wait like an evil monster, hoping to unseat, maim or kill an unwary motorist.

The warning sign for 'Sharp Bend' and the direction chevrons on the bend itself had become overgrown long ago. There was no speed restriction on that stretch of road and 'That Bend' was upon you before you knew it.

Travelling on the scooter, we had been lucky not to have run out of road. More than once we entered this dangerous curve too fast, bike keeled over to the maximum, in the wrong gear, unable to twist the handlebars any further. Rosie, bless her, had likewise been befuddled by this road planners' aberration. Now it was the turn of Mandy Morris, my little wolf in sheep's clothing.

We entered the bend in top gear, doing 40 miles an hour. In a flurry of dubious driving tactics I dabbed the brake, changed down a gear and accelerated, relying on the front-wheel drive and 'Hydrolastic ©' (as advertised) suspension to pull us through.

Back on the straight, a totally unfazed Harry spoke. 'Do you remember the time we went to the kipper factory this way, with Aintree in the back of the old Ford?' He laughed at his own recollection. 'The look on his face when you took that bend! Old Aintree went white as a sheet, then he turned as green as the car. I thought he was going to spew.'

'Beautiful place, Danbury,' I remarked, anxious to move swiftly on from any further discussion of sickness involving Aintree. 'Shame about the fish.' On our solitary visit, the three of us had landed catches but they were miserable affairs, consisting entirely of small, hybrid fish without any fight: dull, stunted, flaccid, uninspiring little things. Harry said that they reminded him of small kippers. Thereafter he always referred to Danbury Park as 'the kipper factory'.

'We're not going past Danbury today, H. I'll be taking a right and driving through Tiptree and Kelvedon.' I much preferred this winding, country route to the flat, concrete miles of the A12 trunk road. Soon we would cross the tidal reaches of the Chelmer, wending its way to join the Blackwater estuary at Maldon.

A short distance beyond Maldon at Heybridge, the Blackwater in its turn succumbs to the siren call of the ocean and the two rivers, in one final, defiant gesture, offer parting gifts of precious fresh water before they surrender to the sea. Diverted by impressive and complex feats of engineering, they feed the arrow-straight, first pound of the Chelmer and Blackwater Navigation Canal. On high tides you can imagine the presence of a frustrated Neptune, deprived of a portion of his bounty, angrily spitting salt spray at the closed gates of the sea lock.

'Kelvedon,' repeated Harry. 'Isn't that where 'Chips' Channon's place is?'

'Chips ?' What was he on about?

'Sir Henry Channon,' explained Harry, 'Paul Channon's father. They've been MPs of Southend for years now, the Channons, one after the other. Wealthy lot. Part of the Guinness family.'

'Maybe he'll invite us in for a pint.'

'He's dead now, Chips Channon,' announced Harry. 'Anyway, he preferred cake.'

'Cake?' I queried.

'Sailor's cake,' said Harry.

'What's 'sailor's cake'?'

Harry laughed. 'The cake they give to sailors in the Navy.'

'I don't know what you're talking about Harry.' He just laughed again and began to sing:

> 'There's a boy across the river, with a bottom like a peach –
> But alas, I cannot swim....'

The patchy results from our recent fishing expeditions, to venues gleaned from acquaintants by word of mouth, (or 'shithouse rumours', as Harry preferred to call them), might have inclined less enthusiastic and robust mortals to the view that not much was to be expected of this, our first fishing trip to north-east Essex.

Rising near Saffron Walden as the River Pant, the River Blackwater between Feering and Coggeshall came highly recommended, (as is the way with the majority of shithouse rumours). What the donor of this particular SHR had failed to suggest were a) good places to park, b) a precise route to the river from the road, and c) specific places to fish along the river bank, should we manage successfully to negotiate a) and b) and eventually arrive at the waterside.

Approaching from Kelvedon, the river reassuringly remained in sight for a while since it ran parallel to the road, but then came a point where the road turned sharply left while the river turned right. We caught tantalising glimpses of water, silver in the distance where the fields fell gently away into the river valley. Frustrated, we drove for more than a mile along the winding road until we approached the outskirts of Coggeshall Hamlet.

'I'm going to turn round and go back, Harry. There was a footpath sign opposite the pub back there. It could lead down to the river.'

'Might as well,' said Harry compliantly. 'We've got nothing to lose.'

Walking briskly between ploughed field and hedgerow for more than half a mile, we flushed several more pheasant. This elicited a rousing encore of 'The Song of the Pheasant Plucker' from Harry. Finally, separated from us by tall and vicious stinging nettles, we came upon the upper Blackwater at close quarters for the first time.

Lines of willow had been planted along the river some ten yards back from the bank and a path ran beside the trees. Following the path for some distance, we came eventually to a point where previous visitors had beaten a route to the river through the shoulder-high nettles, trampling the stems underfoot as they went.

On either side of this narrow passage, the nettles posed a threat. To avoid being stung, I transferred the rod bag onto one shoulder, the duffle and food bags onto the other and held my fishing seat in the crook of my arm. Then I stuffed both hands into my jacket pockets. I advised Harry to do likewise.

'Fuck it! Vicious bloody things!' he yelled from behind me. I had obviously left my advice a bit late.

My claustrophobia grew as we pressed on, surrounded by nettles so tall that I could not see over them. I was starting to panic when, at last, we reached a clearing. The nettles gave way to tall grasses, umbellifers and willow herb. Here an area of bank had been cleared. Reeds fringed the margins.

A meander offered two adjacent swims, each with good water depth and ground cover. With relief, I put my equipment down.

'This looks fine, Harry. Let's get set up.'

I was eager to try out my new purchase, a dual-purpose device consisting of two sections of curved steel tubing with woven red-and-white plastic stretched between, fastened amidships by butterfly screws. It was fitted with wheels and when extended was a luggage transporter. But folded in half, with the racks pulled away from the frame at an angle to act as legs, this miraculous contraption transformed into a low profile, extremely comfortable fishing seat. As a bonus, I could spin the little wheels when I was bored.

The riverbank had fallen away over time and this, combined with the silt build-up on the inside of the bend, provided a small, flat shelf from where to fish. I set up the wonder chair and placed it in position, then assembled my landing net and propped it against the bank. Choosing a cork-bodied, sliding antennae float to carry plenty of shot and armed with a half loaf of bread, I gingerly descended to the waterside with my rod and rod rest and settled in my seat.

By trial and error, I fixed upon a depth where the float sat at an angle, with just half an inch showing above the water. The river was narrow enough at this point to fish the far bank, shielded from the fishes' view by a narrow outcrop of weed where it broke the surface. I baited with bread flake, cast into this channel and awaited results.

Downstream from me Harry was having problems, judging by the language.

'Come here, you snot-gobbling fuck-pig!'

'You all right Harry?'

'Yes, you just carry on, Tony. My hook's stuck in the nettles. Bastard things!'

Carry on I had to, because my float quickly disappeared. Striking firmly, I felt a solid resistance and saw a silver flash. Guiding the fish around the weed and into my waiting net, I landed my first Blackwater roach.

Several more followed in the next half hour. All were around the one pound mark, bright fish with plenty of fight. I could only think that they were bemused; enticed into taking the bait by my cunning use of still-water tactics in a flowing stream. When the shoal moved on and the bites stopped, I lifted my rod from the water and went round to check on Harry.

He at least had temporarily abandoned the decorous, seated, contemplative approach of the lakeside fisherman. Eschewing his fishing seat, he stood firmly rooted with legs apart, humming to himself as he re-baited and cast upstream, not without some skill. The float settled gently and trotted down, nicely cocked. At the end of its run he reeled in and repeated the process.

'Baws,' he said, acknowledging my presence. 'Had any luck?'

'Some nice roach. What about you?'

'Had a few knocks. Can't tell if they're bites or if the float's just catching on something.'

'Well, it looks impressive, Harry. I've just been letting the thing stay there – see what happens.'

'I tried that. Absolutely fuck all. One more go, then I'm going have some coffee.'

With this, he cast in. His float did not gently settle this time, but immediately shot beneath the water.

'Strike, Harry!'

A fish was hooked and Harry's rod bent over. Feverishly, he wound the reel handle but the slipping clutch gave line. He fiddled around the front of the spool, seeking to increase the tension. Instead he succeeded in not only

141

unwinding the locking nut, which fell to the ground, but in pulling the spool completely from its spindle.

'Fucking fixed spool reels,' he spluttered between clenched teeth, as the spool full of line cartwheeled towards the water. 'Bastard invention.'

Now it became a muscular fight between Harry's line and the mystery fish. With admirable presence of mind in the circumstances, or perhaps by accident, he grabbed the line and pressed it against the rod handle. Put under renewed strain, the fish surfaced and flapped. No roach this – an altogether more brassy affair.

'Careful, Harry, don't want to lose it now.'

Harry's face was red with excitement. Beads of perspiration stood out on his forehead. Gradually he gained ground by the simple expedient of walking backwards away from the fish, holding rod and line in a steely grip, until I managed to slip the net under a fine chub.

'Well, that's a first,' I said as we stooped to examine Harry's prize. 'We've never caught a chub before.'

We sat for a few moments saying nothing, allowing Harry to recover his composure and to bask in the unvarnished pleasure of his notable catch.

'Apparently they taste rank,' remarked Harry, breaking the silence.

'What do?'

'Chub.'

'Where did you learn that?'

'Oh it's well known,' he said with a slight air of superiority. 'You never see it on restaurant menus do you?'

I had to admit this much was true, although my experience of restaurants was hardly wide-ranging.

'I've seen a recipe for cooking chub though,' Harry continued. 'Izaak Walton mentions it in 'The Compleat Angler'. Bloody foul. Chavender – that was what they used to call chub – or cheven. Old Walton talks about cooking it in its own blood. Says it's jolly good. Good, my arse!' He was getting up a head of steam. 'Fucking idiot! Fucking dreadful!'

'We won't be eating it then?'

Harry made a noise indicating abject disgust. 'Ptha!'

'We could amend the old sailors' recipe for cooking gulls and try it on the chub,' I suggested.

'What's that, Baws?'

'Well, you put the gull into a pot with a house brick, cover with water and bring to the boil,' I explained, straight-faced, pausing for maximum effect.

'Hmmm? Go on,' urged Harry.

'Then you throw away the gull, and eat the brick!'

'Ah, 'These You Have Loved',' mused Harry, gazing to the heavens and adopting an expression of *faux* piety. I was pleased that the old joke amused him.

The fixed spool nut was soon found and the spool itself retrieved. By some miracle it had come to rest on the bank and lodged in the reeds, only inches from the water. Soon Harry's tackle was re-assembled and the reel tension set to a nicety.

With my soothing words of friendly caution (along the lines of 'Don't touch the bloody fixed spool this time!') lingering in his ears, he began once more to trot the stream. Again his float disappeared, again the rod bent over and another plump chub was guided to the net, this time without mishap and seemingly without much effort. Despite being three times the weight, these attractive chub clearly did not pull and fight as did the lighter roach just around the bend, but Harry was delighted with his catch and I in turn was pleased for him.

The chub ceased feeding as abruptly as had the roach. Warmed by the midday sun, we stretched out on the bank to eat our lunch. The water gurgled beneath our feet and the faintest movement of air through the river valley rustled the tops of the tall grasses and the stands of hemlock where they had set seed. It was easy to see how the pastoral charm of the riverbank had inspired artists and writers over the years.

But a far more prosaic component can invariably be seen to contribute to these creative observations of the aquatic idyll, namely, food. Since Suzie now kindly made my sandwiches (and I made sure to keep them close by), I was freed from the tyranny of those early, twin-pack days, whereby food intended for me had disappeared down Harry's eager gullet.

Equally, Harry's own food box was able at last to legitimately accommodate an expansive supply of produce, entirely for his own consumption. Pork pies, sausages, cured hams and large wedges of cheese now appeared on the menu provided by Billie, in addition to the basic courses of mixed sandwiches and fruit. All were laid out by Harry with a flourish upon a spotless white napkin. Delicately held between thumb and forefinger, with little finger extended, the constituent parts were raised to his mouth and slowly, deliberately masticated.

Despite this grand performance and attention to detail, Harry managed to finish his meal before I was even halfway through my far more modest repast. He must have noticed my wide-eyed and open mouthed reaction at this prodigious intake of victuals.

'This is nothing, Baws,' said Harry, dabbing at his mouth with the napkin and launching into one of his favourite rants. 'George IV – do you know what he had for breakfast just before he died? A pigeon and beef pie,

143

three bottles of fizzy wine, two glasses of port and a glass of brandy. When he went to bed that night, having scoffed his way through an enormous dinner, he rounded it off with two glasses of hot ale and toast. Hot ale! What? That must given him the shits in the morning!'

'No wonder he died young,' I observed acidly.

'That's the point,' rejoined Harry. 'Prinny was still on the throne at sixty-eight. Makes you think, Tony. All that scoff and swog, all that laudanum. Pissed as a rat most of the time, fuck-all sanitation, no real medicine, doctors were quacks. And he manages to live to nearly seventy.'

I kept to the script and posed the question I knew he was waiting to hear. 'So would you have like to have lived in those days?'

'As I've said before, it was all right in court circles,' opined Harry, 'so long as you kept your nose clean and the King found you amusing. Beau Brummell discovered that the hard way. One remark out of place – boom! Out on your ear and no way back.'

He continued in this vein as we tidied away our lunch things.

'It was the same in the Army, Tony. Well, after the war that is. When I was at the War Office, if you kept on the good side of the old man, you had an easy wicket.' Reflectively, almost to himself, he added, 'In wartime it's a different story. No easy wickets there.'

A warm and gentle afternoon brought several more fish to the net; chub for Harry and roach for me. The day drew to a close, the sky turned from blue to orange to magenta. Blackbirds sang as we made our way back across the field; rabbits were beginning their evening feed, foraging along the margins and under the hedgerows, suddenly stopping, alert, ears raised to the hooting barn owl in the distance.

'Bloody good day that,' said Harry, easing himself into the car. 'Smashing spot.' He was asleep within five minutes and did not wake until I gave him a gentle nudge outside his flat.

'Come on Harry, we're home.'

CHAPTER 16

Rare as Hens' Teeth

'Shah! Shtil! Macht nicht kein gevald,
Der rebbe geit shoyn tantzen, tantzen bald.'
'Still, quiet, do not make a noise, the rebbe will soon dance, dance'

Traditional Yiddish *shtetl* song at the procession of the Torah

Warmed by the late autumn sun, we stood contemplating the view from the edge of the field by Rivenhall lake. The day's fishing had been patchy, although Harry swore that he had missed something big. 'It must have been something decent,' he moaned. 'I had a fucking great piece of bread on there, size of a bloody golf ball.'

Such was Harry's way. Where the sophisticated angler might scale down when fishing was slow, in an attempt to outwit their quarry with a discreet hook, and tempt their discerning palettes with offerings of smaller pieces of bait, Harry took an opposite, expansive view. If a single maggot drew no response, he would try 'a great, big bunch of the bastards. No point in pissing about, Baws,' as he frequently remarked.

What had once been a single ornamental lake was now divided into two parts by a reed bed, with fishing allowed only in the smaller section. An ancient, three-span bridge carried a narrow drive across the private part of the lake where we stood. At one time the whole area had been contoured parkland, but it had been ploughed up for agricultural use during World War Two, and was now quite flat. All that remained of the old park were the trees lining the water.

On the far bank stood an imposing rectangular residence of Georgian appearance – Rivenhall Place. I could see that Harry was impressed. 'I bet they held some big balls in there,' I sniggered.

'Very funny, Baws,' he said.

I tried to imagine Harry realising his fantasy as a dancing, prancing, Regency dandy attending a grand ball. He displayed the hand and mouth refinements, and certainly possessed the stomach capacity required for the prandial part of the proceedings, that much was true. But the sartorial style of the period placed particular emphasis upon the waist, which in Harry's case, judging by the tightly knotted old school tie holding up his corduroy trousers, seemed to be absent.

As for dancing, he had only once described to me, (and that in graphic, emetophobia-inducing detail), any activity remotely Terpsichorean, and that was a far cry from the elegance of the waltz or the formality of a quadrille. The event in question took place during his army days. Following several exhausting rounds of the 'Cardinal Puff' drinking game, and already staggeringly drunk, participants were then required to circumnavigate the mess table while balancing a pint of beer on their heads and all the time slowly twirling, egged on by their fellow officers stamping and cheering.

Harry must have read my mind. 'I never had much time for dancing,' he said. 'Even when I was courting; all that jigging around and falling over your feet.' (I had witnessed this style as performed by Harry on numerous occasions, not on the dance floor but on the river bank).

'When you look at some of those Regency prints,' he said, warming to his theme, 'the ones where they're fishing, they're still all ponced up, as though they're out for a gentle stroll around town. Long frock coats, tight breeches, white cravats and shiny boots. They even kept their top hats on. Mind you, I liked the tackle – no reels, bloody good! At least they didn't have to use fucking fixed spools.'

'Then there were the dogs,' he continued. 'There's always a trotter or two, snaffling around an overflowing hamper. And bottles and bottles of swog. They were all piss-artists, even when they went fishing. Probably couldn't see the float half the time.'

'Or maybe they could see two of them,' I suggested. 'They struck at whichever one went down first.'

We sat under an alder tree, smoking our cigarettes. A flotilla of mallards appeared from under the bridge and swam cautiously towards us, hoping for a handout. Harry felt in his pockets. 'I've got nothing for you I'm afraid,' he said apologetically.

'Hold on,' I said, speaking half to Harry and half to the ducks. 'I'm bound to have a bit of old crust lurking around here somewhere.' From the bowels of my jacket I retrieved a piece of ancient crust and flicked it towards the water like a playing card. The ducks paddled furiously after it, but before they could reach their reward, two huge, humped backs broke the surface and scattered the quacking wildfowl.

'Well I'll be Mother Tucker's rubber-ducked,' I gasped. 'Did you see that Harry?

'Bloody good fish, Baws. I told you I missed something big.'

Our enthusiasm revived by this sighting, we hastily made our way back to our rods and eagerly began to fish once more. The large carp however stayed perversely in their private part of the lake.

Cousin Mick had not fished again since his visit to Doggetts, the day he had won his wager with Ray. He was always keen to hear what Harry and I had been up to on the fishing front and listened intently while I regaled him with tales of our most recent outings to the wilds of Essex at Feering and Rivenhall. When I had finished, he suggested that next time perhaps we might like to go fishing on 'his patch', the Regent's Canal between Mile End and Stepney in the East End of London.

Much as I enjoyed working with Mick and Ray, Joe and Ramon, it was time to move on and shortly I would be leaving the firm in Bishopsgate. I had already handed in my notice so Mick and I looked upon this as a farewell outing. A date was fixed for a fortnight's time – the first Saturday after the Rosh Hashanah and Yom Kippur high holy days.

Any fishing expedition filled Harry and me with excitement, and this particular venue had added zest for us both. The East End was an area where my mother and father, and my grandparents and great-grandparents before them, had settled, lived and raised their families. My father's maternal family were Sephardic Jews from Holland, while my mother's ancestors were Ashkenazim from Eastern Europe. Little love was lost at first between these two immigrant factions, the Dutch 'Khuts' and the Pale of Settlement 'Polaks'.

Since Huguenot immigrants had preceded both sets of Jews in settling the area, Harry's family too had lived there. 'The Tenterground' in the East End, such a mysterious word from my childhood memory, was an area used by Flemish weavers to dry cloth. Maybe from this came the term 'rag trade', which everyone assumes to be of Jewish origin.

Harry's grandfather, a clerk at the Public Records Office, (as was Harry, briefly), had lived in Mile End itself, in the days when the area was gentrified. To delight Harry further, there was of course the Regency connection. Mile End was substantially redeveloped in the Georgian era and the canal itself, although a commercial venture, had received the specific blessing of Harry's hero, the Prince Regent, whose name it bears. The foremost architect of the period, John Nash, planned and supervised much of the work.

'I've just been reading this old book about London angling clubs,' said Harry when I went round to tell him of Mick's invitation. 'It mentions the

147

Regent's Canal, funnily enough.'

He rooted around the small bureau which served as a bookcase.

'Yes, here it is. 'Angling Clubs and Preservation Societies of London and the Provinces'. 1883 it was first published, this is a reprint.' He began rifling through its pages.

'Listen to this, Baws. Er, oh yes, here we are. They're talking about specimen fish trophies – glass case jobs – owned by the Westbourne Park Piscatorial Society: 'A very pretty Jack of 16 pounds' – he must mean a pike – 'taken from the Regent's Canal by the late Mr Severn , in which water he recently lost his life.'

'Does that mean he died in the River Severn or the Regent's Canal?' I asked.

'Fuck knows,' said Harry, nicely rounding off our brief literary excursion.

It was agreed that we would drive up to London on the Saturday, rather than take the train. Since owning a car, I had almost forgotten what it meant to travel light. To make matters worse, I continued to add to our stock of equipment in a manner bordering on compulsion. The advertising agency where Suzie worked as a visualiser had acquired the account of Edgar Sealey, a firm of quality rod makers. Through her connection, I acquired several excellent new rods for Harry and myself. We did not really need them, but there they were; such new, shiny, desirable objects – and practically free!

I had become so used to taking this collection of tackle along on every trip, 'just in case', that I was reluctant to pare down my burden and lighten the load. Besides, the vision of Mick boarding the train at Southend, caked in mud, looking 'like an unwashed fucking King Edward potato', as Harry had so delicately described him, made me determined to avoid public transport on fishing trips wherever possible. We piled everything into the car as usual and set off to meet Mick.

'Jessel!' exclaimed Harry as we approached the Green Man roundabout at Wanstead.

What on earth did he mean? A new swearword, perhaps? Had I narrowly avoided an accident?

'I've been trying to think of the man's name since Gants Hill,' he said, leaving me none the wiser.

'And...?'

'Commander Richard Jessel. I've been reading a book about Edward VIII and Wallis Simpson.'

No wonder the shelves of our local library always seemed half-empty whenever I went there – Harry had out half their stock.

'Hold on, H. Let's get round this lot.' As we came out into Leytonstone High Road on the other side of the roundabout, he started up again.

'Anyway, this Captain Jessel...'

'I thought you said he was a Commander?'

'That was his rank, but he was captain of a destroyer at the time. He was escorting the King on a Mediterranean cruise, goes swimming one day off the side of the ship and has both his legs mangled by the propeller of the Royal bloody motorboat. Still goes on to serve in the Royal Navy and ends up a war hero. Commanded a destroyer on the Malta convoys apparently. Rescued hundreds of men from the *Ark Royal* when that sank. Then he was captured by those Vichy French fuckers and banged up in Algeria.'

'So...?'

'He was Jewish,' offered Harry, (as though passing through a *soi-disant* Jewish residential area would automatically trigger in me the synaptic connection necessary to illuminate his diverting tale).

'Well, good for him,' I muttered.

'There weren't many sea-faring Jews in the Royal Navy, Baws, that's the point. Rare as rocking-horse shit they were. Hardly surprising since they weren't allowed to hold a commission unless they converted, and that was only about a hundred years ago.'

'What about the other services?' I asked. 'My Uncle Sid was in the RAF and my Uncle Jack was in the Army. Middle East he was. I've got pictures of both of them in khaki shorts. Very smart they looked too. What about The Jewish Brigade? Didn't you have any Jews in your outfit?'

'I was in an Irish regiment,' said Harry, as though that was explanation enough.

'I've got a couple of Jewish property developer clients,' I countered. 'One of them is Irish. Max Isaiah his name is, comes from Dublin. He's Orthodox, a proper *frummer, and* a very passionate Irishman.'

'That could be confusing,' remarked Harry pensively.

'You know the Feast of Purim, the only date in the Jewish calendar when we're actually encouraged to go a bit wild and drink too much? Max told me that once, when St Patrick's Day fell on the same weekend as Purim, he was drunk as a skunk for days – on kosher wine and Guinness, apparently.'

'Strong stuff that 'Palwins',' chuckled Harry. The dark, sweet, almost sickly drink, a product of the Palestine Wine and Trading Company, had long been the staple, almost the *sine qua non* of Jewish toasts and ceremonial.

'I tell you who I do think are rare though,' I said, reverting to the main theme. 'Jewish fishermen. I've never met any in all the time we've been fishing, have you? There's probably only Mick and me.'

'And those chaps from Galilee,' he laughed.

'All right, apart from them, you silly sod.'

'That's a nice way to address your father-in-law,' said Harry, in mock complaint.

We both sank into silence, trying to think of any of our angling friends and acquaintances who bore, or could conceivably bear, any trace of a Jewish connection. Suddenly a more pressing matter came into my mind.

'Bugger!'

'Who's that, Tony?'

'Not who, what. I forgot to ask Suzie to get any sodding maggots. Oh well, we'll have to pop in to Peek's. It's not too far off our route.'

Along the Mile End Road and through Whitechapel and Aldgate we drove; past Petticoat Lane where 'Tubby' Isaacs ran his (strictly non-kosher) jellied eels stall, past Jewry Street in the East and beyond Old Jewry to the West; through the City of London, with Harry pointing out places of interest like a knowledgeable tourist guide: here an old vendor's sign, there a dark alleyway with a shady past. Occasionally we would pass the premises of one of his prestigious, weekday customers and then he would sink deeper into his seat, fearful that he might be spotted wearing *mufti*.

I pulled in to the kerb by the entrance to Chancery Lane Underground station, opposite Gray's Inn Road. A small parade of Tudor-fronted buildings housed two of my favourite shops. The first was Maynard's sweet shop, whose particular specialities were coloured marzipans, moulded into the shape of various fruits and sold loose, and delicious maple fondants containing whole Brazil nuts, to which Suzie and I were addicted.

The second shop housed a high class tobacconist. Although the owners were not ostensibly Jewish, our passage through the East End served to remind me that Jewish immigrants had been important to the tobacco trade. The factories of Godfrey Phillips, Carreras, Rothman, J Wix and Ardath sold mainly to the mass market, while the smaller firms of Abdullah and Marcovitch catered for those of more refined taste, and deeper pockets. Even Harry's present employers, J Lyons & Co, had begun life as Salmon & Gluckstein, tobacco merchants.

As a paranoid realist I hoped that, in view of increasing concerns about the adverse affects of smoking, these Jewish tobacco barons were matched in equal number by Jewish medical men, who advocated abstention from tobacco products. They might well be needed in due course to counter any accusation of some fiendish plot, some fantastic notion, of a Jewish conspiracy to compromise the nation's health.

'Fancy some fags, H?'

'I'll pay for them,' said Harry, vigorously patting his pockets.

'It's all right, it's my treat.'

Despite my irregular attire, the staff could not have been more charming.

'Hello, Sir, and how may we help you today?'

I scanned the shelves of quality merchandise; pipes, cigars, accessories, loose tobacco, cigarettes and smoking accessories. A day spent fishing on the canal really called for twenty Woodbine Tipped, but such a plebeian product was obviously beneath contempt in this august company. Besides, there was a celebratory aspect to our planned event, which called for something extra.

'Er, twenty Woodbine Export please, and twenty Three Castles.' These would provide a smoking treat worthy of the occasion. And lastly perhaps, a special treat for Harry. 'Oh, and ten Abdullah Turkish please.'

'How much do I owe you, Tony?' asked Harry as I handed over the little box of Abdullah. Just the mere thought of smoking them made me feel slightly queasy, as Harry well knew.

'No, it's my treat Harry. But don't you dare light one up until I drop you off at home.'

In Gray's Inn Road, near to where Suzie worked, was a tackle shop, proudly indicated by the ornately lettered sign above the door: 'Messrs Peek', it read, in shadowed gold leaf on glass, 'Makers of Fine Rods and Purveyors of Quality Fishing Tackle'.

Peek's also supplied bait, including maggots. I had the feeling that this was a service provided with some reluctance, simply to gain an insight into which of their potential customers was a coarse fishermen. A true gentleman would surely use a fly.

As a result, I had developed an inferiority complex about shopping there. I was particularly in awe of the manager. A small, impatient man, with slicked-down black hair, neat moustache and glasses, he always intimidated me. My heart sank each time I faced him. The way he asked 'May I help you?' clearly expressed the exact opposite wish on his part, this despite the fact that he rounded off the enquiry with a perfunctory and not too convincing 'Sir?'

But it was on the basis of geographical proximity to her place of work, rather than as a result of cowardice on my part, that the regular bait run for the weekend was frequently delegated to Suzie. Many is the time on a Friday evening that, unbeknown to her fellow commuters, she travelled from Fenchurch Street to Chalkwell carrying in her unassuming bag a container full of wriggling maggots.

Nevertheless I had become a regular customer at Peek's, which was not to say that their welcome had become any more enthusiastic. My major purchase to date was a Mark IV carp rod, a highly desirable object, hand-built by the respected firm of Davenport and Fordham. I would have thought that by this token alone they would recognise me as someone of merit. Not a bit of it: there was always the impression that they were doing you, (or 'one'), an enormous favour by serving you, (or 'one'), at all.

I parked the car outside Peek's and grabbed my shoulder bag from the boot. The street was surprisingly busy for a Saturday, compared to the almost funereal silence of the City. Gamage's Department Store around the corner was open, as was the Daily Mirror building on the corner of Fetter Lane. Sadler's Wells Theatre was nearby and the sandwich bars and cafés on the east side of Gray's Inn Road offered a welcome break from rehearsals for the directors, stage managers, lighting people and sound engineers – even for the sylph-like performers – of the ballet companies.

On the opposite side of the road stood one of the four Inns of Court, Gray's Inn itself; home to a myriad assortment of lawyers and clerks. Shadowy, sometimes cloaked figures came and went through the archways in the high-bricked walls which guarded their inner sanctum. Beyond, one could glimpse the clipped lawns and the worn, stone pathways leading to their chambers.

If any of Harry's regular customers had chanced to see him this day, it was unlikely they would have recognised him. Gone was the workaday Harry, he of the impeccable dark suit, the regimental tie, the bowler hat, the briefcase and the rolled umbrella. In his place was the fisherman Harry, he of the shabby corduroy trousers, the maroon jumper and the woolly hat. And the black wellington boots.

We strode purposefully into Peek's, only to be faced by my nemesis, the manager. Seeking to delay eye contact for as long as possible, I began looking at floats.

I could never resist the glitter of new floats. No matter how many I had, there was always room for one or two more. I examined the display boards under the manager's watchful and dismissive eye. Harry meanwhile examined the rods in their racks, but I knew that he was paying full attention to the proceedings.

Making my selection in more haste than I would have liked, I placed my new treasures on the glass counter.

'Will that be all, Sir?'

I heard the manager's weasel words and felt myself shrink but remembered that this time Harry was by my side.

'I'd like some BB shot,' I announced clearly, 'and some size 12 and 14 'Model Perfect' eyed hooks, please.'

The manager turned and reached into the drawer where such items were kept. I sensed his disdain, even with his back turned towards me.

'Will that be all, Sir?' he repeated, anxious to dispatch me from his hallowed premises. I could sense that Harry was getting riled.

'Aren't you going to call him 'Flight'? I asked, trying to double guess him.

'Flight?' hissed Harry to me, 'little shit was probably in the Pay Corps. '*Imshi*!' he said, not sufficiently *sotte voce* to evade the manager's acute hearing. '*Yalla!*'

'I beg your pardon, Sir?' The manager looked at Harry in disgust, as though he had crapped on the floor.

'Do you want me to pay, Baws?' Harry asked in a booming voice, glaring at the manager, putting down a marker.

'No, it's okay,' I assured him. Then, to the manager, 'I'd like a pint of maggots, please.'

'A pint of gentles, Sir. That'll be two pounds two and sixpence in all, if you please'.

I placed the money on the highly polished counter

'Does Sir have a container?'

I delved into my canvas fishing bag and handed him a green bait box, which had not seen the light of day since Harry and I last went fishing at Rivenhall Lake a fortnight previously. Impatiently, the manager tugged at the plastic lid. Liberated at last from their confinement, the air was suddenly filled with a huge swarm of hungry, buzzing, bluebottles. Within seconds, every counter and display case in the shop was covered with large flies. Panic rose as the manager and his staff swatted frantically and desperately at the encircling menace.

'For God's sake open the bloody door!' he screamed, red in the face and practically apoplectic with rage.

Into the lunchtime crowd of theatre workers, sandwich eaters and perambulating barristers, was ushered the largest swarm of bluebottles ever witnessed along the Gray's Inn Road. People flapped their hands at them, wrinkling up their noses in horror and shouting, as if that would make them go away. Many ducked in a vain attempt to avoid contact with the flying menace, bumping into one another in the process.

In the ensuing confusion, Harry and I made a swift getaway, almost beside ourselves with laughter. Missing the first right turn in our haste, we cruised contentedly past Sadler's Wells and right up to the Angel, before heading back along City Road and on into the East End. Every so often we were forced to stop in order to evict yet another stowaway bluebottle.

'Funny old life, a fly,' remarked Harry.

'Bluebottles, actually.'

'Born a maggot on some bait farm in Kent,' continued Harry, 'up to Peek's, down to Leigh, out to Rivenhall, turn into a chrysalis and wind up at Peek's again.'

'And now,' I added as we approached Stepney and I stopped to release what I hoped would be the very last one, 'maybe down to a ship at Limehouse dock, heading for Lord-knows-where. Still, I suppose that's better than ending up on a hook.'

'*Sic transit gloria mundi*,' intoned Harry piously, shaking his head slowly from side to side.

'I don't know why Gloria only feels sick on a Monday, Harry. Those vans make me feel ill any day of the week.'

Mick met us at his front door, rod and bag in hand and a broad grin on his face. His mother Betty hovered behind him, twisting her wedding ring, smiling nervously at these two unknown, scruffy men at her door.

At my prompting, Mick had already alerted his mother to the urgent necessity of separately packaging and labelling his sandwiches, in order to dissuade Harry from wolfing his way through everything. 'A bit of a *khazer* is he?' she had asked – a greedy gobbler rather than a pig, (for which was reserved the cruder, Germanic term *schwein*).

Betty's generosity had been further stretched to the limit when Mick asked if she could also perhaps buy us an uncut loaf, to be used for bait.

'I should buy you good bread, so that you can feed it to fish?' was her first comment. Later she reconsidered.

'Maybe you can catch a carp, *efshe*?' she had suggested. 'I could make some really good *gefillte* fish.'

Now she stood looking at us, trying to match the image of Harry in her mind with the reality before her. What was she to make of this man, with his maroon jumper and brown corduroy trousers held up with an old tie? And his woolly hat with a feather? And wellington boots, *noch*. This man was a *schloch* as well as a *khazer*!

Our mumbled 'hellos' were interrupted by Mick. He was as anxious to start fishing as were we. He encouraged us with a Yiddish tongue-twister:

'*Kimt shoyn Shimon, der sin shaynt shoyn!* – 'make haste Simon, the sun is already high!'

In an area devastated by German wartime bombing, few old buildings remained along the canal itself. The towpath ran at the foot of Mick's block, separated from the small grassed patch in front of the flats by iron railings. Here we assembled our rods, observed by a small gathering of boys. Later, no doubt, would come the usual annoying enquiry – 'Have you caught anything yet, Mister?' – but for now they were quiet and good humoured.

The canal was rarely used for boating. With the lock gates shut at both ends of the pound, there was little flow to the murky water. We settled in to three swims some ten yards apart on the concrete towpath in a rare clear stretch between discarded bicycles and partly-submerged mattresses.

I helped Mick and Harry set up and distributed the Peek's maggots between Harry and myself. Mick, who was still squeamish about maggots, decided that he would stick to bread flake, 'thanks all the same'.

'Go on Mick, be a man,' teased Harry good-naturedly. 'I'll put some on for you,' adding, 'you're not meant to do any work on *shobbas*.'

Mick looked away as three lively maggots were impaled on his hook.

Harry could not contain a guffaw at the recollection of our visit to Peek's. 'Those fucking flies, Baws,' he laughed, 'I never saw so many in my life, even in the desert.'

'What's that?' asked Mick.

'*Shtum*! Harry,' I snapped, urging him to be quiet lest Mick was put off maggots for life.

'Oh, never mind, Mick,' replied Harry. 'You cast in and I'll throw some more around to encourage them.'

Encourage them it certainly did since the float sailed away almost instantly, the fish practically hooking itself as an open-mouthed Mick lifted his rod skywards. I shuffled round to his swim and without too much ado, slid the landing net under a smart little roach.

'Got him!' I heard Harry exclaim. He too had a fish; another roach, slightly bigger than Mick's. Having landed it, Harry went over to help Mick re-bait.

Then it was my turn, a bream this time, on bread. Perhaps the fish here were so hungry and lacking in natural food that the absence of any cover and the noise we were making as we moved between the swims were totally irrelevant. Whatever the reason, in that most uninspiring of settings, we three had a brisk afternoon catching roach, bream and perch, with scarcely a break in the activity.

But as the light faded and a mist began to swirl across the water, the bites ceased and it grew quite cold.

'Mum's made us some tea before you go,' offered Mick. It sounded an excellent idea.

As we began to stow the equipment in the car, three men in the black suits and coats, white shirts and large-brimmed hats of the devout, Chassidic Jews, came towards us. The Sabbath was coming to an end and they were returning home for their evening meal, after praying in the synagogue for much of the day.

'Careful – *frummers* approaching,' said Mick, jokingly.

Harry, in distinctly informal attire by contrast, but always on his best behaviour, turned to greet them. '*Shalom*,' he said, 'good *shobbas*.'

'And good *shabat* to you, friend,' said one. They looked at our rods disappearing into the car, and a second one spoke. 'Did you catch anything, Mister?'

Smelling strongly of fish and maggots, we rode the lift to Mick's flat. It took a while for the look of disgust to evaporate from his mum's face as she ushered us into the bathroom. Grinning and laughing, we cleaned ourselves up as best we could. I was proud of Harry for the extreme self-control he showed in settling for, what was to him, a most rudimentary form of washing and self-cleansing. Nevertheless, he grasped eagerly at Mick's offer of a new grooming preparation, 'Brut' cologne by Fabergé, which he gratefully splashed onto all exposed parts of his body.

A splendid spread awaited us: cold fried fish, chopped fish balls, *matzo* balls, pickled herring, pickled cucumber (both new green and *haimishah*), *chrain*, (strong beetroot and horseradish sauce), *gefillte* fish, (both boiled and fried), salt beef and chopped liver. There was a plaited *khale*, bread for the Sabbath, as well as brown bread with caraway seed.

'*Ess, gesunthayt,*' said Mick's mum. ('Eat! Good health!')

The pronunciation of this common phrase sounds like 'S goes into (h) eight.' Mick and I chirruped the juvenile response in unison 'and two goes into four!', a folk-memory from when we children tried to make sense of the garble of Yiddish and Cockney spoken all around us.

All the while, Mick's father sat in an armchair by the electric fire, smoking, saying nothing. 'Dad's done something to his chest – thinks he might have cracked a rib,' explained Mick, offering no real explanation at all for the lung cancer that would kill his Dad within six months. 'He's seeing the doctor Monday.'

'Would you boys like some wine, to finish the meal?' asked Mick's mum.

A bottle of Palwin's was produced.

'Be careful not to get too *shikker,*' she cautioned.

'*L'chaim,*' rang the toast – 'to life!'

CHAPTER 17

One of the Hazards of Angling

'With Bill Brewer, Jan Stewer
Peter Gurney, Peter Day
Daniel Whiddon, Harry Hawk,
Old Uncle Tom Cobleigh and all,
Old Uncle Tom Cobleigh and all.'

TRADITIONAL *Widdicombe Fair*

For the umpteenth time at the AGM, Jenkins the Pharmacist rose to his feet.

'On a point of order, Mr Chairman,' he whinged, waving his copy of the agenda.

A low, dismissive groan arose from the audience, followed by mutterings and muted suggestions and the sound of shuffling of feet, as Jenkins droned on and on about some minor point in his thin, whining voice.

'Sit down, Jenkins,' pleaded one anonymous voice from the back of the room, louder and clearer than the rest, 'or we'll be here all bloody night!'

I sat with my fellow club officers at a long table facing the rank-and-file, (whose number included Harry in the front row, grinning at me in an unsettling manner). As Treasurer I did not have much to do except collect subscriptions on the night and illuminate the odd query on the accounts when my time came to speak. This followed the same pattern year after year: what was included in sundry expenses, why was the printing, postage and stationery item so high and how could we generate more income without raising the fees?

The elephant in the room was the decision by the local council to build a by-pass, which would cut across one corner of the Res. There had been no question of the club mounting an effective fight against the proposal since the majority of residents were in favour of it, and the club merely rented the

158

water from the council. The best that could be hoped for was that when the time came, damage would be minimal and as many fish as possible would be saved.

Having discharged my duties and been re-elected (despite arriving with every intention never to stand for office again), I joined Harry downstairs at the public bar of The Horse and Groom.

'Did you get a chance to speak to old dog-face about the swamp by the Bobbing Float?' he asked, pushing a half pint of beer towards me. 'It'll be a bugger when that road comes through.'

I knew what he meant. Occasionally, when the inlet sluice at the Res was left open in heavy rain, the outlet into the River Roach could not drain water away quickly enough to prevent a rise in level over the reservoir as a whole. At such times the shallow corner by the club hut became water-logged. If you were fishing on the wrong side you either waded through the knee-high water, or were forced to trudge all the way round the lake.

'Yes, I had a word.'

'What did he say?'

'He said, and I quote: 'That is one of the hazards of angling, Mr Baws.' Very proper he is – never calls me Tony.'

'Proper old sod you mean,' remarked Harry somewhat uncharitably. 'I don't suppose he cares one way or the other. You never see him fish.'

It was true. Neither the chairman nor the secretary here, nor the respective officers of the other local club where I was treasurer, ever actually went fishing. While they often threatened to do so (particularly when expounding some controversial schemes which they averred would be in the interest of members), they were never witnessed putting line to water.

Like trade union members, the fishing club rank-and-file were grateful that the burden of negotiation, paperwork and fighting their corner was regularly taken on by others. They were happy enough to constantly re-elect the same people to these unpaid and, it must be said, often unrewarding and frustrating posts. Pareto's Principle – the so-called 80/20 rule – also applied to work parties. In my brief experience, the same faces turned up time after time.

But also like trade unions, the positions of power were open to abuse: political contrivance, incompetence, suppression of truth and sheer despotism. All could be seen at work in these microcosms of society. Harry had concocted a Spoonerism for one such errant officer at another club:

'What's the difference between Alf Nugent, and North Sea fish migrating to the Riviera?' he asked.

'Go on – I don't know.'

'One's a sunning cod, and the other's a ...'

159

I tutted. They were getting worse. Harry looked at me almost apologetically.

'Still,' I said, pressing on, 'I have been put in charge of work parties, and I'll bloody do something about that swamp one day. One of the hazards of angling, my arse!'

'Well that's certainly true,' noted Harry. 'Fancy another beer, boy?' he asked, patting his pocket. 'My round.'

It was not that long since that we had trouble finding somewhere to fish; now we were spoilt for choice. The angling clubs of Chelmsford, Kelvedon and Billericay all offered open membership and gave excellent value, with access to rivers, lakes, ponds and pits over a wide area of Essex. But night fishing remained our passion, and for that we stuck to places nearer home.

The by-pass publicity spurred the local clubs into action. While the debate about Doggetts dragged on endlessly, a lake in Hadleigh had become available. Known to locals as 'The Blue Lagoon', it had been neglected for years. Being on Salvation Army property, stewardship was in the hands of their farm manager. As the incumbent of that post changed frequently, likewise did their plans for the water. For now they were happy for the club to rent it on a yearly basis. We could do what we liked within reason to make the place fishable, using whatever materials we found on site.

I had mixed feelings. On the one hand I had been born in the Salvation Army Mother's Home in Clapton and so from my very nativity I had an affinity for that movement as a whole, strengthened by the fellowship and friendship shown by members of the Hadleigh Citadel towards our family, especially to my father. It would be an appropriate way to show my respect by working on their land, to our mutual advantage.

On the other hand the site held painful memories. When I was aged ten and living in nearby Benfleet, an older friend had lost his life doing casual work there. The brickworks had recently ceased operation and only a skeleton staff remained, to clear the fuel dump and store room and to salvage some of the equipment. On a lunch break, the newspaper he was reading had blown into the water and my friend 'Mump' Jarvis, at sixteen the oldest of three brothers, and the family breadwinner, had reached for it, overbalanced and fallen into the deep water unobserved. Some said that he had a heart attack, others that he was unable to get a grip on the steep, wet clay sides, and drowned.

A survey one Sunday morning quickly revealed the work ahead of us necessary to make the place fishable. The few accessible areas of water were solid with weed. Thick vegetation and trees grew up in the middle of such paths as there were and out from the sheer quarry walls themselves, frustrating any attempt to make a circuit of the lake. To do so while carrying fishing equipment would be impossible. The areas we had been able to reach, apart from the deep pool where the unfortunate Mump had tragically drowned, were depressingly shallow and dredging was not a viable option.

My plan of action was firstly to indicate the presence of the club, to ensure that the benefit of any work done by the club would be reserved for members only. The next was to organise sufficient labour to clear a path the entire way round the lake and to build secure swims far enough out to be able to cast into deeper water.

Up until now I had worked only in public practice, although I had been an auditor and prepared the accounts for a wide range of concerns. To gain some commercial and industrial experience at first hand before branching out on my own, I became financial assistant to the Company Secretary of a quoted public company making machine tools. When the travelling became too much, I settled closer to home as the financial accountant with a small firm of metal engineers not far from Hadleigh.

I suppose I ranked as middle management. Above me were the board of directors, being the two owners, (both ex-public school), the company secretary (who was also the financial director) and the sales director (who had previously sold aeroplanes). On the same level as myself were a legal assistant and a work study engineer, a time and motion enthusiast.

Various administration staff were ostensibly below me, but I immediately fell foul of the payroll manager, a mid-thirties, flame-haired harridan who ruled her department with a rod of iron and woe betide any who stepped in her way. I observed that she was very cosy with one of the directors. My comparative innocence of office politics after leading a relaxed and sheltered life in public practice saw us soon at loggerheads.

The company's costing strategy was based on a report by a prestigious firm of management consultants, commissioned some years previously at huge expense. It did not take long for me to identify why profitability fell far short of expectations. While it was no doubt a splendid report at the time, the directors had failed to update it regularly, and to recognise that its critical assumptions and calculations no longer applied. The firm was incurring a loss on every item it manufactured.

The director/owners did not take my announcement of this state of affairs too kindly. They called me a 'black crow', a harbinger of doom, and were happy to shoot the messenger. They angrily referred me to the Duke of Wellington, the Battle of Waterloo and the playing fields of Eton. The context was totally lost on me. Since I had blotted my copybook early on by parking in a space reserved for directors and also by innocently using the 'directors only' toilet, I sensed that my time there was limited.

The shop floor, by comparison, was an oasis of calm. My occasional white-coated forays into the land of the manual workers were usually to observe physical checks on stock and work-in-progress, either alone or in the company of the firm's auditors. Sometimes, to escape my job's tedium, I would accompany Derek, the work study engineer, as he visited each machine and process on some arcane measurement and timing expedition. He was the closest I had to a friend in that miserable company.

Although Derek thought I was odd, and my addiction to fishing particularly so, we did share an enthusiasm for tinkering with cars. His great passion was fuel economy and he drove by reference to a vacuum gauge installed on his dashboard, rather than by checking the speedometer or rev. counter. When I told him of my plans for the lake at Hadleigh, he insisted that I make the signs myself in the factory one lunchtime, using off-cuts of sheet aluminium for the signs themselves and chicken-wire mesh to protect them.

Kitted out for the task by Derek, in the brown coat reserved for manual staff, I nervously accompanied him onto the empty shop floor. Donning industrial gloves, and under his watchful eye, I fed a large sheet of uncut aluminium into the foot-operated guillotine. The protective gate descended as I pressed the foot pedal, but in my nervousness I did not apply sufficient downward thrust. As a result, the blade scored the metal but failed to sever it.

The sheet began to oscillate and give off a loud noise, like an Australian wobble board. This disturbance attracted the attention of the storekeeper and a small crowd of factory workers, who, sandwiches in hand, gathered round to watch this twit from upstairs make a pratt of himself. Amid smirks and giggles from the assembled workers, and after several attempts, I succeeded in cutting the sheet into six pieces measuring roughly fifteen inches by ten. Worse was to follow.

Shaking and sweating from my public performance on the guillotine, I was led to the pillar-drill, bearing my precious cargo. Here I was to sink screw holes in the aluminium sheets; one hole in each corner and one in the centre of each side.

My folly with the first piece was that, instead of holding it firmly in place by an edge, I merely pressed down on its surface with my gloved hand. As the drill bit contacted the unsecured metal, the aluminium sheet spun round. It was only the gloves that prevented me being injured by the fast revolving, razor-sharp edges.

I eventually drilled all 48 holes. The crowd followed me back to the guillotine, where I managed to cut the requisite wire mesh without further mishap. To an ironic round of applause, I trudged off with my spoils. I could sense Derek behind me half-turning to the work force and rolling his eyes, to indicate his solidarity with them and his despair with me.

A small group assembled at the gated entrance to The Blue Lagoon on Saint Crispin's Day in October. Here were the Barrett's, father and son, Freddie Frobisher, Dusty Miller, Don the fireman (who had helped with the pumping operation at Greenacres and had the strength of two men), 'Jack' Russell, 'Slapper' Collins (bald as a coot), Aintree Forbes, Harry and me. 'We few, we happy few.'

Suzie had made a handsome job of painting and lettering the signs. In no time we had removed the encroaching bramble from the five-bar gate at the entrance and proudly affixed to it the first of the notices announcing these club waters as 'Strictly Private – no day tickets'. We would affix the others as we made our way round.

Beyond the gate was a brick building, its large doors wedged open and, like the front gate, overgrown with nettle and bramble. I peered cautiously inside. At the far end was a mezzanine hay loft, still containing a few bales. The roof had collapsed in places, scattering red tiles onto the dust floor. A few rolls of fencing wire were propped up against the wall.

Otherwise the place was empty, apart from an ancient piece of wooden farm equipment, about twenty feet long and probably used to lift and lower bales to and from the loft. One end was supported by a pair of rusted iron wheels. The other housed a geared crank handle and a roller to wind a rope, both jammed solid. It might take some work but I saw before me a partial solution to our lack of swims.

Harry joined me as I was making a fuller examination of the hay conveyor. He looked at it with apprehension, reading my mind. 'You're not seriously thinking of moving that thing, are you, Baws?'

The other work party stalwarts gathered round, to hear details of Tony's latest hare-brained scheme.

'What we're going to do,' I told them confidently, pointing to the conveyor, 'is to move this thing down to the water and use it as a jetty, so that we can cast out to where it's deeper.'

'How are going to do that?' asked Freddie. 'The place is totally overgrown.'

'We'll just have to cut our way through, and see how we go,' I answered. It was hardly the rousing speech that Shakespeare's Henry V had used when addressing his troops on this day, but there were no complaints.

Armed with machetes, axes, and bow saws, we began clearing a path to the water, sufficiently wide to take the old conveyor in due course. Where we encountered trees of a manageable size, we decided on the spot whether to by-pass them and leave them as cover or to fell, trim and stack them, for use in the future to construct swims. Some of the thinner birches had keeled over naturally and needed moving out of the way. It was hard work and by the time we stopped for a coffee break some two hours later, we had advanced maybe twenty yards.

'What are we going to do if we can't get those conveyor wheels to work?' asked Barrett Junior.

'We could make rollers out of those birch stems,' I suggested ambitiously, 'and manoeuvre it along with ropes, like one of the uprights at Stonehenge.'

'Why stop at Stonehenge?' teased Harry. 'The Great Pyramid at Giza, that's what you should be aiming for. No point in pissing about, Baws!'

Everyone laughed.

'It'll be like that bloody film, 'The Ten Commandments',' joked Don. 'Anyone see it?' It seemed that everyone had.

'Who's going to play Charlton Heston, then?' asked Freddie.

Barrett Senior nodded in the direction of his good friend, the woolly-hatted Slapper Collins. 'Well,' he said, 'at least we know who's going to be Yul Brynner!'

By the end of November, working every weekend, we had cleared a path half way round the lake. Here we were forced to halt by a water-filled gulley ten feet across. This trench formed one side of a promontory guarding the deep pool – the Blue Lagoon itself. It was time to move the conveyor into position.

The wheels still worked, as far as we could judge from rocking the machine back and forth. They could no doubt be persuaded to turn, with a liberal application of oil. The seized crank handle and rusted gearing however would not budge. This latter problem was soon solved by Don. From the boot of his car he produced a fourteen-pound sledgehammer, which he wielded as though it weighed no more than a golf club. He cautioned us to stand clear as he set to work demolishing the gears.

Harry, meanwhile, leaned against the outside wall, smoking a cigarette, looking thoughtful. He may not have been to the fore in all the physical effort, but he had played his part; clearing scrub, retrieving fallen branches from the water or lending a hand on a rope.

'A penny for them, Harry.'

He looked down at the front of his muddied greatcoat, then lifted up each arm in turn and examined the sleeves, noting the places where thorn and thicket had left their mark. 'I don't know, Tone. Being on a farm I suppose, seeing that old machine being broken up, got me thinking.' He took a puff of his cigarette and exhaled loudly. 'I've been fucking lucky – lots of blokes weren't.'

I remembered that he had been captured on a farm and he had vaguely mentioned something about working on a farm as a prisoner-of-war, but now I was taken by surprise and a bit embarrassed. I thought of the few things he had let slip about his time on active service; posted to North Africa, landing in Italy, captured in the fierce fighting at Monte Cassino and transported eventually to a camp in Southern Germany. 'You did your bit, Harry,' I said, lowering my voice. 'Anyone who served in that war did, as far as I'm concerned. Think where me and my family could be by now. You know I'll always be grateful. You know that.'

Don continued to smash away at the iron gears in the background. Harry stubbed out his cigarette and we rejoined the others.

CHAPTER 18

Boot-laces and Horse-shoes

'Hush children, what's that sound?
Everybody look what's goin' down.'

STEPHEN STILLS *For What it's Worth*

The world of retail marketing was changing rapidly and Harry knew it.

'I just do it all myself now, Tony. Go in, check the shelves, see what's needed, make a list and bugger off. No need to sell anymore. Just fill in the form and the stuff gets despatched.'

To me, who disliked the notion of being a salesman, this seemed like a positive move, but it depressed Harry enormously. His whole working persona was built around the role of the salesman as actor – happy in the spotlight, dressed for the part and delivering his well-rehearsed lines. As the company realigned existing staff to accommodate their changing corporate needs, so offers of promotion for Harry came and went.

'Billie wouldn't put up with it. They've offered me the manager's job in Bath. Nice place to live, more money, but she won't go. She's not really a businessman's wife,' he remarked sadly.

It was not my place to interfere. Besides, what could I say? Theirs was a strange relationship, at least it appeared so to me. Maybe in the early days their lives had been one mad whirl of romance, excitement and adventure. By the time I met them they did very little together. No visits to the cinema, no theatre outings, no dinners with friends. No holidays. Christmas seemed to be their only break from routine. Harry worked and brought in the money and Billie did the domestic chores, paid the bills and provided Harry with pocket money. That was it. They accepted the apparent limitations of their lives, what some describe as English reservation or the English way, and others as quiet desperation.

Then again, what the hell did I know? Harry had enlisted in the army in the same month and year I was born. He had been a prisoner-of-war by the time he was in his late twenties – not much older than I was right now. As a couple, Billie and Harry seemed to behave no differently to the majority of people of their age at the time. Perhaps the solidity and comfort of domestic routine was really all that mattered to them after the deprivations, the dangers and the desolation of wartime.

My former boss at Bishopsgate had called to say that his son had become manager of a band called The Pretty Things and asked if I could do some accountancy work for him. I loved music and it seemed too good a chance to miss. The engineering firm and I had at any rate reached the parting of the ways.

There would be some holiday pay to come and so before starting the new venture, and in an attempt to head off Harry's increasingly depressed mood, I arranged a fishing holiday. I bought the *Angling Times* and found in the holiday section a guest house offering 'good fishing' on the River Avon. As well as Harry, Suzie and me, we invited Aintree, who insisted on making his own way down on his Honda motorbike, while the three of us roared off in Mandy the Morris, road-hog style.

The white-painted guest house had at one time been a working mill, although there was little visible sign of that now. The water wheel at the back had been removed, as had the sluice, and over time the disused backwater had spread out into a wide, shallow run, overhung by tall trees. (Harry was later to refer to this stretch as 'Nutters' Reach'). A large conservatory had been added at the front to serve as both lounge and dining area. From this, one looked out onto a formal lawn running down to the river where the water flowed over a diagonal weir, a lasting reminder of the working mill heritage.

On our arrival the owner, a self-confident, handsome, blond fellow called Graham, bounded forward eagerly to open the car door for Suzie, giving her an alpha male smile, which immediately put my jealousy radar on high alert.

We stood around the car without even unloading our bags while he lengthily explained that he had only taken over the 'hotel' recently and this was the first time he had advertised the place as a fishing venue. We learned how he had converted an outhouse into a tackle and kit room for the purpose, and how we would be the first guests to christen it. But the jewel in his crown (he said), was the large barn which he had converted into a discotheque, and for this he had great plans.

'I thought that maybe helicopters could land on the lawn,' he announced grandly with a sweep of his arm. 'It would be great for pop groups, film stars, those sorts of people to stay here. I'm hoping to get The Beatles or The Rolling Stones to come down. They could do a bit of fishing, relax – even play in the club maybe. '

Such was the man's utter self-confidence that it was hard to gainsay him. 'Good idea' and 'best of luck' we muttered, by way of lip service.

When he did at last remember his primary duties and offer to help with our bags, I waved him aside, remembering the shifty way he had smiled at Suzie. 'No need,' I said, ' I'm sure we can manage. Just tell us the room numbers and give us the keys.' He wasn't coming anywhere near my bedroom for the duration if I had anything to do with it.

We soon located our room, which had views over the river. Harry had the twin-bedded room next door; he would be sharing with Aintree, who was due to arrive later that evening.

Holding back the curtain to survey the view, Suzie reflected on the owner's little *spiel* and asked me if I could seriously imagine either John Lennon or Mick Jagger turning up in a helicopter and fishing off the weir out there. 'No chance,' I snapped. 'Man's an idiot.'

Suzie considered for a moment. 'What about Jimi Hendrix?'

'You silly goose.' We giggled and I pulled her onto the bed, remembering to close the curtain.

Exhausted by the journey and feeling relaxed after a pleasant supper, Suzie and I retired early. Aintree had arrived safely and we left him and Harry chatting amiably in the conservatory.

It must have been around 5.30 or 6 o'clock the next morning that we became aware of raised voices from the room next door, followed by the sounds of a slamming door and heavy footfalls along the passage and down the stairs. Through the wall, we could hear Harry humming and singing cheerfully to himself:

> *'If I had the wings of an angel – and the balls of a big buffalo,*
> *I'd sit on the edge of creation, and piss on the buggers below!'*

Throwing on some trousers, I went down to see what the commotion was about. Aintree stood in reception, dressed in full motorbike kit, suitcase and fishing rod bag at his side.

'Everything all right Aintree? ' I enquired carefully.

'No, it's not bloody all right, Tony.' He was agitated, and trembling slightly. 'I'm not putting up with that!'

'Putting up with what?' I had no idea what he was talking about.

'That's queers' practice that is,' said Aintree, 'queers' practice.'

'What is?'

'All that nancy-boy stuff your father-in-law gets up to. He's been at it since four o'clock this morning. Woke me up with it.'

'He's only washing Aintree. He always does it.' I sought to calm him down, but he was having none of it.

'That's not normal washing, Tony. That's queer's practice,' he repeated. 'I'm not staying in a room with him.'

'Well, I'm sorry you feel like that Aintree. Maybe they can find you another room?'

'No. I'm off home. Sorry, Tony' he said, yet again, 'but that's queers' practice.'

'So Aintree, 'I asked him, without realising immediately what I was saying, 'you're leaving without wetting your tackle?'

Without another word to me, he turned on his heels and left.

The three of us enjoyed our breakfast. Harry was bemused by Aintree's departure. Why should the sight and sound of a naked man, singing and splashing and dabbing at himself with a variety of cosmetics, for a couple of hours in the dawn light, disturb anyone? Suzie and I fell to sniggering about my parting comment to Aintree, and so his precipitous exit passed into our family folk-memory.

The owner wandered over and asked us cordially how we had slept, whether we were enjoying breakfast and so on. His gaze fell on Suzie.

'Have you chaps got any plans for today?' he enquired breezily.

'I thought we might try some fishing,' I replied, trying to sound ironic. Ignoring me, he turned to Suzie.

'Are you going with them, Mrs Baws?'

'Er, we hadn't got that far,' Suzie replied hesitantly.

'Well,' continued the owner, with an ingratiating smile, 'if it's okay with your husband, I could take you out for a while in the car to see a bit of the countryside. I have a few things to do in the next village. Is that alright with you, Mr Baws?'

The smarmy git. What could I say? My jealousy antennae were buzzing but I knew that a wrong word now could lead to us all upping sticks and following Aintree back to Essex before the holiday had even begun. Suzie's beauty drew many unwanted admirers and despite her unswerving loyalty,

I invariably found myself rising to the bait. I managed to keep calm.

'Do you want to do that, Sue?'

'Well, it'll give you and Harry a chance to settle in won't it?' she suggested in all innocence.

So that was me, stymied. Caught between my wife 'Beauty' and Mr Smooth 'the Beast'.

'Have you got any idea where we should start along the river?' I asked in a low, flat tone, feigning disinterest, a futile attempt to indicate maximum displeasure while graciously allowing things to stand.

'Oh, yes,' he replied bouncily.' God, I hated him. 'If you head upstream across the lawn, there's a gate at the end, goes into a grassed field. No cows in there at the moment – nothing to worry about. Right at the far end where the trees thin out a bit, there are some good spots – plenty of reed cover there too.'

At least he hadn't sent us miles away in order to allow himself more time to have his wicked way with my wife.

'Well, Sue, it's ten o'clock now – so we'll see you back here around one for lunch? That suit you, Harry?' I saw no point in addressing my rival directly.

'Fine with me, Baws,' said Harry jovially. This potential threat to my honour was passing right over his head. Had he no protective feelings at all towards his stepdaughter?

A short while later we reassembled on the small gravelled parking area in front of the house. Suzie looked stunning in a printed summer dress, no stockings and flat shoes, her long black hair flowing down her back. I was dressed in green, ex-American Army jungle-combat fatigues. They were ever so slightly smelly. Harry was clothed entirely in khaki. With trousers tucked into black water boots and a *kepi* on his head to protect the back of his neck from the sun, he stood, arms on hips, looking like an extra from 'Beau Geste'.

Around the corner roared an open-topped MG sports car finished in British Racing Green, complete with knock-off wheel nuts and wood-and-aluminium steering wheel. Here was the hotel owner, all open-neck shirt and sunglasses, blond hair swept casually back. He leaped out and bustled Suzie into the car.

'Good luck with the fishing you two,' he grinned. Dropping the car into gear, he was off in a cloud of gravel and dust.

Somewhat stunned by Suzie's speedy departure, Harry and I turned and made our way slowly across the lawn as directed. This felt slightly odd, since few guests were actually there for the fishing. Tables and chairs were arranged on the lawn, as were several sun-loungers and deckchairs. Some people were finishing a leisurely breakfast, some were reading, others were already sun bathing. Through this relaxed and civilised gathering strode myself and Harry, rod bags slapping against our backs, fishing boots rasping against each other, Harry smelling strongly of aftershave and Lord knows what else, and my jacket exuding its usual vague aroma of fish and maggots.

'Morning!' offered Harry politely to left and right, as we wove our way across the manicured lawn between and around the guests. 'Morning!'

Down by the river bank we stopped to look at the weir. Spaced at intervals across the weir wall were some half a dozen youngsters all facing downstream, the water rushing over the backs of their bare feet. Although it was summer-low, it still took skill and concentration to fish in that spot and keep your balance. The tactic they all employed was to drag their hooks up the weir wall, gathering the green weed which grew there, then cast out into the turbulent water below the weir. Before our eyes, we watched these youngsters hook roach after roach, shimmering silver and red in the bright light of morning.

'Fancy giving that a try, Baws?' asked Harry cheerfully.

I remembered Harry and the lake at Corringham, when he lost his torch and nearly his life. I remembered the thunderstorm at Rochford and our hazardous ice walk. I remembered my near miss at Star Lane. I tried to picture Harry and me balancing on the weir, him in his black wellington boots. We had played against the fates before and won. Why tempt them again?

'No, I think we'll push on, H.'

The sun was warm on our backs as we made our way across the field, doing our best to avoid the cow pats. We tackled up in the cover of the trees before moving into the swims. The river was about eight foot deep and flowing quite fast. We were not experienced river fishermen and this wide, majestic River Avon was a world away from the slow-flowing, narrow rivers in Essex. It required some added weight and float adjustment to get the measure of the stream. An hour passed without a bite.

'He's a fly geezer, that Graham,' said Harry, out of nowhere. 'You want to watch him, Tone.'

For Harry to make this observation, things must be serious. Not that Harry didn't often refer to 'geezers' being shifty or fly, but he rarely entered the marital space inhabited by Suzie and me. He was an ideal stepfather, there for support when Suzie needed it, but otherwise remaining in the background.

'Yes, I figured that, Harry. You having any bites?'

'Fuck all ,Tony. You?'

'No, nothing. I might give the worm a try.'

'Good idea, Baws,' encouraged Harry. 'Be a man!'

A worm usually signalled the last act of desperation. The unwelcome attention of greedy small perch and eels was all that ever came of it as a rule, and this day was no exception. Within minutes my float disappeared and I felt the sickening sideways lurch of an eel bite. With horror I watched as a bootlace eel, about a foot long and half an inch round, wriggled and knotted its way around my line, covering it with slime. I groped for the slippery swine with my outstretched hand as it swung towards me but I missed, allowing it to deposit slime on my jacket and trousers as it flailed around.

Harry, observing all this, chortled from the next swim. 'Go on Tony, you love jellieds. Those little ones are viewed as a great delicacy aren't they?'

'That's elvers,' I groused, 'not bleedin' bootlaces.'

'West Country's the place for them though, Tone,' mused Harry. 'They trap them up the Severn at night with nets. You just think. All the way from the Sargasso Sea they come, even travelling overland. Slithering across fields, swimming through ditches. Marvellous really. Then they go all the way back to the Sargasso the same way to breed – if they don't end up on Tubby Isaacs's Stall .'

'If you love them so much, Harry,' I said, 'why won't you eat them?'

'Not likely,' said Harry, 'horrible fucking things.'

Eventually I pinned the little wriggler to the ground, removed the hook and released the eel back into the water. It looked back at me, reproachfully, as if saying 'I'm gonna tell my Dad about you.'

It was a perfect, early summer day. Bees buzzed, damsel flies flitted through the reeds, swallows swooped across the river. The glug and gurgle of the water marked the occasional rise of a dace or chub. Since we hardly ever went fly fishing, this was of academic interest only to me, entrancing though it was, but Harry always became excited. 'Was that a rise, Tony?' he would ask energetically, as though every time was the first time he had ever witnessed the event, as though, even if it were indeed a fish rise, that alone would make an impact on our success. If only Harry's repetitions and enthusiasms could conjure up bites.

The morning wore on, getting hotter as the sun rose high. There were no bites at all now. We packed our things for the short walk back to the guest house. Distracted by a particularly loud 'rise', Harry did not see the cow pat ahead of him as he turned to look back at the river.

'Shit!' he cried.

'Quite so,' I said, before I too, with my very next step, planted my right foot firmly in a squidgy deposit.

Luncheon was being served when we arrived back on the hotel lawn. If we had offered the merest suggestion of fish aroma on our outward departure, we were now giving off a powerful pong of eel slime and cow shit to the assembled diners. Noses were upturned, faces averted.

'Afternoon!' beamed Harry to left and right, smiling engagingly. 'Afternoon!'

We put our gear in the tackle room, removed our boots and went off to change. In the bedroom I found Suzie, gazing out of the window overlooking the weir. On the dressing table were two horseshoes.

'Hello pussycat, have a good time?' I say, giving her a kiss, tight-lipped and curious, loving her, trusting her but with uncontrollable jealousy already raging. Not really wanting to hear an answer, I force myself to ask. 'Where did you go?'

'Oh, I don't really know. Graham just drove us around.'

'Where d'you get the horseshoes, Sue?'

'We went to a smithy and Graham bought them for me.'

I grab the horseshoes and go looking for the fly geezer. I find him in the dining room, simpering to assorted guest. I march up to him, put my face in his:

'Did you buy these for my wife?'

'Yes,' he said, 'is there a problem?'

'How much did you pay for them?'

'Oh, I don't know,' he replies.

'HOW MUCH DID YOU PAY?'

'They were only a couple of quid. It's just a small present.'

I reach in my pocket, peel off two one-pound notes and thrust them at him.

'There you are – two pounds.'

At first he does not want to accept, but I force the money on him.

'We can pay our own way thanks!'

I give him a final, mean look, then turn on my heels and walk off. By now Suzie has made her way down to the conservatory, where shortly we are joined by Harry. No one says anything.

'Everything all right, Tony? asks Harry eventually, breaking the silence.

'It is now,' I snarl.

'What on earth is the matter?' asks Suzie. 'Have I done something wrong?'

'Done something wrong?' I repeat. 'Letting that bloke buy you horseshoes?'

'What's so wrong with that?'

'What's wrong with it? WHAT'S WRONG?' I can hear my voice getting louder. I sigh and speak more quietly, as a measure of my self-control and also for maximum sympathetic effect. 'Honestly, Suzie.' I say, shaking my head with dejection, 'you'd let anyone shit on your head!'

I catch Harry's face out of the corner of my eye. His mouth is screwed up, trying not to smile. He searches for words to placate me.

'Oh, I don't think she would, Tony' he says solemnly, 'Suzie's very selective.'

Suzie giggles, I chuckle, and we all three begin to laugh.

CHAPTER 19

The Great Eel

'These shall ye eat, of all that are in the waters:
whatsoever hath fins and scales.
And all that have not fins and scales, in the seas,
and in the rivers, of all that move in the waters,
they shall be an abomination unto you.'

LEVITICUS 11: 9-12

According to my treasured copy of 'Mr Crabtree Goes Fishing', which was our veritable fishing bible at that time, 'there is no river in England which is more exciting to the imagination of the coarse fisherman than the Hampshire Avon.'

As an introduction to serious fishing, Harry and I had been informed, amused and infuriated in turns by the wonderful cartoon strip/graphic novel-cum-fishing instruction manual, written and illustrated by the legendary Bernard Venables. I had even relied on his recommendation when booking this holiday, all the more so since I chose it from the pages of the *Angling Times*, which he had co-founded. I simply made a small geographical error. We were in fact currently fishing on the Bristol Avon.

So here we were, holiday dabbling in the noon-day sun on the wrong Avon. Gudgeon and small roach had been plentiful all week, but we had caught nothing to match the size of the fish taken regularly by the young-sters on the weir. We had changed tactics, moved swims, altered depth. We had experimented with baits in the hope of luring the odd chub – elder-berries, wood grubs and the like, but all to no avail. Harry did become extremely excited one time when his float shot under, only to discover that somehow he had hooked a large water snail.

Often when the fishing was quiet, when bite-less hour followed bite-less hour, Harry would play out dialogues based on the easy success and the early post-war style of the fictional Mr Crabtree and his young son Peter. Published in 1948, their fishing adventures were full of drama and colour and inspiration, but so much had changed in the intervening years. The way the pair dressed seemed especially outmoded. Although Harry wore a suit for work, Mr Crabtree wore one to go fishing – and a hat and a tie and a jumper, in all seasons. And he was never seen without a pipe in his mouth. Peter was like a smaller version of his Dad, but with short trousers and without the hat and pipe. There was, however, one distinguishing feature that Mr. Crabtree, Peter and Harry had in common: their ubiquitous black wellington boots.

The clock at Bathampton struck three, and still neither of us had registered even the merest hint of a bite. As a comment on the day's proceedings, and by way of comparison, Harry launched into an ironic impersonation of the Crabtree's unremitting success, as catalogued in their eponymous book:

"I had been fishing for thirty seconds," he reported. "Suddenly my float shot under and I was rewarded with a three pound roach."

He settled into the performance.

"I re-baited with a large slice of salami and was quickly into another fish. This time it was a six pound chub. I urged Peter to try different baits and see what he could do.'

"Peter, there should still be some of that Roquefort left from Aunt Peg's sandwiches. Stick a lump on and see how it goes.'

"Okay, Dad. Look, I've got a bite already!'

"Good boy, Peter. Hold on while I slip the landing net under him. Another fine chub. Why, it's even bigger than mine!"

'Yes,' I interrupted, 'and he's only twelve.'

'What a filthy mind you have, Baws,' said Harry with pretend affront, before continuing in character:

"Jolly well done Peter, it looks all of seven pounds to me. Let's put it back to grow even bigger." Here he rounded off the performance with a barrage of colourful expletives.

'You had enough then, Harry?' I asked innocently.

'Well Tony,' he replied, gazing into the river, 'I reckon we could fish here from arsehole to breakfast time and still not get a bite.'

I tended to agree with him. 'I think I'll take Suzie for a stroll. She hasn't seen much of the surroundings. What are you going to do?'

'Oh, I'll settle down and have a read I think.'

We split up back at the hotel. I went off to change and find Suzie. She and I spent a pleasant summer's afternoon walking along the disused canal that ran nearby. In the spirit of romantic reconciliation after the episode with the horseshoes, I tried to keep my mind off fishing, but the fact was that Harry and I had spent all week on the river with little to show for our efforts, and this canal, which we hadn't explored at all, looked so tempting. None of that river rush, bustling eagerly to reach the sea, but lovely, still, calm water that called out to me: 'Here be fish'. Another time perhaps.

Harry had decided against reading. Instead he had set off to explore the old mill backwater in our absence. We returned to find him standing in the shallows mid-stream, shouting abuse and flogging the water. This was the infamous 'Nutters' Reach'. Looking at his body language, it seemed that he might welcome some encouragement.

'Caught anything, Harry?' was my opening innocent gambit. He was not encouraged by this.

'Don't be fuckin' daft, Baws! By the Jesus,' he ranted, 'why won't they just take the fucking thing!'

I tried again. 'Getting any bites?'

'Stacks of fucking bites, but I can't connect.'

'What bait are you using?'

'I've tried every fucking thing; bread, maggots, worms. Fuck all use! Must be pissers. Mouths as small as a rat's armpit!'

Harry had got up a fair old steam. I looked at Suzie and we both stifled a laugh. Moving a few yards downstream in the direction of the main river and then looking back towards where Harry was thrashing about, I could see a disturbance in the water. I bent down for a closer look. Here was the answer to Harry's frustration – minnows, great shoals of them. I thought it best not to let on.

'We were thinking of giving that 'Old Barn Disco' of his a try tonight. Fancy it?'

'Yes, okay.' He snapped the line violently. 'Enough of this soddin' misery!'

The barn conversion had been tastefully done. The original barn timbers had been carefully restored and exposed. Great oak mainmasts, salvaged from a Bristol schooner, served as additional bracing to the old roof beams. The bar, the sound system and the dance area were at ground level. Above was a mezzanine floor where one could take drinks and find a comfortable place to sit and chat. There, despite the fashionable disco sound played at high volume, it was still just possible to hold a conversation without having to scream directly into the adjacent person's ear.

The cellar extended under the river, which was were they kept the barrels of draught Guinness. I was not yet a drinking man - a pint or two could make me feel quite merry - but I could tell a good pint from a bad one and the beer there was sublime; smooth, chilled, a perfect creamy head and plenty of body. Suzie maintained that her doctor had recommended stout to help her put on weight, so she was drinking 'purely for medicinal purposes'. Her medicine here was certainly something special.

Harry, on the other hand, had been a prodigious drinker in his youth. How often had he regaled me with lurid tales of times when he had drunk vast quantities of beer, wine or spirits, (possibly all three together), of army drinking games such as 'Cardinal Puff' when he had consumed industrial-level intakes of alcohol, with the prize apparently going to the last man standing? 'The trick, Baws,' he would say, 'was to go outside and spew, then go round to the other bar and have a tomato juice to settle the stomach. Then you could start all over again and nobody knew.' How many times had I explained my emetophobia to him and it failed to register. 'Oh I forgot, you don't like being sick do you?' he would ask unctuously, having made me feel queasy once again.

Soon our fishing disappointments were forgotten as the music, the lights and the Guinness weaved their spell. Since the fashionable style of dancing did not involve a readily identifiable partner, Suzie and I dragged Harry onto the dance floor and the three of us frugged the night away.

Our ears were still ringing from the loud music as we sauntered back, slightly unsteadily, across the lawn to the hotel. It must have been around one o'clock. The night was clear and warm and the only sounds were those of the river nearby. The air smelled of balsam.

'Fancy some night fishing, Tony?' asked Harry. I suspected he was only half-joking.

'No thanks, Harry. I think we'll call it a night.' I squeezed Suzie's hand and she squeezed back.

Unfortunately, by the time we sank into bed, whatever mildly aphro-disiac effect the draught Guinness might have had was now wasted on Suzie. Within minutes she was asleep; not only asleep, but snoring loudly, in a most unladylike manner.

All my plans of a woozy romantic interlude had to be abandoned. Whenever I nuzzled up to her, she sighed briefly, only to begin snoring again. I lay on my back, trying to ignore her snores in the hope that I myself might drift off to sleep, but it was hopeless.

Maybe Harry's suggestion of night fishing was not such a bad idea after all?

Reluctant to admit defeat, but being a realist, I dressed again and made my way along the corridor and down the stairs to the tackle room. I was still feeling the effects of the Guinness, so locating what I would need without knocking anything over in the dark took great concentration. Luckily my carp rod – the Davenport and Fordham MkIV 'Farstrike' from Peek's (with which I had in fact landed surprisingly few carp, and none requiring a strike at any great distance) – was still set up. It was short and manageable, ideal for night fishing without a float.

But there was one problem – I had no bait.

Harry had used all our maggots, feeding them to the minnows at Nutters' Reach. We would be leaving in the morning and had we fancied a quick dabble before we left, we planned to purloin some bread from breakfast.

In the meantime I'd have to settle for worms from the lawn. I tried hard not to think about worm-happy eels, particularly the annoying bootlace catch from earlier in the week. Full of resolve, I picked up my rod, rod rest, my landing net, a bait box and my torch and made my way outside.

Gathering lobworms from a lawn at night can be a difficult enough task when sober, but it is fraught with problems when one is slightly squiffy; footfalls are heavier and a delicate touch is absent. Added to this, the necessary lowering of the head towards one's quarry in the torchlight tends to make the loose marbles rattle and the head swim.

Fortunately, worm gathering was a skill I had gradually honed. Some practitioners insist on waggling a fork into the ground to entice worms to the surface. Others, what might be called 'the exotic tendency', swear by an application of diluted mustard or similar worm irritants over the target area in order to drive the worms upward. I am a purist and follow a simple technique:
- locate basking worm in diffused light of torch (direct light frightens them and they disappear down their holes at vast speed)
- advance towards worm
- place finger gently but firmly upon worm where it exits from worm hole
- place torch gently on ground and with spare hand grab free, wiggly end of worm and tug gently (too fierce or rapid a pull will result in

the capture of half a worm only).

Within ten minutes or so I had about a dozen worms in my box. Turning to pick up the rest of my stuff from where I had left it propped up against the conservatory wall, I bumped into and almost flattened Harry.

'What the hell – ?' I spluttered.

'Sorry, Baws,' Harry apologised, 'I came out to see what was up. There was this flashing light coming in my bedroom window. Thought it might be burglars. What are you up to now?'

'Just gathering some worms.' Now it was my turn. 'Thought I might do a spot of night fishing. Fancy it?'

'No thanks,' said Harry, 'still feeling a bit spinny. I'll come and watch you though.'

There didn't seem any point in staggering through the gate and across the field in the dark, with both of us feeling unsteady. It would be simpler to fish directly off the lawn.

There was a certain amount of cover where a reed bed had established itself and reached out a short distance from the bank. I set my rod up just to the right of the reeds, downstream of the weir. Unable to free-line due to the pull of the current, I ledgered with a small Arlesey Bomb, stopped by a single shot placed one foot from the hook.

Baiting with a whole worm, lightly nicked at two points along its length, I cast into the tail of the weir pool and reeled up the slack until the line was stretched taut against the rod. There was no need for a bite indicator or a torch, because in the dim light still coming from the hotel I could make out the rod tip quite clearly – if that moved, I would know that I had a bite.

Harry and I pulled up a garden chair apiece, lit our cigarettes and awaited events. It was a warm, still night and the sound of water rushing over the weir had a soporific effect. Coupled with the efforts of my worming expedition and the remaining afterglow of the splendid draught Guinness, I was finding it difficult to stay awake.

'Are you asleep, Tony?' asked Harry, in voice loud enough to wake the dead.

'Yes.'

'Did you ever hear of Beau Nash?' Harry had a disquieting knack of starting a conversation in the middle, but he had succeeded in rousing me from my stupor.

'What about him?'

'Master of Ceremonies in Bath,' offered Harry, by way of no explanation.

'Was that the same Nash who built the Regent's Canal?'

'No, that was John Nash,' he said carefully.

'What did this one do then?'

'He made arrangements for society dos,' explained Harry, 'dances, weddings, that sort of thing.'

' What made you suddenly think of him?'

'He had a place not far from here. Bit of a character – eighteenth century.'

'What, his house?'

'No, Nash.'

'Beau Nash?' I was totally confused. 'You sure you don't mean Brummell?'

'I'm sure, Baws. Beau Brummell came a bit later. His real name was George.'

'They were all called George in those days weren't they?'

Harry chose to ignore what I thought was a very perceptive comment.

'Regency dandy he was, Brummell. Wore elegant clothes; silk shirts, cravats. Used to take five hours to wash and dress.'

That sounded familiar – no wonder Harry was interested in him. A role model indeed.

'Apparently he was one of the few people at that time to wash regularly and clean his teeth,' he continued.

I put my hand up to silence him as I peered at the rod tip.

'Had a knock?' asked Harry, lowering his voice to a stage whisper.

'False alarm. Anyway, these blokes you were on about. What happened to them?'

'Nash was buried in a pauper's grave and Brummell died of syphilis,' said Harry crisply.

'Washing didn't do him much good then?'

Harry pulled on his cigarette, looking thoughtful.

'Maybe he just missed a bit!'

A sudden plop put an abrupt end to our musings. Shining my torch into the water, I caught a glimpse of a water vole swimming briskly toward the reed bed, just by our feet.

'Look, Tony, a ratty man.'

Harry and I had a soft spot for these lovely creatures, with their sleek coats and beady eyes. They are voles of course, but to anyone who has read 'The Wind in the Willows', they are 'Ratty'. Whenever I saw one my heart leapt with pleasure and appreciation.

On this singular occasion I was suddenly possessed by a moment of folly which I can only ascribe to the lateness of the hour, and residual drunken whimsy. Reaching out with my landing net to trawl after the diving vole, I never dreamed for an instant that I would catch it. But here it was, struggling furiously in my landing net as I lifted it from the water.

'Bugger that, Baws!' exclaimed Harry, 'he doesn't look happy.'

My anthropomorphic love of the sweet little animal quickly turned sour. 'I didn't think I'd actually catch the bastard!' I complained, as I swung the net onto the grass.

I bent down to assess the situation. The water vole was restrained by the net, but engaged in vigorous vertical leaps in an effort to free itself. What was needed was for me to grab the vole, present the net to the water and turn it upside down. With luck, the bugger would simply drop out.

An angry vole is not something to be grabbed with bare hands. Using a doubled-up handkerchief, I grasped animal and net combined. Holding the handle in my left hand I carefully positioned the net above the water. At the point I was about to release the water vole, there came a loud shout from Harry.

'You've got a bite, Tone!'

My rod jumped in its rest and the tip curved steeply around.

'Here Harry, grab this,' I shouted. Harry reluctantly accepted responsibility for the net, and with it the still struggling vole. He picked up my torch in his other hand to take a closer look.

'Ratty's bloody cross,' he hissed.

With both hands now free, I picked up the rod. There was no need to strike as the line flew off the reel against the anti-return ratchet. I did not know what I had hooked, but it was big and powerful and it was pulling towards the weir. I risked a break as I applied pressure to turn it. Gradually I retrieved line, and as I worked the fish to the surface I was aware of an unsettling side-to-side pull on the other end. Oh no, not a jellied! But it was. An enormous eel.

'Fuck!' I swore in annoyance.

'Big one by the looks of it,' whispered a voice I did not recognise.

Turning to see who had just spoken, I noticed to my horror that we had been joined by several hotel guests, dressed in pyjamas and dressing gowns. Awoken by the disturbance and the flashing light on the lawn, they stood quietly in a small group, awaiting events.

Gradually I drew the great eel towards the bank. 'Harry, get the net under it will you, please?' How polite I had become, playing to the watching crowd.

'Can't Tone – still got a rat in it.'

'F ... never mind the rat Harry, just slide the net under.'

The eel slithered across the frame of the net but it was far too big to fit inside.

'Try again Harry – get the tail in first.'

On about the fifth attempt, Harry managed to ensnare the lower half of the eel in the net. Without ceremony, we swung the rod and the net out of the water and manhandled the brute onto dry land.

Greatly relieved, and using the handkerchief I had pressed into service to catch hold of the water vole, I grabbed the eel amidships, only to be given the fright of my life as from under the eel shot the terrified and slightly slimy vole. It dashed into the water, a very relieved animal. The problem now was, how to placate three foot of thrashing eel.

'Have you got your cheive, Tone?' Harry enquired. He tended to employ foreign or old English words whenever strangers were around, in an attempt to either confuse them or, as in this case, to protect their assumed sensibilities. Cheive. Here was a word that his friends the Nashes might have used.

I felt in my jacket pocket. Yes, I had a knife. But a beheaded eel was not a tranquil eel. I had a better plan.

'What we need is some newspaper, Harry.'

A voice arose from the gathered guests. 'I've got the *Telegraph* in my room. Would you like me to get it?'

Normally I would not have gone anywhere near this bastion of the Tory shires, but trying times called for stern measures. Besides, as a broadsheet it carried far more raw material in terms of eel-controlling paper than its Labour competitor the *Daily Mirror*.

'Yes, that would be great, thanks,' I answered.

The slippered figure in pyjamas and dark blue dressing gown moved silently across the lawn and re-appeared shortly, bearing a copy of the *Daily Telegraph*. I thanked him and opened the paper out on the grass, dividing it into two sections. The first I used to cover the wriggling eel, in order to get some sort of grip. Grasping its head in one hand and its tail in the other, I deposited it diagonally across the other section of the newspaper.

There was no point in trying to release the hook right then, so I employed my 'cheive' in a modest manner and cut the line close to the hook. Then I rolled the eel up tightly in the *Telegraph*. Later I would think of cleverly dark political metaphors about eels and Tories, but for now I was thankful that the episode had a successful outcome. Like a crowd leaving the scene of an accident, the guests began to quietly disperse, muttering observations such as 'hmm, interesting' and 'bloody big eel!'

'You going to eat it, Baws?' asked Harry.

'Course I'm going to eat it. No point in letting a good eel go to waste.'

In fact I had no idea what I was going to do with it. It was three in the morning and soon it would begin to get light. I packed up the tackle and sprinkled water sparingly on the eel. Cocooned in the rolled-up newspaper, it was practically motionless, but still very much alive. What to do? A sharp blow on the head? It seemed wrong to end such an eventful but rewarding session on a note of violence. Harry and I smoked our final cigarettes and said goodnight. Rather than leave the eel for others to discover the next morning, I took it with me to my bedroom and put it in the bottom of the wardrobe.

Slipping into bed next to her, I disturbed Suzie. She rubbed her eyes and wrinkled up her nose.

'Tony Baws!' she gasped, 'you smell dreadful.'

Blearily I looked at her. 'I had a quick wash before I came to bed, poppet. It was a bit late.'

'You need more than a quick wash. You need a bath. Off you go.'

With that she pushed me out of bed. I staggered into the bathroom and ran the shower. I heard Suzie's raised voice.

'You've polluted the entire room Tony.'

'Won't be a minute love.' I towelled myself off and applied a liberal splash of whatever was in the bathroom cabinet – anything to absolve myself from the crime of fishy pong. Returning to the bedroom I found Suzie sniffing around the wardrobe.

'It's coming from in here,' she said anxiously, and opened the wardrobe door. The smell of eel was overwhelming. 'What's that in the corner, in the wet newspaper?'

'Er, it's an eel, love. Caught it last night.'

'Well, get it out!'

'I haven't decided what to do with it yet. What do you think?'

'How should I know?' she said impatiently, 'I don't eat the ruddy things! Just go and put it in the car boot – we're leaving later today at any rate.'

I removed the soggy newspaper package from the wardrobe, took it down the stairs and placed it in the boot of my car. Later that day on the journey home, I stopped the car in a lay-by, somewhere along the A34. There, after removing the hook, I deposited the torpid but still alive eel in a water-filled ditch. It faced a long, long journey back to the Sargasso Sea.

CHAPTER 20

The Dreadful Smell

'When the last rose of summer pricks my finger
And the hot sun chills me to the bone
When I can't hear the song for the singer
And I can't tell my pillow from a stone
I will walk alone, by the black, muddy river
And sing me a song of my own'

ROBERT HUNTER/JERRY GARCIA *Black Muddy River*

It was all we could do to clean the mud off the tools and stack them in The Bobbing Float, so exhausted were we by our efforts.

'Bloody good job,' said Harry admiringly, surveying what had been a swamp but was now a raised path of timber, puddled clay and turf. 'Tony's Bridge. You said you'd do it, Baws. It'll probably outlast us all.'

Finally, we would be able to walk all the way around the Res, regardless of the water level. I thanked those who had contributed to the day's work party, the usual suspects: Freddie, 'Dusty', the Barretts, Don and 'Slapper'. Laughing and joking, weary but happy, we parted in good spirits.

But as Harry and I headed for the car, as soon as I was no longer distracted, I became aware once more of the feeling of nausea which had haunted me almost constantly for months. All the tests had come back negative; the medical opinion was that I was suffering from overwork, nervous tension and a delayed reaction to the loss of my mother – in other words, it was 'all in the mind'. For a lifelong emetophobe, that may as well have been a sentence of death, as each long day and even longer night turned into a struggle against my worst, primordial fear.

Luckily a new fishing season would soon begin. Our holiday the previous year had succeeded in taking Harry's mind off his problems for a while: maybe it could work for me too.

Trawling through the *Angling Times* for inspiration, I came across only three holiday insertions; two were in Ireland, on the Shannon, and the other was in Somerset. The latter read as follows:

Farmhouse B&B: Ideal base for fishing holidays:
River Parrett, River Brue, Huntspill,
King's Sedgemoor Drain, local lakes.
Packed lunch and evening meal available.

I was hesitant at the prospect of river fishing. Much as we had enjoyed our time in the West Country (with the possible exception of the horse-shoes episode), we were ultimately relieved to leave behind the incessant rush of the weir and the flow of the river, to return to Essex and our natural habitat of still-water indolence. On the other hand, these Somerset venues were well-known and would present us with a fresh challenge. As a last resort, we could always fall back on the lakes.

I read out the details to Harry. 'They give a phone number here, I could give them a ring. What do you think?'

He gave his usual reply, full of boundless enthusiasm.

'Might as well Tony, we've got nothing to lose.'

I stopped the car in a lay-by opposite the farmhouse and walked across the road. Through the door I could hear a woman's voice giving disciplinary instructions:

'Get down will you, you're all muddy!'

I pondered for a moment. Who was she talking to?

The latch turned and I was greeted by the buxom and jovial Grace Trenton. Together with husband William she ran a small dairy farm, with a few chickens, geese and pigs kept as a sideline. Pulling an eager young German Shepherd puppy behind her, she ushered me inside to make our introductions and complete the few formalities.

'This is Tess,' she said, fondling the dog's ears. 'Pest more like! We've got a border collie as well, Sheba. She's in the yard. She's fine, but she will try and round you up. Anyway, let me show you over the place, then you can get your things.'

A quick tour followed. In the beamed dining room were comfy looking, chintz-covered chairs and a splendidly polished oak table set for four. An inglenook fireplace, decorated with horse brasses and hunting horns, bore sooty signs of recent use. A glimpse into the kitchen revealed a cosy, quarry-tiled room with a well-used Aga range at its centre, a good place to sit and chat.

Upstairs, the passages and rooms sloped every which way, like The Crooked House in Southend's amusement park. Studying the angles made by the furniture against the picture rail, the mirrors hanging on the walls and the lighting flex descending from the ceiling, nothing at all appeared to be geometrically square.

'Well, this is your room and the one next door is for your friend. Harry is it?'

'He's my father-in-law actually.'

'Oh, sorry,' said Grace, colouring slightly. She conducted us down the stairs. 'Mind these as you go,' she warned, 'they're very steep.' At the front door she directed me to the yard. 'There's a place round the back you can keep your fishing things and muddy boots; I'll meet you round the back and show you where. Ignore the dogs.'

I drove the car through the gate, past the apple orchard and into the yard. As I turned off the engine, Tess from one side and Sheba from the other leaped at the car doors, barking and scratching.

'She told us to ignore them, Harry.'

'What about those?' he asked, pointing to a flock of geese advancing menacingly towards the car; heads forward, necks straight and honking fiercely.

We were rescued from this pandemonium by Grace, who shooed the geese, shouted at the dogs and restored some semblance of calm to the proceedings. I introduced Harry and we started to unpack.

'Over there,' said Grace, pointing to a slatted wooden door in a brick lean-to. 'You can put your rods in there, and your boots. Well, I'll leave you to it. Come down to the kitchen once you've unpacked and I'll make you a cup of tea.' With that, she strode towards the back door of the farm, calling out to the dogs. 'Here girls, come on.'

The two dogs followed eagerly behind, wagging their tails and nuzzling each other, with backward glances at us, as if to say 'we sure frightened the hell out of those visitors!' The geese were gathered in a corner muttering darkly, no doubt discussing tactics.

I was unprepared for what happened next. Over time I had become inured to the smell of horse or cattle manure, was even fond of the smell of pigs, but the rank odour that assailed me as I opened the lean-to door made me instantly nauseous.

'Christ, Harry,' I yelled, quickly closing the door. 'What the fuck's that?'

'What's up, Tony?'

'That fucking smell. What is it?'

'I can't smell anything.'

'Well, your snout must have packed up. It's making me feel sick.'

Harry looked bemused. 'Do you want me to put the rods away?'

'Please, if you don't mind. I'll take my clothes up and see you later.'

I was glad to have something to take my mind off the dreadful smell as I hung my clothes in the cupboard and organised my few things. The odd slope of the floor, combined with the high polish which Grace had vigorously applied to the sideboard and bedside table, meant that any object placed there had a tendency to slide off. I made a mental note to take particular care with my glasses at night.

In the room next door, Harry began the long-winded process of unpacking and stacking his washing and make-up paraphernalia. Every so often I heard a noise of something hitting the floor, followed by an outburst of Harry swearing though gritted teeth. I popped in to see him.

'Everything all right, Harry? Bed okay?'

'Fine thanks, Tony,' he answered, carefully balancing another cosmetic item on the sideboard, 'except the furniture's not straight.'

'I think it's the floor. Anyway, what did you make of that smell?'

'I couldn't really smell anything, Tone. Smelled of apples a bit, that's all. You could ask when we go down.'

Grace welcomed us into the kitchen and sat us at the table. I could see her looking thoughtfully at Harry, who still bore just enough trace of Man Tan and eyebrow pencil from home to give a stranger pause for thought.

'Your rooms okay?' she asked, pouring the tea.

'Fine thanks, Mrs Trenton.'

'You call me Grace,' she said, 'everyone else does. Have you thought where you're going fishing? There's plenty of places round here to choose from.'

'We've got a map,' I said confidently, 'but since we have to go in to Bridgwater first to get our permits and some bait, we thought we'd ask at the tackle shop about the best spots to fish. We did think perhaps we'd give the King's Sedgemoor Drain a go tomorrow night, as our first outing.'

'What?' asked Grace in disbelief, 'all night?'

'Oh yes,' replied Harry jovially. 'Night fishing, that's what we like best.'

Grace made no comment, but opened her eyes wide and raised her eyebrows to give us a look which implied 'you're mad, but please yourselves!'

That welcoming cup of tea in the kitchen was all I had to eat or drink until the following morning, so distressed and confused was my stomach by the smell lurking behind the out-house door. This was a great pity since we had pre-booked dinner.

Grace had prepared for us a wholesome meal of short crust steak and ale pie, with great piles of vegetables, lashings of gravy, half a loaf of thick, farmhouse bread and a dish of home-made butter. She was disappointed that I had no appetite. I struggled to make my apologies, but thought it polite to refrain from voicing the reason for my discomfort, at least until some later date. Also, I knew that Harry could be relied on in such a situation. He duly stepped into the breach and polished off the entire pie and all the vegetables and gravy single handed. Nor was there a scrap of bread left. I could probably have forced myself to eat the sweet course – rhubarb crumble and thick custard – but by then my appestat was confused between nausea and hunger. I looked on as Harry happily demolished enough crumble for two.

Tired from the long journey, and exhausted by my constant fight to keep the nausea at bay, I went to bed early, but slept restlessly, my tummy rumbling with hunger. The night brought strange noises, as though someone were rolling marbles or playing skittles in the wainscoting. I assumed it was mice but I was not quite sure. I was relieved to see the dawn through the drawn curtains.

Grace bustled around serving breakfast. We were the only guests.

'Would you like a packed lunch?' she asked.

'Yes please,' I answered. 'And could you please make up another meal for tonight, when we're out fishing?'

'Of course,' said Grace.

'And would you please make up four packs, and label two 'Tony' and two 'Harry' in very large letters?'

She looked at me wide-eyed, shaking her head slightly. She said nothing, but I could imagine her saying to herself 'these Townies – strange folk.'

'What about something to drink?'

'Just a bottle of cold drink please. We'll take our empty flasks and have them filled up somewhere later on – they'll be cold by the evening otherwise.'

Grace disappeared back into the kitchen. I managed to eat most of the excellent, full English breakfast which she had prepared, except for the fried egg, which I had left till last. There was something about the yellow viscosity and the slightly runny white which put me off. In an attempt to take my mind off the egg, I left the table and began studying the horse brasses and hunting horns above the inglenook fireplace.

'Go on, give it a blow, Tony,' said Harry, in jest.

I took down one of the hunting horns, put it to my mouth, formed my lips into what I thought passed for an *embouchure* and blew. The instrument, much to our surprise, emitted a long, piercingly shrill note.

Even more to our surprise, there arose from the direction of the kitchen the sound of wailing, like a tormented choir of ghosts and ghouls on All Hallows Eve. The door burst open and into the room bounded the two dogs, Tess and Sheba, barking furiously and snapping at the hunting horn which I still held in my hand. They were soon followed by a distraught Grace. It was the only time I ever saw her angry.

'Please don't do that!' she snapped. 'It sets off the dogs for hours.'

Shamefaced and embarrassed, but smirking like naughty schoolboys, we crept off to pack the car. Harry opened the lean-to door to get our rods. The weird smell was overpowering and I nearly retched. I just couldn't place it and what was frustrating was that Harry, whose sense of smell was normally as keen as mine, noticed nothing unusual.

'Smells like a farm Tony – cattle, pigs, goose shit, apples.'

I went into the kitchen to collect our packed food. It was time for answers.

'Grace,' I started, 'I know I've got a bit of a tummy problem at the moment, but what's that awful smell in the lean-to?'

She looked innocent and slightly hurt, as one would expect. 'What sort of smell?'

'I don't know, it's sort of chemical and fruit – goes right to my stomach.'

'We did have a wasp problem in there,' she said thoughtfully, 'maybe it's the stuff we used still hanging about. Cyanide I think it was. I can't think of anything else.'

('Hmmm,' I thought, 'cyanide – that's encouraging!')

'Anyway, here's your food. Where are you off to now?'

'Bridgwater first, then who knows?'

'Well, good luck,' said Grace, wiping her hands briskly on her apron to signal the end of the conversation. 'I'll see you later. Sounds like you're in for a long session. The front door's always open, so you can let yourselves in if you decide to pack up early.'

The Trentons' farm lay midway along the base of an isosceles triangle formed by three main roads, with Bridgwater at the apex. In this attractive market town, constructed around the estuary of the River Parrett, we soon tracked down the all-important tackle and bait shop.

Announcing ourselves to the owner as tourists from Essex, more specifically Southend, we were treated to the usual saws about knees ups, kiss-me-quick hats, cockles and whelks and jellied eels. When we asked where we might find a good place to go night fishing, his immediate recommendation was a stretch of the King's Sedgemoor Drain, which he assured us carried a fine head of fish. It had the great benefit, he said, of being easily accessible from the road, at a place called Greylake Bridge.

'It's not too far to walk,' he said enthusiastically. His final recommendation could not have fallen on ears more deaf. 'It holds some bloody good eels too. You boys'll love 'em, I bet!'

Bearing maps and permits, full of well-meaning advice, provisioned with loaves, maggots, worms and ground bait, we left town by the western route, heading for the village of Burrowbridge where we aimed to have lunch before doubling back to find the fishing spot.

'Chedzoy, Westonzoyland, Middlezoy.' Harry read off the curious sounding village names from the signpost at the cross roads.

'What about 'mach azoy'?' I asked (Yiddish for 'do it like this'). 'Or maybe there's an 'Oy vay' in there somewhere?'

'Westonzoyland,' repeated Harry sombrely, ignoring my pathetic wit. 'I wouldn't fancy spending a night there.'

'Why's that?'

'That was the actual site of the Battle of Sedgemoor, the final battle of the Monmouth rebellion. A nasty do – muzzle-loaders, swords, pitchforks, pikes. Fuck that!'

'You don't believe in ghosts, do you H?'

'You can never be too sure, Baws. Something like that, a big battle, hundreds dying – it must leave some trace.'

A large sign with flaking paintwork announced 'RAF Weston Zoyland'. On a whim, I swung the car off the main road into the wide driveway, expecting to face a gate or barrier and be challenged by perimeter guards. Instead we were able to proceed unhindered onto the apron of a disused airfield.

The field was so overgrown that in places the scrub and bramble stood several feet high. To our left I could see a control tower and some abandoned outbuildings, gaunt and windowless but otherwise intact. Ahead stretched a concrete runway, weedy but serviceable. To a suppressed boy racer, the pull was irresistible!

I put Mandy the Morris in gear and accelerated. We must have been doing ninety when a go-kart, invisible below the line of scrub, shot out from our left and disappeared to our right down the transverse secondary runway. We were obviously not alone. I slammed on the brakes and in a screech of burning rubber, the car slewed to a halt.

'Bawdrip!' shouted Harry.

'Sorry,' I mumbled apologetically, 'I didn't see it coming.'

'That's where the Duke of Monmouth launched his night attack from,

Bawdrip. It's a village just north of Bridgwater.' Harry had not even noticed our near miss.

After our dice with death at the airfield, I was relieved to arrive safely in Burrowbridge and find somewhere to park. We clambered up the ancient earthwork of Burrow Mump and settled under a small oak tree to eat a late lunch. My appetite was poor and I nibbled at the crust of a cheese sandwich without much enthusiasm.

Below us we could make out the high, muddy banks of the River Parrett at its tidal limit where it ran under the single span of the stone road bridge.

'I once had a friend called Mump,' I recalled. 'Drowned at the Blue Lagoon in Hadleigh.'

'Cheer us up Baws, why don't you?' said Harry, munching vigorously on an apple. I thought of my earlier request to Grace that she label our food carefully; now I would not object if Harry did indeed finish every morsel, such was my dis-ease with the notion of eating.

'That river down there looks a bit depressing too,' I continued, 'all that mud. I know we live on an estuary – it's all bloody mud off Southend – but there's something foul about salt tide where it washes up mud onto fresh-water reeds. Yuck!'

Harry was silent for a while, contemplating my opinion of the view. 'Do you want to move off then?'

'If you're ready. Anyway, we've got to find somewhere to fill our flasks for tonight.' As I stood up, I reached in my pocket and took out a penny piece. 'We'll probably never come back here, to this exact spot,' I said. 'Let's leave something for the future.' With that I pressed the coin into a deep fissure in the bark of the oak tree.

'Tone's Treasure,' beamed Harry. 'I wonder if someone will find it years from now. You never know.'

More to the point was finding somewhere to fill up with hot drinks for the night ahead. There was nowhere in the village so we headed out towards Street, keeping our eyes peeled. Just beyond the junction on the road to Glastonbury we came across a lay-by in which was a prominent 'A' board sign. In handwritten characters it announced 'Café – Hot meals all day'. A crudely-drawn hand pointed in the direction of a large caravan.

I parked the car and we ascended the unsteady stairs. Inside the caravan were two fixed rows of bench seats and tables, with a gap between the rows leading to a serving counter at the far end. On one side of this counter stood an ancient hot-water boiler, hissing with the sound of escaping steam, and on the other a glass case, in which sat two round rolls of indeterminate content, a cake with a shredded coconut topping and a few bars of 'Kit Kat'. A blackboard on the wall listed the table d'hote: a range of fried, chips-with-everything attractions, supplemented by jam sponge and custard, tea and a slice.

Harsh neon lights illuminated the unsmiling faces of the clientele. Facing us between the glass case and the boiler stood the proprietor, a small man with wispy hair. He wore an off-white coat, with greasy marks down the flanks where he habitually wiped his hands.

As he saw us approaching, he shovelled three spoonfuls of tea into a large, steel pot. This he positioned under the spout of the boiler while simultaneously, with the practice born of years, opening the spigot with his elbow. A jet of fiercely scalding water shot into the teapot.

'What can I get you gents?' he asked briskly.

It seemed churlish to request our normal coffee, confronted by such a demonstration of the tea-maker's art.

'Could you fill these two flasks, please? Strong, with plenty of sugar.'

Behind me, Harry launched into a practised recitation of the available varieties, which he often did when the word 'tea' was mentioned.

'There are many kinds of tea,' he intoned, in a professorial manner. 'Ceylon Tea – plenty of body but little smell; Effayar Tea – plenty of smell, but little body; Essaychai Tea – lots of smell and plenty of body…'

The owner busied about preparing our flasks, the hiss of the boiler making it impossible for him to understand what Harry was saying. 'Anythin' else?' he asked.

I looked questioningly at Harry, who turned down his mouth and shook his head.

'No, that'll be all thanks.'

The filled flasks were handed back. 'Call that three and six.'

'Are we right for the King's Sedgemoor?' I asked, handing over the money.

'This is it,' he said, gesturing with his thumb, 'over the back of the car park there. Fishermen are you?'

'That's right.'

'Aimin' to stay all night?'

'That's the plan'

'Best keep an eye on the levels then. There's been people workin' on the clyces lately.'

(Classes? glasses? I didn't know what he was talking about, but thanked him all the same.)

'I'm open till seven tonight, then again from five thirty in the morning, if you need anythin' else.'

The eponymous Drain ran arrow-straight to the horizon. Although it was only late afternoon, a hint of mist was already creeping over the low lying expanse of sedge and moor.

Pausing for a moment a few hundred yards below the bridge, I could see why Harry might feel disquieted by this place. I too sensed an almost tangible panorama; the sights and sounds of warring men. To have fought centuries ago on this barren and boggy wasteland, whether as a soldier of King James II's superior and well-trained forces or as a conscript in the ill-assorted and poorly equipped troops assembled by the rebel Duke of Monmouth, must have been a gruesome and terrifying experience.

I was grateful to be transported back to the present by the sound of water rushing through the steel sluices and for the reassurance they gave of industrial presence and modernity. Downstream the second of two tributaries flowed into the Drain, but right where we stood the water was slow-moving and the banks were shallow, sloping, and lined with reeds.

We set down our bags and tackled up, our two swims separated by a small clump of stunted trees. For two bite-less hours I stared at my motionless float, before going to see how Harry was faring a few yards away.

'How's it going, H?'

'Not a bloody knock. And they call this one of the premier fishing venues of England. Whoever 'they' are must be fucking easily pleased!'

'Maybe it'll be better after dark,' I said, trying to remain positive.

'You heard what that bloke said in Bridgwater – eels. A bloody jellied in the dark, that's something to look forward to!' He ranted on. 'And I could do without this mist. Gets up your snout and makes you feel gobbly.'

Normally I was able to diffuse Harry's rare negative moods, as he was mine, but now neither of us could find words of encouragement for the other. I returned to my swim, sensing it would be a long night.

The light was fading as I positioned my flashlight. I poured myself a drink, considering what best to eat. Confronted by the onset of anorexia, I still acknowledged the need to keep up my strength. I wound in the line and reaching in Grace's food box, located the hard boiled egg.

I delicately removed the shell and, finding a thoughtfully provided sachet of salt, sprinkled some on the blunt end of the egg and took a bite. The undercooked white parted easily, too easily, between my teeth and the cold, yellow, semi-solid yolk dribbled slowly down my chin.

Fighting back nausea, I sought to distract myself, by pulling on an additional jumper to ward against the chill night ahead and by changing my float and shot for a heavier model, in anticipation of casting in the dark. Neither stratagem worked. Paralysed with emetophobia, I sat rigidly in my chair, smoking cigarette after cigarette, as night fell on the moor. The line remained embedded by the hook in the cork handle of my rod. I did not fish that night.

Waking in the pitch dark from a fitful sleep, I imagined I heard the sound of battle. Close by was the sound of metal rasping on metal. All around were whispers of anguish; gurgling death throes and muffled cries. I stifled the urge to scream and felt down at my feet for my torch.

Sweeping the beam in a broad arc revealed only sedge behind me and only mud ahead; there was no water. Where not long ago I had been fishing, the reeds lay collapsed in the mud. In the torchlight beam swarmed a myriad flies and other winged insects.

I ran round to where Harry sat sleeping and there I stayed, close by him till the dawn. Bleary eyed in the cold light of day, we could see where the sluice, the clyce, had slowly fallen shut, trapping the water behind it. Without fresh water entering, the water in our swims had drained away.

We stowed our belongings in the car and sought the sanctuary of the transport café on the bridge. The place was full, even though it was barely six o'clock. Each table was occupied by burly drivers, wading enthusiastically into their breakfast. The smell of fried bacon stimulated my taste buds and my stomach rumbled from hunger, yet I had no appetite.

'Hello gents,' said the owner, recognising us from the previous day. 'Have a good night?'

I was aware of Harry engaging him in conversation but then their voices faded into the background. My intestines cramped and I suddenly found myself needing to concentrate on restraining my bowels, for fear they might suddenly part company with what little I had digested of that foul, cold, soft-boiled egg.

'Tony, what will you have?' asked Harry.

The pain was severe, and food was the furthest thing from my mind. For no reason other than simplicity, I placed my order. 'Just a 'Kit Kat' please.'

This vocalisation was enough to make me fractionally lose concentration, and my sphincter marginally relaxed. Thankfully there was no evidence of a solid nature. Instead a smell of overwhelming pungency, a noxious *melange* of fruit, meat, cheese, egg and the demons of Hades, silently permeated the entire café, borne aloft and dispersed by the heat of the cooking range and the hot-water boiler.

I stared straight ahead, well versed in the ways of disavowing a silent but noisesome fart. I knew also that I could rely on Harry who, realising it was not him, would suspect that it was me, and would cover my back, so to speak. The café owner had no option but to serve us without comment, although the look of disgust on his face and his contorted nose indicated that he had his suspicions.

Harry paid and we turned away from the counter, heading towards the exit. On our way out we noticed that on the tables were scattered utensils, half-eaten meals and unfinished cups of tea and coffee, as though there had been a pressing emergency requiring an immediate mass exodus. Of the voracious customers, so recently relishing their repast and imbibing with vigour, there was not a sign, save for some deep ruts in the car park, where their vehicles had accelerated away at high speed.

CHAPTER 21

The Sargasso Sea of Somerset

'Oh man of the sea! Come listen to me!
For Alice my wife, the plague of my life,
Has sent me to beg a boon of thee.'

<small>TRADITIONAL</small>

Harry's eyes were watering. This was possibly a direct result of my antics in the café – certainly my gruff was enough to stop a buffalo in its tracks, or perhaps it was the physical price he was paying for his appreciation of that nostril-ripping, café-clearing event as pure theatre, since he had hardly stopped laughing during the entire journey back to the farm from Greylake bridge.

To add to this, there was the amusement he derived from a careful study of the empty 'Five Boys' chocolate-bar wrapper he now held in his hand. Somehow one component of Grace's packed meals had escaped his attention during the night.

Produced by J S Fry & Sons Ltd of Bristol, this iconic packaging depicted the face of a young boy, illustrated to reflect him in marginally different emotional states, beginning with despair and culminating in joy as he was rewarded with the chocolate treat. Underneath each illustration was a single word, intended to describe the changing facial expression. The wrapper seemed to give far more joy to Harry than the chocolate content inside (although he did manage to tuck that away too, swiftly and with relish).

Harry read the words aloud, in the style of an old time theatre actor-manager, elongating each syllable for maximum resonance:

'Desperation – Pacification – Expectation – Acclamation – Realisation – It's Fry's!'

'Look at him, Baws,' he spluttered, trying to snarl and laugh at the same time, all the while waving the wrapper at me. 'Miserable little sod! Doesn't deserve any treats. And here, and here – he's hardly cheered up at all. Bastard only breaks into a laugh at the end. I wouldn't give him fuck all!'

We were not to know at the time that the message of the wrapper could serve as a parable of our early days at Durston, but with the iconic words re-arranged in reverse order.

William's tractor stood throbbing at the open gate, coupled up to a high-sided trailer. I nudged the car into the farmyard, carefully negotiating the gap between the tractor and the gate-post, and pulled up alongside. Stepping out, it was a case of the biter bit as I, purveyor not long since of the foulest smell in Somerset, sniffed that pungent aroma; that foul, noxious smell which I recognised as the one that had plagued me since the day of our arrival. It came from the trailer.

'Christ, William!' I complained. 'What have you got in there? It smells bloody vile.'

William Trenton looked at me, puzzled.

'That's just slabs of apple mush – from our cider pressing. We's got too much for our few pigs, so I'm takin' some down the road to Potter's place.'

'And that's all that's been making me feel so ill? Rotten apples?'

William lifted his flat cap and scratched his head. ''S'pose it is a bit strong if you ain't used to it,' he conceded, putting the tractor in gear. 'All I knows is, it makes damn good cider and the pigs love it.' He gave a cheery wave as he turned into the road. 'Oh well,' he said, 'see you soon.' Harry helped me unload the car and we stacked our equipment in the lean-to. Already the smell had begun to clear. The back door opened and Grace appeared, Sheba and Tess jumping and snapping at her heels.

'Mornin' gents, have a good night?'

I recounted our miserable experience on the King's Sedge Moor; the ghostly sounds, the drained waterway, the mud, the flies. Harry studied me while I spoke, a hint of a smirk playing around his lips, wordlessly urging me to mention the fart, but I resisted.

'Shame,' she said. 'Maybe you should give the old canal down the road a try. It's not very far and hardly anyone ever goes there now. My old Dad used to say it was the best fishing for miles around. William's just gone that way now with the tractor to take some mush down to Kirby Potter. His farm backs onto the canal. I can give you directions if you like. It's easy enough to get to.'

Loath as I was to follow the dreadful smell of the apple mush down to Potter's Farm, Grace's promise for the new water momentarily served to dispel the haunting memory of the mud and the flies on the King's Sedgemoor Drain. I was bolstered by the *Realisation* that a better spot was to be found not far away.

'What do you think, Harry? We can go and have a quick look and then come back for a clean up and rest. We could go back this evening if it looks any good.'

'Might as well, boy – we've got nothing to lose.'

The disused Bridgwater and Taunton Canal ran north-south, to the west of the farm, some two miles beyond the Trentons' fields as the crow flies. An abandoned railway ran for a short distance alongside the canal and a humpbacked bridge carried a country lane across the track, past the imposing Victorian station building (now a private residence) and onto a small marshalling yard flanked by a row of terraced houses.

We caught glimpses of canal over the hedgerow as we made our approach and excitement gripped us. We left the car in the yard and hurried towards the water, as though it might disappear if we did not move quickly enough.

At the far end of the yard, a dirt road led to an aluminium bridge, the front access to Potter's Farm. Here we stood, absorbing for the first time the charm of the canal which was to sear itself into the shared memories of our fishing friendship, and which we referred to always and with great affection as simply 'Durston'.

We headed off along the towpath, away from the main road, trying to get a feel for the water. It was clean and the channel was well scoured but there was some colour to it. There were no signs of other anglers having visited recently – no obvious, down-trodden swims, no forgotten or abandoned rod rests. There were no signs of boating either and the reason for this became apparent after a few hundred yards. Here we came to a broken and abandoned lock, the jammed gates overgrown with weed. Despite the absence of any signs that others than ourselves had shown an interest, this canal had a distinctly fishy feel to it.

'I think I saw a rise, Tone,' urged an excited Harry.

To be sure, some coarse fish do rise; a dace or chub will take an insect much as a trout might do. Then again, a fish might rise to the surface, flick its tail and be off, for no apparent reason. Nevertheless, taking one thing with another, and having observed Harry's reported 'rises' over many outings, I felt that most could be put down to the activities of amphibians, voles, water-boatmen, falling bird-droppings, skimming swallows or the heralding splash of a shower of rain.

'I can't wait to get into the water, can you,?' said Harry, with such vigour that I imagined him doing just that. 'Looks good doesn't it?' he went on. ' I reckon it hasn't been fished much.'

'Well, shall we give it a go later on?' I enquired, giving rein to his boundless enthusiasm. 'We can get some bread at the farm. What do you think?'

'Worth a try isn't it?' said Harry. 'After all, we've got nothing to lose.'

When we returned to the canal, late that balmy afternoon, the picture which greeted us was even more inviting than when we had first seen it a mere few hours ago. The surface of the water was unrippled and the reed tops barely rustled in the warm, summer air. Swallows appeared as if from nowhere and were silhouetted briefly against the almost violet sky, before dipping low and skimming the water for insects.

We chose two swims on a gentle bend, opposite a line of huge elm trees. We began to assemble our rods, taking our time, trying to keep calm. I settled in my low chair and poked the rod through a gap in the reeds. The float hardly had time to settle before it lifted unhurriedly and slid majestically under the water.

I struck and felt a solid resistance, moving to my left, away from Harry's swim. I stood up, the better to lift the rod clear of the reeds as the line whirred off the reel and the rod curved over. The fish travelled 20 yards or more before I recovered some semblance of control. I began to manoeuvre it back into my swim but then it turned straight towards me, wedging itself into the muddy limit of the reed bed. I desperately wound in line and passed the rod once again over the reeds to make a straight pull between me and the fish. Extending my arms as far as possible I effectively attempted to *push* the fish back into open water.

'Have you got one?' shouted Harry.

I felt it was the other way round, that this one had got me.

'Do you want me to come round, Tone?' yelled Harry.

'For fuck's sake, Yes, H!'

'Coming!'

Thus was the halcyon scene shattered, as the urgency to land the fish became all-consuming. Harry grabbed the landing net and peered hopefully at where he thought the fish might be. Suddenly the mighty tench was free again, moving off and taking line. One more run, and then I had it more or less under control. I say more or less because, grateful as I was for all his help over the years, Harry waving a landing net around added no certainty to a successful outcome and did little to inspire confidence that any fish would be landed with greater facility due to his intervention. Often where the fish was, Harry was not. This time though, the prize was netted, with much splashing from the fish and back-slapping from Harry.

'Look at that,' he beamed in *Acclamation*. 'What a beauty.'

We gazed admiringly at the bulky tench, its green-gold-tinged body glistening in the sun, set off by an iridescent red eye. I had no weighing scales but guessed it was around six pounds. I looked about for something to measure it against which would indicate its size in a photograph. My rod and reel would have been ideal but instead all I could think of was a cigarette packet, which proved no help at all. Looking at the photo later, with the fish laid out on my chair, it was about the size of my left buttock.

Neither of us had any further bites. The exhaustion of the previous session began to tell and we decided to have an early night. In the event, my night turned out to be somewhat earlier than Harry's.

'Whatever is he doin' up there?' asked Grace in the kitchen, referring to the sound of stomping, splashing, slapping and tra-la-la'ing coming from Harry's room above. 'I was up there a short while ago,' she said, 'and it smells like, like, like I don't know what. Ladies stuff sort of, only quite nice in a way.'

'Yes,' I said soberly, 'Harry likes to keep clean when we're not fishing.'

My appetite was still poor but Harry tucked into dinner with gusto. We had just finished when William came into the dining room.

'I'm goin' down The Monmouth Arms for a pint. Would you gen'l'men like to join me?'

'My tummy's still a bit rough, thanks all the same. You go though, Harry.'

'Just one then. You sure you don't mind, Tone?'

'No, it's fine. See you later.'

Harry did not appear for breakfast and Grace was not her usual bubbly self.

'Bloody men,' she hissed, 'excuse my French. Work to do, then comes back all soppy like.'

I gathered that William and Harry had stayed rather too long at the pub, quaffing cider. But Grace could not stay cross for long.

'Would you like some toast after? I'll be takin' Harry up a strong cup of coffee in a bit.'

Rather than set off fishing on my own directly after breakfast, I decided to explore the farm and the fields which lay behind it. Now that the pungent smell of the cider mush had been dispersed, it was really quite enjoyable. The Trentons' teenaged son Jack pulled up beside me on a blue tractor, towing a trailer. On the trailer was an ancient black motor-bike.

'I'm goin' down the bottom field to have a run on the bike,' he said. 'Fancy a go?'

Technically I held a licence to drive anything with wheels, although this did not seem to be a situation which would call for a licence. It would just be a bit of fun.

'Yes, I'd like that.'

'Jump on the trailer then,' said Jack cheerfully, and off we went, bumping down the track.

On the way, we passed a decidedly non-agricultural gathering. In a field, standing in the manner implied by their generic name, or else leaning drunkenly against each other, were congregated between 15 and 20 upright pianos. I wondered if there was a collective noun for such a number.

'Sedgemoor Fair soon,' said Jack, noticing my interest. 'They's for the piano smashing contest. You 'as to break 'em up into pieces small enough to pass through a tractor tyre suspended from a tree.'

It was re-assuring to know that I had been justified in giving up my lessons early in life – obviously piano playing was merely a passing fad.

'Here we are,' said Jack, cutting the engine. The motor-bike was wheeled proudly off the trailer and I immediately noticed a singular deficiency; it had no saddle, just the saddle fixings, pointing skywards at a rectum-threatening angle.

'You can 'ave a go after me,' announced Jack, kicking over the bike and revving the engine, 'so's you can watch where I go.' With that, he dropped the bike into gear and roared off, making sure not to sit down.

When it came eventually to my turn, I realised that I had been spoilt by the only two-wheeled vehicle I had ridden up to this point, namely a Lambretta Scooter. Deemed competence on that most sedate of machines had somehow qualified me to ride all types and classes of motorcycle, up to and including the monsters of the Isle of Man TT, if I had so wished.

I did notice some important dissimilarities between my cherished Lambretta and the gruesome and gnarled beast which I was now being invited to ride. For a start my scooter had a proper saddle – no contest there. Secondly, the scooter gears were on the handlebars, whereas the bike gears were 'somewhere down there'. Thirdly, the footbrake on a scooter is visible and easily accessed, whilst the brake on this motor-bike was also 'somewhere down there'.

I ruminated briefly over the other things in life for which I had volunteered and for which I was actually ill prepared and basically bluffing and realised I had usually come a cropper: refereeing a match at the local rugby festival while I was still at school and had only a scant knowledge of the offside rules; offering to play drums in a traditional jazz band when the drummer failed to appear, (I had never so much as picked up a pair of drumsticks before that night); insisting on driving someone else's left-hand drive car in the hubbub of Brussels city centre at night, only days after I passed my test in England. Now I was about to try my untrained bluffer's hand again.

'Here you are,' urged Jack, handing me the bike after roaring up and down the field several times. 'Your turn.'

I remembered, from observing Jack, how to select first gear and even managed to get it into second, all the while desperately trying to remember not to sit down on the non-existent saddle. At the junction of the two fields I ran into a problem. Either I had not been paying sufficient attention at the time, or Jack's negotiation of the water-filled ditch running transversely between the fields, but hidden by the slope, had been remarkably smooth.

Having only a split second to react, I was faced with the stark choice of staying with the bike and risking serious injury to my genitals on the saddle-stumps, or baling out. I decided to jump off.

I thought that Jack would never stop laughing as I went one way and the bike the other. But I had known worse, in the ditch with Harry on that dark night coming through Bicknacre in Essex.

Jack ran forward to cut the engine, all the time roaring with laughter. Mustering as much dignity and *sang-froid* as a slight limp and multiple bruising would allow, I thanked him for the bike ride and helped him to man-handle the cause of my downfall back onto the trailer. It was time to rouse Harry and go fishing.

'Still feel a bit gutty, Baws. You just carry on. I'll stay in the car for a while.'

I had managed to bring the horse to water, but he was as yet in no fit state to drink. Or maybe it was the drink that had brought him to this state. Rather than disappoint Harry with a return to the scene of yesterday's triumphs while he was still feeling poorly today, I headed the car for a different location along the canal, to the lock beside The Harvest Moon pub.

The water in this pound was shallow and clear. Had Harry been *compos mentis*, he would have warned me against ever trying to catch fish you can see. There were many of his well-worn phrases to choose from if I were ever forced to select a single one for his epitaph, but 'You never catch fuck all in gin clear water' might well have been a contender.

But here I was, landing a lively tench which I had fortuitously spotted in about a foot of water just by the pub car park. I had simply dropped a bread-baited hook in front of it and – *voilà!* It had even shown the decency to remain stationary for the ten or so minutes it took me between tackling up from scratch and actually hooking it

'Harry! Harry! Come and look at this.'

There was no response from the comatose figure snoring soundly in the back seat. If a decent tench did not make him stir, he really was in bad shape.

Like a bored schoolboy, I mooched off, taking my rod, landing net and duffle bag. Maybe I could track and catch another tench. Instead, I spotted the most enormous pike, lurking immobile in the shadow of the tow-path.

I do not know to this day how I kept my hands steady enough to remove the float, shot and hook used for the tench and attach in their place a lifelike imitation frog, which I had bought on a whim at the tackle shop in Bridgwater.

Stealthily I crouched down with the great pike still in sight. Carefully I swung the frog lure into the water ahead of it. The massive jaws eased open as, unbelievably, the frog settled on the pike's snout. Time seemed to stand still before, in a split-second, the pike made a dart for the frog and an over-anxious angler struck.

There was a fleeting moment where I felt a glorious resistance before the frog flew over my head and landed in the hedge behind, where the shock of the recoil parted line and lure, thus leading me to lose my expensive, imitation frog on its maiden voyage.

Harry was standing, stretching and yawning outside the car when I returned,

'Had any luck, Baws?'

I recounted the tale of the tench and the pike . After I finished my story with the dramatic and tragic loss of the rubber frog, Harry spoke.

'Do you know what I fancy?' he said, gazing towards the welcoming portal of the pub. 'A pint and a pork pie.'

Whatever they served to Harry at The Harvest Moon that day should be patented as a hangover cure. By the time we arrived back at the bridge leading to Potter's Farm, Harry was raring to go. Flying in the face of his personal protocol and casting into midstream with a single maggot, letting the float trot down, he landed fish after fish.

'Got 'im!' shouted Harry as he hooked yet another fine Durston roach.

How many did that make? Twenty, twenty-one? As to my own tally? Precisely zero. *Zilch, nada, niente, rien, gornisht.* Not only had Harry discovered the whereabouts of a fishing Shangri-la, but he had arrived there while going through a Purple Patch on his Red Letter Day. Those same hands which I had witnessed demolishing many a fixed-spool reel or creating the most inextricable birds' nests, now caressed the line to tease the tackle many yards downstream, until the float shot under and a powerful strike picked up the line to hook the fish.

Harry continued to land roach until the light faded. I was pleased that he was pleased.

'Coming back here tomorrow, Tone?' he asked excitedly.

'Yes, fine,' I answered, the two of us full of hope and *Expectation* at the promise of another memorable session.

Arriving early at the canal the following day, conditions were perfect. For the first half hour we both caught roach steadily, but then quite suddenly the bites ceased and the shoal moved on.

'Gone a bit turpsy, Tone,' Harry complained miserably.

I could never get from him what 'turpsy' meant exactly. I reasoned that it had something to do with the paint thinning property of turpentine, since he similarly employed the word 'thin', as in 'having a thin time of it'. He might describe a chill winter wind as 'thin'. If there was a long period without a bite, Harry would tilt his face upwards to the Heavens and yell; 'THIN!!'

We took our lines from the water and stood around, smoking cigarettes.

'Let's walk on a bit,' I suggested after a while. 'We can take our rods and stuff with us. See if we can't find some fish.'

Actually finding fish was not the real problem. Below the lock and all the way to The Harvest Moon, the water was wide, shallow and clear. Huge shoals of weighty roach could be seen, nervously hugging the far bank or sheltering behind fronds of mid-water weed.

It was the catching of them that proved impossible. As soon as we approached with our tackle they were gone. We were careful not to cast shadows and our footfall was considerate, but despite all precautions we could not keep them in a swim. We followed the shoals all morning but they continued to elude us.

The hot mid-day sun bore down on our futile quest. We both grew increasingly frustrated.

'By the prophet's beard!' hissed Harry in annoyance as yet another roach shoal took flight. 'By the scrotum of John the Baptist, this could drive you *meshugge.*'

As a last resort, I suggested to Harry that he stayed in one spot while I attempted to resurrect my very best Baden-Powell tracking skills, (which had lain dormant since I was in the 2nd Hadleigh Cubs), in a final effort to bag one of these elusive fish.

Crawling low on all fours, holding my rod by the butt with the tip behind me, I reached the cover of margin reeds some twenty yards away. I waved cautiously to Harry, whom I could see as he sat quietly smoking. He gave me a thumbs up. Slowly, very slowly, I raised my head – the roach were still there. Carefully I attached a small piece of flake to the hook but as I half crouched to cast in, the roach shoal sensed my presence, turned as one and headed at speed down the cut.

'*Genug!*' I shouted. '*Das ist genug!*' I heard Harry laugh and pick up the cry – '*Genug!*' Then I stood bolt upright and began flailing at the water with my rod. '*Genug!*'

Harry made his way toward me as I whipped the water with increasing vigour. He was laughing hysterically by the time he reached me and I decided to go for broke. Judging the water to be not too deep I took my first hesitant step from the bank.

Within three strides, the water was up to my waist, but there it stopped. With one final blow of my rod on the water, I vented my frustration not only on these roach, but on all fish who had frustrated me over the years with their selfish, avoiding tactics. Losing my balance, I tripped head first and went right under.

Harry found it hard to keep a straight face as we trudged back to the bridge, my boots squelching at every step. In the back of the car, the only dry item of clothing I could find was an orange, woollen, knitted dress belonging to Suzie, which she had somehow failed to unpack from our previous weekend away visiting Uncle Sid in Brighton.

'I must say it suits you, Tony' grinned Harry as I took off my wet clothes and pulled on the dress. 'It's quite your colour.'

'Do you think it goes with the boots though?'

At least the tight knit covered my essentials. I draped my own clothes over the car, hoping they would dry in time for the short drive home. It was not so much embarrassment at the prospect of being seen in a dress, but the fear that I would not be able to operate the car foot pedals without hitching up my skirt in a brazen manner.

We made our way onto the bridge, peering into the water. I was hoping that no one would come by. As if to taunt us, a large shoal of roach weaved this way and that under the bridge supports, chasing down the odd snack. The adrenalin rush of my impromptu diving display had worn off. Now I felt depressed that the early promise of the day had come to this.

Footsteps in the distance jolted me from my self-pity. Walking along the station road towards us was a girl and I decided then and there that I would rather not be seen in public (or in private for that matter) wearing my wife's dress if it could be avoided. I motioned Harry quickly to join me and we hastily clambered back into the car.

It used to amuse Harry greatly that I gave more than a passing interest to women's breasts. He took advantage of my interest in bosoms by instituting a parlour game, of which he was the quizmaster. It was basically a variant of the 'twenty pounds cash or a twenty pound carp?' dilemma.

When the fishing was exceptionally good, Harry would pose a question, such as: 'What would you rather be doing now, Tony? Fishing, or groping Brigitte Bardot's tits?'

Now Harry obviously knew what was going through my mind as I watched Farmer Potter's daughter approach. Even at a distance, it was apparent that here was a big girl.

'Fine set of tits, Tony!' was his observation as she drew closer.

A strange expression really, 'set of tits'. Some people might find it offensive but I find that it has a certain appeal as a collective noun, with a nice, rustic ring to it – a brace of pheasant, a flight of ducks, a set of tits.

At least the arrival of Potter's daughter afforded some degree of *Pacification*, a temporary, mental diversion from the damp and increasingly itchy state in which I found myself.

We hunkered further down in our seats and tried to make ourselves invisible as the girl reached the bridge, hoping she would not focus on the odd sight of mens' underwear and clothing laid out to dry on top of the car, stop to investigate, and find one of us wearing a dress! To my great relief she quickly disappeared up the short road to the farmhouse.

Opening the car door to check on my clothes once the coast was clear, I could hear raised voices coming from the direction of Potter's place, followed by the sound of breaking glass and crockery, then heavy thumps and more shouting. Harry leaned out of the door as we strained our ears, trying to make out what was going on. We could only discern the occasional word:

'....staying out all hours...',

'...don't need you tellin' me what to do...'

'...I'm your father...'

'See, what did I always tell you, Tony?' said Harry, tapping the side of his nose knowingly. 'Big tits, big trouble.'

To her great credit, Grace Trenton made no comment on my dress (or rather Suzie's dress) as Harry and I made our way upstairs. Although her jaw dropped and her eyes opened wide, no comment passed her lips, either at the time or later. Serving us dinner that night, she was most solicitous as to our piscatorial progress, pausing briefly only to mention she hoped that the annual weed-cutting on the canal would not inconvenience us greatly.

The following morning we stood on the bridge at Durston, appalled and speechless, surveying the scene. Downstream we could make out the top of the lock gates in the distance, while upstream we could see as far as the bend before the road bridge, with its row of elm trees. Here I had caught the large tench on our first day. What we could not see, no matter how hard we tried, was water. In its place was a solid green mass of cut reed and weed, snaking into the distance in both directions.

'Bloody hell!' fumed Harry, 'you could walk on that bastard!'

It certainly was solid. As if accepting Harry's invitation, two moorhens strutted out from the bankside and strolled casually over the weed, pausing occasionally to pick up this or that piece of appetising detritus.

The visit the previous day had been frustrating enough, and now this. Harry, it must be said, was an extremely well-read and articulate man, for all his pretences of coarseness. But now, gazing glumly at the weed, he could summon only one phrase. This he repeated for emphasis:

'Well, I'll be fucked! Well, fuck me!'

It certainly summed up the situation while doing nothing to alleviate it.

'Come on, Harry. Let's have a look a bit further up. It might be a bit better there.'

We began walking in the direction of the lock but it was no use. The canal we had left not long ago – the swims where we had landed those fine, fresh, silver-and-red, dashing roach, had all disappeared. The Sargasso Sea of Somerset had crept up and covered it so thickly that it was hard to imagine there had ever been any water there at all. We stared at the weed in *Desperation*.

'Well, I'll be fucked,' muttered Harry. 'Well, fuck me!'

CHAPTER 22

Westward Ho The Wagon!

'From ghoulies and ghosties
And long-leggedy beasties
And things that go bump in the night,
Good Lord, deliver us!'

<small>TRADITIONAL PRAYER</small>

Eventually the redundancy axe fell, as Harry had feared it would. Although he put a brave face on his predicament, patting his pocket to show he could still buy his round, beneath the façade he was a worried man. He was treated with scant regard, despite his dedicated service, after more than twenty years with one firm: no pension, no gold watch, no office farewell.

He did not have a desk to clear apart from the wooden trolley at home. Without the paperwork to fill it, he used the space to extend his collection of cleansing and cosmetic preparations. With unwelcome time on his hands, he expanded his washing rituals to take up large parts of each day. He invested most of his modest severance pay in six bespoke suits, 'the better to fit me out for a new position'. He also acquired a wickedly sharp, Regency swordstick, for reasons less apparent.

Finding work was not easy. He was used to the outdoor life of a travelling salesman and apart from the compulsive work pattern of his paperwork (which he himself had initiated), he was also accustomed to being his own man.

An old friend did find him a job in the foreign currency department of an insurance company – Harry left after two weeks: 'They sat me in a little cubicle with this machine,' he groused. 'You have to turn a handle and it converts foreign currency into sterling. It was decent of old dogface to arrange it for me I suppose, but honestly Tony – all bloody day turning a sodding handle. It's enough to drive you round the fucking twist!'

On occasion, he was kind enough to run one or two business errands for me – collecting records from clients, delivering urgent letters to the tax office and so on. I also imposed on him to perform the odd clerical service. Although I could not expect from him much in the way of accountancy skills this late in the day, he soon mastered the rudiments of a bank analysis and he had all the attributes of a valued employee: reliability, smart appearance, pleasant manner, good speaking voice. His military bearing and attention to detail were additional assets.

Rather than let him feel that I was taking advantage, I made him a formal offer of employment. He was reluctant to accept, suspecting I was only doing it out of the goodness of my heart. To find a way out of this *impasse*, he insisted that I accept as a cash loan the last of his redundancy pay, which I used to fulfil a longstanding ambition.

My uncle Ben, who somehow managed to combine a career as an opera singer and music teacher, while at the same time selling leather coats, had driven me to the cemetery on the day of my mother's funeral in his prized possession, a Lotus Cortina. Despite the solemnity of the occasion, he delighted in showing off and putting the car through its paces on the narrow Essex roads. I fell in love with it on the spot and determined to buy one someday. Thanks to Harry's loan, that day had now arrived.

Unfortunately, the model I bought was a disaster. Ignoring my own unwritten rule, which broadly states 'never travel long distances to part with money', and tempted by her siren call, I bought a vehicular pig-in-a-poke - in Bournemouth – for cash.

By sheer serendipity, my partner had acquired that very week as a new client a car-dealer who was the local Lotus agent. He was pleased to examine the car, the myriad defects were soon identified and costed and a deal was struck. The dealer agreed to fix my car in return for equal value in accountancy and tax services. I trust that our professional input matched his mechanical competence, because the car he handed back to me six weeks later was a mighty, hairy beast.

My choice of substitute vehicle while the Lotus was being repaired suited perfectly an expression my mother often used: 'From the sublime to the Gawd Blimey!' For seventy pounds, at Alexandra Palace Car Auctions in North London, I bought an ancient Morris J4.

'Molly Morris' was mainly painted green, with only her red roof remaining as a clue to previous life as a Post Office delivery van. Someone had glued Beatrix Potter posters along both sides and someone, (possibly the same culprit), had painted the entire interior a bright, sky blue. With a couple of old mattresses and a camping stove installed in the back, the van had quite a hippy ambience.

Suzie and I were hardly hippies but we were happy to be swept along by the *zeitgeist*. Harry too joined in with enthusiasm. He appreciated the music of the time and furthermore was discerning in his taste. He enjoyed dancing and was not averse to the odd toke. He soon gained a reputation among our friends as being something of a mature 'groover', both for his non-judgemental approach and for his willingness, within reason, to 'try anything once'.

Being close to the music business, not only did I come to view smoking joints as commonplace, but I became something of a cannabis connoisseur. I also discovered that the plastic containers used by tackle shops to supply and dispense lead shot provided a convenient means of storage and transportation of my personal supply of hashish. However, it was very important that I labelled the containers clearly, since the contents of the six separate compartments were as follows:

Fishing Container: Dust shot – No.4 – No.1 – BB – AAA – Swan shot.
Smoking Container: Moroccan Ketama – Red Leb – Paki Gold Seal – Bombay Black – Nepalese Temple Ball – Afghani Twist.

I noted that the lead shot supplied by tackle shops was packaged in the containers in ascending order of weight and effect. On reflection, the same could have been said of my hash!

To celebrate our new working arrangement and to christen Molly Morris as our fishing transport, we made a swift return to the west country, heading this time for Evercreech near Glastonbury, where our good friend Belinda had a cottage.

'Beedie' was the girlfriend of someone I knew in the music business. Dark haired and beautiful with an infectious laugh, she was Belinda only to her family. To everyone else she was Beedie, a happy conjunction of her given name and the little Indian smoking sticks of which she was so fond.

On the journey down we discovered that our smart new van had one drawback. The centrally-mounted engine, with a metal cover, positioned between driver and passenger, became unbearably hot on a long run. By the time we were half way along the A4, the heat was stifling.

I stopped to open the small windows fully for ventilation but we were still boiling hot. Stopping once more, I drew open the sliding door on my side. This induced, in Harry especially, a holiday, coach-outing atmosphere.

He became more and more excited reading the names on the signposts as we travelled westward, launching into a song or a limerick where appropriate:

'*There was a young man from Devizes,*
Whose balls were of varying sizes.
One ball was small, almost no ball at all –'

He paused at the crescendo, urging me to join in the finish.

'Go on,' he chuckled.

We sang the last verse together:

'*but the other was large and won prizes!*'

'I love Bath,' he shouted, above the roar of the wind and the noise of the engine. 'Do you think we can go to the Roman Baths? The Pump Room? It's all lovely and warm in there – clears your snout right away.'

I would have thought that if a hot snout was all that was required, we could simply close the van windows and door again and let Molly do her worst.

He closed his eyes in ecstasy. 'Hmmm, *Aquae Sulis* – can't beat it, Baws!'

The miles rolled past. Occasionally the engine missed a beat but I put this down to age and strain. Our visit to the tourist traps of Bath was pleasant enough and allowed Harry to briefly indulge his Regency fantasies. We peered into the Avon by Pulteney Bridge, excited more by the fish than the history or the architecture. In the Pump Room, Harry widened his eyes and smiled a wicked smile, in case I had missed the point that the sulphurous odour was redolent of farts. At the Roman Baths, he pointed to a dripping portal guarding a dank doorway, with nothing but darkness beyond.

'That's where the Minotaur lives,' he announced jokingly, with blatant disregard for Roman and Greek mythology.

He had packed his Regency swordstick for the journey west, 'just in case' and produced it for our slow perambulation along Royal Terrace. His measured gait was every inch the Regency dandy, even though his apparel might be better described as Essex fisherman.

We headed south out of Bath in the late afternoon. 'It's all military around here,' observed Harry, reading again from the roads signs. 'Devizes, Westbury, Warminster, Shepton Mallett – all army towns. Near Salisbury Plain you see. People are always saying they see flying saucers in the sky around Glastonbury. With all that fucking ordnance being thrown about, it's hardly surprising.'

'Were you involved in exercises on Salisbury Plain then?' I asked.

'No, I never had that pleasure. Ampthill was where my lot were drilled, the Beds and Herts. I was at RAF Cardington for a short while – they had a captive balloon parachute trainer there. Bloody thing! You all stood in a wicker basket, shitting yourselves, while they let the balloon out on a cable.

When you got to the top, they opened a gate in the basket and you had to jump, hoping you didn't 'Roman Candle'.

'Roman Candle? What's that?'

'Oh, you know,' explained Harry with considerable *sang-froid*, 'when the parachute doesn't open. Then there was an assembly place outside Stranraer,' he continued, without giving me time to further question his parachuting exploits. 'After I was transferred to the Royal Ulsters, I got posted to Belfast. Used to go backwards and forwards a lot between Scotland and Ireland across the Irish Sea.'

'Was it rough?'

'It was always fucking rough. I can't remember a time when it wasn't fucking rough.'

'Did you get used to it?'

'Did I bollocks! No, I was sick as pig every trip.'

Observing a road sign announcing the City of Wells, he began to sing, to the tune of 'A Life on the Ocean Wave':

'*The Bishop of Bath and Wells,*
Was fond of peculiar smells…..'

I interrupted to suggest it would be too dark to look for Beedie's cottage tonight, and that we should find somewhere to stay before we reached Frome, which I pronounced to rhyme with 'home'.

'Froom,' corrected Harry. 'Rhymes with broom.'

'And are they?' I asked.

'Are they what?'

'*Frum.*' (Orthodox Jews)

'Could be,' said Harry thoughtfully. 'Jewish refugees from all over Europe made their way through the south of England at one time or another. Some of them might have stayed put, you never know.'

The local sign announced that we were entering the village of Norton St Philip. I reflected that I once worked with a Norman Norton, when I was the Saturday cashier in the menswear shop. He was certainly Jewish. Maybe Harry had a point, although the 'St Philip' part might be a bit of a stretch. Parking the van in a cul-de-sac, we made for the village pub.

If the draught Guinness served to us at the guest house near Bathampton represented the apogee of the brew master's craft, then according to Harry, the beer of Norton St Philip, only a matter of a few miles away, was the nadir. He would always refer to it when a damning comparison was needed, viz: 'it's not as bad as that bloody beer at Norton St Philip.'

'Fucking awful tack!' he moaned as we set off the next morning on the journey to Evercreech. 'Thin, flat, bitter bastard. Only had one half and I felt cloopy – stuff came down my fucking nose. I could have gone outside and shot the cat, but I know you don't like it.'

We would have no such problems concerning malt or hops or yeast while in the company of Beedie, who was a staunch supporter of the local cider. After meeting up with her and her mother Esther and being given a lightning tour of the building-site chaos that was their cottage, we motored out to Stourhead, a formal park and garden owned by the National Trust.

The estate comprised a grand house, landscaped gardens, a vast lake, woodland and farmland, and the entire village of Stourton. By mid-day, the three of us were ensconced in the snug of the village pub, perched on high stools, eating sausage rolls and drinking strong cider.

We were soon in mellow mood. Harry crooked a finger to summon the barman. With a smile of innocence approaching piety, he nodded towards the window and enquired: 'Do they allow fishing in that lake over there?'

He may as well have asked the Dean of Westminster if they had a snooker table in the Abbey. The gardens of Stourhead House were considered the finest landscaped gardens in England. The ornamental lake, which had been formed by damming the River Stour in the 18th century, was the jewel in the crown of the estate. Reproductions of classical temples and Gothic ruins had been purposefully dotted here and there around its banks, to create a romantic and exotic character and to afford spectacular views across the water.

The barman cleared his throat and picked up a glass to wipe, using the distraction of busy fingers to help him maintain his composure. 'I don't think so, Sir,' he replied, carefully enunciating each word. 'I've seen big fish in there, goldfish and the like, but they're purely ornamental.'

Harry and I looked at each other, tongue in cheek, avoiding Beedie's amused gaze.

The barman continued. 'If it's fishing you're after, you could always try the River Brue, or the lakes at Dunwear perhaps. They're not far away.'

Harry drained his glass, stretched his arms and started to sing:

> *'Fish Dunwear, it'll make you queer,*
> *Or try the Brue, if you want to spew......'*

Beedie and I giggled. The barman removed Harry's glass and with admirable self-restraint enquired, 'Would Sir like another?'

215

Our poaching expedition began with a stroke of good fortune. The white, five-bar gate at the entrance to Stourhead Gardens was open and unmanned when we arrived at dusk. All the visitors had gone, as had most of the staff, save for the few who had adjourned to the house to complete their paperwork before locking up for the night.

We could glimpse the lake between the trees and bushes, beyond the manicured grass which now constituted the village green. My heart instantly beat faster as I drove through the gate and pulled the van off the road between two mature trees. Here I parked on a promontory, the van hidden by the huge rhododendron bushes which lined the road on one side and cascaded into the lake on the other.

We could not risk using lights so there was no question of float fishing. Harry, who had never got to grips with ledgering, assured me that he would be happy to sit and watch me free-line.

The ground underfoot felt spongy and the water at the lake edge was extremely shallow, due to the accumulation of leaf drop over many years. Using a large lump of bread as bait on a size 10 hook, I cast as far as I could underhand. On this clear night and with the moon almost full, the silver paper bite-indicator stood out nicely on the sheet of green tarpaulin. Harry positioned his chair a few yards away. Carefully cupping the match, I lit my cigarette and took it across to him.

'Thanks Baws,' he whispered, lighting his own. 'Lovely night. Wonder what's in here?'

There was no time to answer before I heard the rustle of silver paper as the line went taut. Dashing back to my seat I struck, expecting to feel resistance, but there was none.

'Did you get it?' came Harry's stage whisper.

'No, but it must have been something decent. It wasn't a small piece of bait and something took it alright. Oh well, try again.'

And try again I did, and again and again and again. Every single time the line flew across the tarpaulin, each time I struck and missed. After an hour of frustration I decided to take a break from feeding the fish.

'Must have bloody great mouths for you to keep missing them,' commented Harry. I appreciated the implied compliment, but I was stumped.

'Perch wouldn't take bread like that,' he observed sagely. 'What do you think they are?' I knew he was trying his best to be helpful but he was only succeeding in making me more agitated.

'Fuck knows, Harry, but they're bloody irritating. I'd rather not have any bites than keep missing them like this.'

'Maybe someone put some Bigmouth bass in here.'

Now I might have believed the man at Hockley who told me there were cod in the pond when I was about ten years old and I might have believed the boys at Greenacres when they told me I had caught a sea-bream there. But Canadian bass in Wiltshire?

'Don't be daft Harry.'

'Stranger things happen, Baws. What about those huge catfish in Woburn? Ugly bastard things. They only arrived in the late nineteenth century from Europe. Then there's zander in Norfolk – they originally come from the Caucasus. There's even been talk of Russian sturgeon in English rivers.'

We fell silent, contemplating the possible nature of tonight's elusive quarry. After some time without speaking, I became aware of a faint, regular chirruping noise, coming I thought from the rhododendron bushes to Harry's right.

'Can you hear that, Harry?'

'What?'

We both listened.

'It's stopped now.'

After a few minutes the noise started up again.

'There it is, Harry'

'What?'

Again I strained my ears. Nothing. Minutes passed. Suddenly the noise began again. Very carefully I rose from my chair and edged towards where Harry sat. It was definitely coming from his direction. I was almost up to him when the noise stopped.

We listened again. Nothing.

I returned to my chair and cast in once more. Just as before, the bite indicator shot up the line and I struck firmly. Nothing. Then the chirruping noise started up again. Backwards and forwards I went, trying in vain to track down the irksome sound and to catch fish. Each time I reached Harry, the noise stopped, and each time I arrived back at my chair I had a bite, struck and missed. This insane performance continued for at least half an hour. As I missed yet another bite and the noise began again, I clenched my fists and pounded the ground.

'Surely you can hear that, Harry?' I half shouted through clenched teeth.

'Did you have a bite?' he asked disingenuously.

'Yes, yes – but what about the noise. You must be able to hear it.' I stood up and walked over to him. Needless to say, the noise stopped as approached. I placed my hand on his shoulder.

'What does it sound like Tony?'

'Like a cricket. No – more like a cicada.'

'Like this?' He chuckled as he rubbed a brittle rhododendron leaf rhythmically against the taught underside of his woven plastic seat.

'Harry, you rotten sod!'

At least the mystery of the noise was solved. We never did discover the identity of the phantom monster fishes of Stourhead lake.

Molly had begun to misbehave rather badly. Every ten miles or so the engine died and I had to stop, pull over and try the ignition again. This produced an irregular clicking sound when I first turned the key before pulling the starter but by some miracle she would always re-start.

Although we had some success fishing both on the River Brue and at the lakes at Dunwear (despite Harry's musical words of caution in the pub at Stourhead), and we were enjoying our stay, I decided it would be best to head for home before the van broke down completely. Beedie wished us well with a parting gift of a cardboard box containing several lemonade bottles of cloudy, green scrumpy, which she bought at the village store for sixpence each.

At the major crossroad in the centre of Warminster, Molly stalled once more, only this time she refused to start again. Opening the engine compartment I checked all the electric connections I could trace, before focusing on the fuel supply. I opened the carburettor and noted that the chamber was empty and dry. We had plenty of fuel so it must be a problem between the tank and the carburettor. Fuel pump!

Luckily the pump diaphragm had not died completely but it was failing. Lying under the van, with traffic passing inches from my outstretched feet, I uncoupled the metal fuel pipe leading to the tank and sucked hard to create a vacuum. Spitting out petrol, I reconnected the pipe as fast as I could. Clambering back into the van I allowed a few seconds for any spillage to evaporate, then fired the ignition. *Voilà!*

'Rinse your mouth out with this,' said Harry, passing me a bottle of scrumpy.

The flat, green liquid was not the best thing I had ever tasted but nevertheless I swallowed rather than spit.

This became the pattern of events over the next few miles. The van would stop, I would suck petrol and drink scrumpy, and on we would go. Harry eschewed the petrol chaser but chugged away at the cider 'to keep me company'. By the time we came to a sign in Wiltshire which said 'The Langfords', the combination of petrol and rough cider had made me feel distinctly woozy. I urgently needed to get off the road and have a rest.

So when a further, hand-written sign appeared, bearing the beguiling words 'Fishing – Day tickets – 300 yards down lane', it was like a gift from the gods. We could see what appeared to be a large lake over the hedgerow, but annoyingly the only entrance we could find bore a large sign saying 'Riding School – Lessons and Livery – BHA Approved Instructor'. Then came a bridge over a river and beyond that the road curved sharply away.

Too tired to investigate further, I turned the van before the bridge and parked hard up to the stable entrance. I wrote a hasty note of apology in case I was causing an obstruction and wedged it in a heater vent against the windscreen, facing outwards. Harry and I crawled into the back and settled down on the mattresses. Within a few minutes we were both soundly asleep.

CHAPTER 23

All is Vanity

'Matilda told such dreadful lies,
It made one gasp and stretch one's eyes;
Her Aunt, who, from her earliest youth,
Had kept a strict regard for truth,
Attempted to believe Matilda:
The effort very nearly killed her.'

HILAIRE BELLOC *Matilda*

I awoke to what I thought was the sound of a horse's hooves, a suspicion confirmed by the sight of a large, equine face poking in the open window! Hastily exiting by the back doors, I went round to the front of the van and introduced myself to the attractive young rider. It transpired that she was the owner of the riding school and stables and adjoining land, including the lakes.

'My name's Jill,' she announced in a pleasant, well-spoken voice. 'You can come in and park up along there if you like,' indicating a grassed area fronting the river. 'As long as you don't disturb the horses, they won't disturb you.'

'That's very kind of you. I'm with my father-in-law, actually – he's asleep in the back.' She did not question this, which was a relief. 'We were on a fishing holiday,' I explained, 'but we're having trouble with the van.'

'There's a garage in the next village,' she said. 'He's very good. What's the problem? Maybe he can fix it for you.'

'It's the fuel pump.'

'And what van is it?'

'Morris J4.'

'I'll give him a ring and let you know. Anyway, make yourselves at home. There's a toilet on this side of the stable block – you're welcome to use it. Make sure you shut the gate after you.' She made a clicking noise while pulling gently on a left rein and the horse moved off.

Fortunately the van started first time without the need for me to imbibe any more of the ruinous petrol and cider cocktail. I drove though the gate and parked facing the River Wylye. Opening the back doors, I gave Harry a shake to wake him from his stupor.

'Baws,' he muttered blearily, as though meeting me for the first time after many years. Then followed a string of questions. 'Everything all right? Where are we? Can I smell horse-shit? Is that running water?'

I explained what had happened.

'I could do with a piss!' said Harry.

I showed him where to go and he staggered off in the direction of the stable block.

Lighting a cigarette, I perched on the van floor with my feet on the ground, listening to the gurgle of the river, taking in the scenery of the lake and the rolling downs behind. When a relieved Harry returned, he was chatting cheerfully to Jill.

'I'm glad you two have met.'

Jill smiled. 'I've had a word with the garage,' she said, 'and you're in luck. Geoff can come and fit a new pump tomorrow afternoon – unless you're in a rush to get off before? He says it'll only take him about half an hour.'

'That'll be great thanks, as long it's no trouble us staying overnight.'

'No, that'll be fine. What's tomorrow – Thursday? Should be fairly quiet. Might be different if my boyfriend was here, he's generally not too keen on fishermen.'

'And where is he?' I asked cautiously. I thought it best to be clear, in view of the implied problem.

'He's in hospital. Be there for a few weeks – had a bit of an accident at work.'

'Sorry to hear that. What sort of work does he do then?'

'Oh, he's a soldier. Parachute Regiment.'

'Go on, you can bugger off!' said Harry, clapping his hands. 'You're a very fine bird but you're a blasted nuisance.' It was his turn to be pestered by the swan.

The morning had dawned bright and warm. Harry, to his credit, had made light of the fact that his cleansing ritual was temporarily put on hold, settling instead for a quick hand-wash in the stable toilet. Now we sat one either side of a narrow, reed-covered spit of gravel which jutted out into the larger of the two lakes. The swan glided round and round, being inquisitive rather than aggressive, approaching first me and then Harry. Fishing in the company of swans always made us anxious because of the risk posed to them by the line. We later learned that this particular spot was where our swan came ashore in the nesting season and we were sitting in his front room, as it were.

A breeze ruffled the surface of the water. My float lifted and lay flat – a typical tench bite. I held my breath and felt my heart rate rise as the float slid across the water and disappeared. There were no obstructions and I delighted in feeling the pull of the fish and allowed it to run more or less unchecked. Gradually it tired and I brought it to the net. Although not of great size, it was a handsome fish, a lighter green and gold than the Durston canal tench, due no doubt to the gravel and chalk habitat of the lake.

Several more tench followed. Harry meanwhile had located a rudd shoal, again of no great size, but their colouring was superb. Then the sport died, as abruptly as it had started.

'Best get back, Harry. That chap from the garage will be coming soon.'

We made our way round the *manège* and strode along the gravel drive behind the stables. Horses' heads poked out from several of the stalls and we stopped to pat them. An altogether more vigorous response was required when we reached the van.

'Hey! Get out of there!' I yelled, addressing the hindquarters of a horse, poking out from the back of the van. I had not had that much contact with horses but I was fairly sure that it would not be a good idea to approach the rear end of one in an attempt to pull it out backwards. Instead I dropped the rods and bags to the ground, ran up to the van and beat on the side panels. The noise sufficiently frightened the horse to make it reverse out. Alerted by the din, Jill came running up to see what was wrong.

'It didn't get anything did it?' she asked anxiously.

'No, I don't think so. There isn't much in there anyway'. I was sure I'd closed the doors. Belatedly I remembered – horses love apples. Cider? Apples? With some apprehension I examined the floor of the van for tell-tale signs of broken glass but thankfully there were none. The last unopened bottle of scrumpy remained intact in its cardboard box.

Relieved that there was no harm done, Jill invited us to join her and a few friends when we were ready. We made our way round to the front of the stable block, where she and her boy-friend lived in a small, blue caravan.

Seated on the grass were several young people, drinking, laughing and passing round a huge joint. They became slightly furtive as we approached, but Jill soon put them at their ease.

'This is Tony and Harry,' she said. 'They own that van over there.'

This was a sound move politically, since the red and green paintwork of Molly Morris, and the Jemima Puddleduck posters with which she was adorned, firmly nailed our colours to the mast. We were made welcome as everyone shuffled round to make space.

'Would you two like a drink?' asked Jill. 'John brews his own beer – it's quite strong.'

It would have been rude to refuse, even though we had not eaten since we got up. Jill went off and soon reappeared with two earthenware mugs and a brown quart bottle with a stone stopper.

'You have to decant it into that jug first . There's a bit of sediment.'

'Here, let me,' offered one of the party. As he began slowly to unscrew the stopper there was a hissing sound and with practised aim he pointed the bottle at the jug to catch the contents as they gushed forth. 'Bit lively this lot, Jill!' he observed.

'Cheers,' said Harry, raising his mug. He took a deep swallow. 'Very pleasant,' he commented. Coming from Harry, this was high praise.

The beer did indeed taste fine. Dark and somewhat sweet, it was, as John was often to describe it, 'more of a food than a beer.' It was however, pretty potent.

'Do you blokes smoke?'

'Cheers,' said Harry, moving his mug into his left hand and accepting the joint in his right. He took a couple of puffs, inhaling deeply, and passed it to me. Grass, not my favourite. I was more of a hash man but again, it would have been rude to decline.

Rather than be forced to smoke grass, I went to the van and returned with my little container. I explained it's original use, which amused everyone. I rolled a three-skin joint of Red Leb and passed it around. The home brew continued to flow.

'I've made some chilli con carne,' announced Jill enthusiastically. Would anyone like some?'

'Cheers,' said Harry.

'There's some bloke asleep in the back of your van.'

Geoff had arrived with the replacement fuel pump. At some stage in the afternoon's proceedings, Harry had discreetly 'done a Captain Oates'. Whether the home brew or the grass or the Red Leb or the chilli con carne or a combination of all four had been responsible, he had graciously withdrawn, looking slightly green, and had not reappeared.

'Can you work round him?' I asked.

'Yeah, shouldn't be a problem. I'll make a noise quietly.'

Half an hour later Geoff returned to say that the pump had been fitted. 'I didn't want to start the engine without you in case I woke that fella in the back,' he said. Somewhat unsteadily I accompanied him back to the van. I turned over the engine and noted that the ominous clicking sound had gone. Just to be on the safe side I decided to give it a short road test. I dared not go out onto the highway and so I drove up and down the length of the gravel drive several times. Satisfied with Geoff's sterling work, I parked the van, paid and thanked him.

It was only at this point that Harry awoke. Considerately, I poured him a cup of water.

'Would you like a drink, H?'

'Cheers,' said Harry.

When reluctantly we took our leave, Jill gave us her telephone number and assured us that we would be very welcome to return at any time, despite the *caveat* regarding her partner John and his distaste for fisher folk. Once home, Harry took up the entire first day washing, no doubt making up for lost time.

Back on our local Essex waters, we experienced a brief, golden period of outstanding fishing, although Harry was not altogether pleased with his personal attainment of piscatorial *nirvana*.

At a deep gravel pit in Southminster, on the edge of the wildness that is the Dengie Peninsular, he had somehow unlocked the key to landing the bream. One after another these huge, slab-sided fish, six, seven, maybe eight pounds in weight, slid into the net. In a reversal of our usual roles, Harry was catching the fish and I was wielding the landing net.

He must have caught twenty or more until eventually he gave up wanting them in his keep net and we simply released them as soon as they were unhooked. Fishing in the swim next to him, I had not a single bite, yet his remarkable catch failed to make him happy.

'They may be big,' he complained 'but it's no fun really. It's like pulling in a lump of wet carpet. I'd rather be catching roach at the Res. At least they put up a fight.'

Visiting the same Southminster venue the following week, we fished, in all innocence, a lake stocked solely with trout and reserved for syndicate members only. Furthermore, unaware as we were of the nature of our prospective quarry, we blithely offered the usual menu of bread and maggot, which the trout woofed down with great gusto.

To our enormous surprise, we caught half a dozen very edible trout, in fairly short order. These energetic fish fought to a standstill, sometimes leaping right out of the water in their effort to break free. Once released, they floated on the surface of the water and resisted all efforts to revive them. Rather than hide our guilt under the bushes, we merrily carried them home. Grilled with a knob of butter, a twist of lemon and a sprinkling of black pepper, they were absolutely delicious.

Next we visited Corringham, where we had not been for some time. The weather had been hot and settled for several days and the water was warm as bath water. I had recently acquired yet another float to add to my collection – a thin, green plastic reed design, finished with a delicate white antenna about one inch long. It carried a single BB shot, and promised to be highly visible by torchlight. This was to be its maiden voyage.

Using bread flake as bait, I had bites from the moment I cast in. One after the other, crucian carp of a pound and over came to the net. Many times the bait was taken on the way down. By dawn I was utterly exhausted. I had filled my own landing net to capacity and having commandeered Harry's, had filled that too. When the taciturn Canadian owner came round for his money, he was taken aback by the size of the three figure haul.

'I have to get this in the local paper,' he enthused. 'Can you send me a photo?'

I had not forgotten my dislike for this man nor his racist remarks about

225

Danny and his family but I still succumbed to the flattery. I did not want to admit that I did not have a camera with me.

'Of course.'

'That's great,' he said. 'You guys can have this one on the house.'

Harry, who had not had a single bite all night, was barely awake. I gave him a nudge. I remembered what had happened to my reel the last time we were here and although Danny and Danny Junior had moved on, it was better to be safe than sorry.

'Harry, could you keep an eye on my stuff please?'

'Why? Where are you off to, Baws?'

'Just popping home to pick up my camera.'

Harry always swears that he heard the sound of the Lotus engine roaring the entire ten miles from Corringham to Leigh and all the way back. It was only when I set up the keep nets and prepared to take the shot that was to guarantee my fleeting moment of fishing fame (in Corringham at least) that I discovered there was no film in the camera.

While trying hard not to be too boastful, we were nonetheless happy to bring our tales of recent fishy success to the next club meeting at The Horse and Groom. Harry had his bream catch to relate and I my crucian haul, while the story of the ill-begotten trout amused everyone.

Several new members were to be proposed at the meeting that evening and there were faces we did not recognise. A large, imposing man with a beard walked in, ordered a pint and sat down behind us. He began holding forth to Freddie and Slapper, who were already seated at that table. Harry and I pricked up our ears as we recognised a familiar tale:

'Yes, they say it was the biggest carp at the Priory for many years,' announced the bearded man. 'Leather carp it was, well over twenty pounds. Lord, it put up a fight! Took over an hour to land. I had to wade in and guide it into the shallows by the sluice there. A young lad helped me pull it out. Everyone standing and looking on gave a big cheer.' He took a sip of beer and smacked his lips, pausing for effect before delivering his punch line. 'Best fish I ever caught, that was.'

Hearing this, Harry's mouth fell open. He looked questioningly at me, arching his eyebrows and rolling his eyes from left to right. I nodded quickly to show that his message was not lost on me and turning round, I addressed the bearded man.

'Excuse me, is your name Chris?'

'No, it's Roger.'

'Aren't you the bloke who waded in and helped our friend Chris land that huge leather carp at the Priory a few years back? We were there too, Harry and me.'

I turned to indicate Harry, whose face was expressionless. He was looking directly at Roger. To be more precise, he was looking at a point just above Roger's eye line, at the middle of his forehead

Red faced, Roger mumbled something, picked up his drink and left.

Slapper too got up, a grin on his face. 'Guess we won't be sponsoring him as a member then. Drinks anyone?'

CHAPTER 24

The Cleanest Man on Earth

'Water, water, see the water flow,
Glancing, dancing, see the water flow,
O Wizard of Changes, water, water, water.'

ROBIN WILLIAMSON *The Water Song*

'Won't be long, Tony. There's some sherry there – help yourself, I don't have to tell you.'

The sound of Harry's vigorous facial slapping as he applied aftershave and Lord-knows-what-else put me in mind of that (usually losing) act often seen at talent competitions, where someone plays a rough approximation of a piece of music – almost invariably 'The William Tell Overture' – on their cheeks.

'Thanks,' I said, declining the invitation. 'I've just been speaking to Alf Nugent. There's to be a committee meeting soon to discuss putting high fencing around Eastwood Rise, to deter the vandals.'

'So wags the world, Baws. We'll soon have to pay at the turnstiles to go fishing.'

Eastwood was by no means our favourite venue and the fishing there had always been patchy but we had a certain fondness for 'The Rise'. My most notable catch had been a totally unexpected chub, which submitted one night to floating crust! Fortunately I did have my camera with me that time and was able to produce the evidence to doubters, of whom there were many.

Approached along an unmade road, the pond backed onto an outback of overgrown scrub and gnarled trees. It was a place where, by substituting East for Wild as the descriptive of the lawless wood, the famed weasels in 'The Wind in the Willows' might easily have lived.

Harry appeared from the kitchen to retrieve yet more grooming applications from the trolley. He was still in his saggy white vest and pants, his thinning hair wet and spiky, his face covered in shaving foam.

'Have a look at that paper, Tone,' he said, pointing. 'They're advertising a magic bait – just what we've always wanted. I've circled it.' He picked out some bottles and disappeared into the kitchen again.

I studied the advertisement:

HOOK-EM FISHING BAIT ADDITIVE
The secret formula in Hook-Em is known only to the manufacturers.
Attracts fish like a magnet!
Simply add a drop of harmless Hook-Em to your normal bait.
Previously ignored baits suddenly become irresistible!
Never experience again the disappointment of returning home biteless!
One bottle holds enough for 500 applications.
NB. Hook-Em has proved so effective, it is banned from competitions.

'You always said you wouldn't want an irresistible bait Harry, that it would be no fun just to sit there and pull fish out, one after the other.'

'Don't suppose it works anyway,' he laughed. 'You think of all the things we've tried. What do you reckon was the worst bait?' Without waiting for an answer, he went on, 'Do you remember that cheese stuff you bought one time in a tin – mixed with cotton-wool? That was pretty foul.'

'That was only because I left it in the boot for months after I'd opened it.'

'Keeyugh,' said Harry in disgust, recalling the horror of it. ' It turned green – fucking dreadful!'

'So what do you think of this Eastwood Rise fence idea?'

'Like I say, Baws, we've seen the best of it.'

It was not the first time that he had made this remark in recent times and I knew exactly what he meant. The *laissez-faire* style of fishing that we enjoyed so much was now under threat from several quarters. Whilst recognising that the rural idyll of which we were so fond only existed thanks to man's intervention over an aeon and that our beloved gravel pits began their lives as commercial enterprises and not as gifts of nature, the rapid pace of change was a worry.

Mindless vandalism and litter were increasing, but so was corporate vandalism. In the name of speed and convenience, new roads were being built everywhere, slicing great swathes through the countryside. Councils had become besotted by the unholy trinity of Access, Convenience and Tidiness, uprooting established trees and shrubs and pruning into ugly, unnatural, rectangular shapes those which were left. Both the Res and the Priory had suffered badly from such corporate interference.

To add to the environmental problems, commercial fisheries and private syndicates were on the increase, outbidding the modest subscription revenues available to local clubs when competing for rented venues. Some of our friends were so disillusioned that they gave up fishing altogether. Chris, our skilful young friend from Star Lane, the same Chris who caught the mighty leather carp at the Priory and had refused to boast about it, took up archery instead.

Happily, not all was doom and gloom. Near to home, we discovered a new water at Barling, one in the long line of pits which exploited the rich gravel deposits along the Thames Valley. This one lay hard up against the sea wall between the River Roach and the backwaters of those secretive Essex islands: Potton, Havengore and Foulness. We still belonged to the open membership clubs we had first joined when we began fishing in earnest. And finally, there were venues and friends old and new in the west country; Beedie, the Trentons, Durston, Langford. Only distance and time prevented us from visiting as often as we would have liked.

From the kitchen came the sound of Harry singing, as he often did when washing. He was putting his own, interesting words to the tune of 'The Skaters' Waltz':

> *'Fucking around, fucking around,*
> *I spent a lifetime fucking around.*
> *Pissing about, pissing about,*
> *I spent a lifetime just pissing about...'*

'Anyway, Harry, I really came round to ask if you wanted to go down to John and Jill's for a few days – this Friday to next Monday?'

If he had answered 'Might as well Baws, we've got nothing to lose,' one more time, I think I'd have screamed. Luckily he simply said 'Fine'.

Any fears we might have had about Jill's boyfriend John turned out to be totally unfounded. He was a tough man for sure, who had not allowed his severe injuries to cramp his style. He refused to accept the medical opinion that he would not walk again and now managed unaided, even though occasionally he had to steady himself against some solid object. He also continued to drive with considerable enthusiasm and *panache*.

John had apparently undergone a sea-change from his original objective on joining an élite regiment, (which, as told to me, was 'basically because I wanted to kill people'). Now he was a staunch supporter of the rights of the working man and a keen observer and commentator on local, national and international politics, not afraid to take action when the need arose. Professing scant regard for 'fucking hippies and hangers-on', he seemed to take a selective approach when actually dealing with them face-to-face. Those whom he judged to be 'a complete bastard and a waste of time' (and there were many) were either given short shrift or allowed to remain purely for entertainment value at 'The Court of King John'; riotous week-end assemblies at the lakeside involving verbal and occasional physical jousting under the influence of large intakes of alcohol.

Only those whom he respected, or who amused him, were given the time of day. I think he respected us and I hope that we amused him. Either way, he made us very welcome, despite the drawback of us being 'southern softies' and in my case 'a neurotic freak.'

Between this ex-paratrooper and his new-found Jewish accountant friend there existed an unlikely bond; a mutual love of the music of The Incredible String Band, especially the early recordings. The counterpoint to this was his obsession with Leonard Cohen, whom I could take or leave. As for Harry, while he could not perform his usual trick and make John snap to attention as he had so many other military men, there was obvious mutual respect for their army past. But drunk or sober, neither man would ever discuss details of their time in the service.

We arrived in Wiltshire in the late afternoon one glorious day in July. I parked the van facing the river as usual and we made our way across the paddock to the caravan where we found John attacking the wooden steps with a hammer.

'Hello, you two,' he said, with his back to us. 'Come to torture those poor bloody fish again?'

'How are you, boy?' asked Harry, ignoring the barb. 'Still on the home brew?'

'Yes, why? Do you fancy one? The jug's over there.'

'A bit later maybe.'

Alcohol of one sort or another was a staple of our visits. I duly handed over the bottle of whisky I had brought as a gift.

John grinned. 'Cheers! Have you two eaten? I'm just going to do some egg and chips for myself. All you'll get from Jill is fucking wog food.'

Just then a somewhat flushed Jill appeared in the caravan doorway, dressed in sweater and jodhpurs, her hair in plaits. Having just given her last riding lesson of the day and aiming to eat before changing, she exuded a slight whiff of horse.

'Oh hello, just arrived? Have you eaten? I'm about to fry up some courgettes.'

'See what I mean?' said John. 'Out of the way woman,' he joked, 'I'm making these blokes some real men's food!'

Although the old blue caravan had been replaced since we were last there, and the current model was larger and more up to date, the combination of cooking chip fat and calor gas lighting still made the air thick and the inside temperature rise dramatically. For those unused to that particular environment, the only way to breathe was to lie on the floor, open the door, or leave. Harry and I chose to wait outside until the actual moment we were called to the table.

'This is no hardship,' remarked Harry, the master of the understatement, as we sat contentedly smoking, drinking in the view. The sun filtered through the spinney of alder and willow on the edge of the paddock. Beyond lay an expanse of calm water, glowing like a burnished bronze mirror in the early evening light, framed by the reflection of the tall trees on the far bank. Swallows and martins swooped across the water, chasing insects, and in the stillness we could hear the crystal song of warblers in the reeds. As if on cue, gliding majestically by, came the swans who gave their name to White Bird Lake.

'Should be a good day's fishing tomorrow if it stays like this.'

The smaller lake next to White Bird was an altogether more enclosed affair. Thorn bushes guarded many of the swims, moss grew on the bank side trees, lily pads and reed mace abounded – a 'tenchy spot' if ever I saw one.

I set up two rods in one of the few clear swims, with Harry fishing beside me. It was an odd juxtaposition, the two of us looking out with huge anticipation at the still water of a perfect coarse fishing lake while the River Wylye, that peerless bastion of game fishing, burbled gently behind us. In Essex, many gravel pits were converting to trout fisheries (as witness our illicit but welcome haul at Southminster). Reservoirs had always adopted a 'fly-only' policy, lest a worm or maggot used as bait should sully the drinking water of the Great British public. Harry often remarked that 'since wildfowl are usually resident on reservoirs and visit in their thousands, there must be a plentiful supply of bird shit on the bottom of every reservoir so what harm can the odd maggot do?' But we had made our decision many years ago – we were coarse to the core.

'Got 'im!' yelled Harry. A plump, glistening tench came to the net.

'Me too!' My float had trailed across ten yards of open water before disappearing from sight.

'Another one, Harry, on the ledger. Oh bugger, there goes the float, can you get this one?'

'Can't, Tone, got one myself.'

It was the most sublime chaos. One after the other, or in pairs, tench after fat tench came to our nets. All fought like demons and none were lost.

At the end of two hours the keep nets were bulging and we were exhausted. Harry had excelled himself with five good tench; I had over forty. As we carefully released them there was no thought of comparison, no consideration of whether this fish was larger than that one. We embraced as we had all those years ago at the Priory on our very first adventure, from our sheer joy and exhilaration at the catch and to signify the pleasure we found in each other's company.

We were tidying up the breakfast things the following morning when Jill appeared at the back of the van. 'We're going for a swim,' she said. 'Care to join us?'

'You go ahead, Tony,' said Harry. I hesitated, considering whether this was another of his Captain Oates moments, but could see nothing in Jill's offer that required self sacrifice on his part. Then things became clearer. 'I'm going to have a bit of a wash and brush up. I'm feeling a bit manky.'

'Well, a swim will soon sort that out.'

'I'm going to have a shave , do my hair – you know.'

'Okay,' I told him, 'we'll see you later. Come up and join us when you've finished.' Knowing Harry's routine as I did, I did not bank on seeing him for some time.

Jill's father owned a further series of lakes the on the other side of the River Wylye. No fishing was allowed and it was here that Jill and John swam, along with their invited friends.

'Give us a hand, Tony,' said John, passing me a crate of home brew.

'Should be enough. There's a few more coming over later. Here Jill, grab the record player and I'll sort out some music.' The battery-operated record player was a great asset; not only did it provide music in the caravan, which had no mains electricity, but it was portable, at a pinch.

I was not a confident swimmer. As a child I had almost drowned on two occasions which I recalled with great clarity and which I recounted to anyone who would listen until Suzie had become sick and tired of hearing about it. On holiday in Denmark as a teenager, I had attempted to repeat the trick in the low salinity of the Baltic Sea. At grammar school a prefect had drowned, caught up in the weeds at Flatford Mill, and to round off my catalogue of watery doom there was the sad death of my friend Mump in the Blue Lagoon at Hadleigh. So after paddling about a bit in the shallowest, most weed-free portions of the lake, I soon returned to dry land, happy to be put in charge of the music for a while.

Complying reluctantly with John's request for 'Songs from a Room' by Leonard Cohen, I put on side one and escaped to see how Harry was doing, since he had still not put in an appearance. After years of experience, the scene that greeted me back at the van should not have surprised me, but it did.

Harry stood naked, whitely pale, up to his knees in the River Wylye, rubbing himself all over with a flannel. He was singing what seemed to me a distinctly inappropriate song for a fine July morning:

> *'Just a song at twilight,*
> *When the lights are low…'*

He elongated the 'ow' in 'low' and 'shadows' and 'go' as a pastiche on the common perception of an upper class 'o', as voiced perhaps by Bertie Wooster to Jeeves, in the phrase 'oh I say!':

> *'And the flickering shadows*
> *Softly come and go…'*

Importantly, there were no modifications by way of swear words to disturb the sensibilities of the two middle-aged ladies peering at him from the parapet, whose remarks I could hear but which were lost to Harry in the rush of water gushing through the stanchions of the bridge:

'He's certainly very clean, Veronica, I'll grant you that.'

'I do believe, Bethany, that he could be the cleanest man on earth.'

Epilogue

Much happened in a short time after our visit to Langford. Suzie and I moved to London, we were blessed with our darling first child, Gideon, Suzie became unwell for a long time and the rods were stowed away.

Harry meanwhile still yearned for a life in the great outdoors and took a job in the Parks Department, which was administered in a relaxed manner and staffed by a merry crew of eccentrics. Happy to be able to dress on a daily basis in black wellingtons, his old cords held up with a school tie and wearing a pheasant feather in his hat, Harry apparently spent much of his time brewing beer in the mess-room and sharing the odd surreptitious joint in the shrubbery. When I asked what work he actually did, he described it as 'massacring roses.'

In a mad moment, I bought a small cruiser on the Thames, the redoubtable *Annie May*. In this splendid little craft, I soon discovered that Harry's initial incompetence at fishing was as nothing compared to his ineptitude at boating. But that is altogether another story.

On that last visit to Langford, with the sun setting over the lake, the white, resting swans bathed in ultraviolet light, with the assembled friends mellow on home brew, from the battered record player came a song by 'The Incredible String Band':

> 'May the long time sun shine upon you,
> All love surround you,
> And the pure light within you
> Guide you all the way on.'

Everyone joined in that final coda as it repeated over and over, swept along by its expression of love and hope for the times. Perhaps it also summed up what was great about fishing with Harry – that despite the differences in our ages, our background, our culture and our aspirations, we shared an optimism which even our innate cynicism could not quite bury, a joy of living we hoped would see us through.

Vocabulary

Harry used many words and phrases which I had not heard before, or at least not in the context that he chose. If fishing was very quiet, with no activity, he would say it had 'gone a bit turpsy. If the weather was uncomfortably cold, it had 'turned a bit clawry'; if things turned really grim, he would raise his fist to the heavens and shout 'thin!' A fusk is a cat, a fusko or trotter being a dog. 'Pissers' are small-fry or tiny fish. To assuage my sensitivities, he had various colourful euphemisms for 'not feeling too well', viz: gobbly, wobbly gobblin, gobbly wobblin', cloopy and shot the cat.

I have introduced a smattering of Yiddish/Hebrew/Russian/German words. *Shtetl* was a small Jewish community or village settlement in pre-WW2 Europe. A *khazer* is a greedy person: originally meaning 'pig', it is a derogatory observation but not quite as insulting as it would be in English. A *frummer* is a devout or observing Jew and a *schloch* is a very untidy person, almost a tramp. *Meshugge* means 'crazy' and *shikker* means drunk or a drunkard. *Efshe* is a re-inforcing word meaning 'maybe, could be, perhaps'. I have heard my mother say '*efshe* p'raps' which is something of a tautology!

Noch in German means 'again', 'also' or 'as well as'. It means the same in Yiddish but the usage is tinged with irony - 'can you believe that?' I think many people recognise that 'to keep *schtum!*' is to 'say nothing'. Likewise, *gefillte* fish is quite well known as being chopped and seasoned fish (predominantly carp in Eastern Europe.) *Matzo* balls are dumplings made using meal from unleavened bread. *Chrain* is a strong beetroot and horse-radish sauce. *Haimisha* means 'homely' rather than 'home-made' and is particularly applied to a sweeter variety of pickled cucumber. *Khalle* is the plaited, white bread, glazed with egg, eaten at the Sabbath meal, where you might hear the exhortation '*ess guzunthayt!* Eat with good health!' *Shobbas/Shabbat* comes in at sunset Friday and departs at sunset on Saturday.

There are a few words of Arabic derivation. *Mufti* is the civilian dress of one who wears uniform when on duty. '*Imshi*' is 'go on!' but '*yalla*' is 'come on! - the two are often strung together as a phrase, thus '*Imshi! – Yalla!*' indicates a pressing need to get on with things.

Acknowledgements

Suzie for her endless love and patience and her wonderful ideas and drawings.

Kenny (Richard Kenworthy of Shynola) for the beautiful cover artwork and for being, with his wife Mia, together with Jason and Chris of Shynola, Gideon's good and constant friends.

Kitty Carruthers of Medina Publishing Limited for editing my work so thoughtfully.

Karen Harris ('Little Karen') for help and support with the illustration artwork.

Ramsay Wood – author of 'Kalila and Dimna' – for encouragement and friendship.

Roz Lamb of the Sarah Moore for the loan of her mother's book and for her unquenchable good humour.

Bili Rocke – 'probably the best landlady in the world'.

Karen, **Merlin** and **Jo** at Merlin Unwin Books for their faith in bringing my book to publication. Their cheerfulness and enthusiasm has made the process relatively pain-free.

To all the above, my love and thanks.

Permissions

Some of the lyrics and poetry quoted in the book are still in copyright and are re-produced with the kind permission of the licence holders:-

'For What It's Worth' by Stephen Stills © 1967 (renewed) – all rights administered by Artemis Muziekuitgeverij B.V. 'Black Muddy River' words and music by Jerry Garcia and Robert Hunter © Ice Nine Publishing Co. Inc. – all rights administered by WB Music Corp. 'Matilda Who Told Lies and was Burned to Death' by Hilaire Belloc, published by Jonathan Cape and reprinted by permission of The Random House Group Ltd. 'The Water Song' by Robin Williamson © 1968 Warner-Tamerlane Publishing Corp – all rights reserved. 'A Very Cellular Song' by Mike Heron © 1968 Warner-Tamerlane Publishing Corp – all rights reserved.

Notes:

1. The song 'Wake up little Susie', a hit record by The Everly Brothers, was written by Felice and Boudleaux Bryant in 1957.
2. The authorship of 'Sixteen Tons' seems to be disputed between Merle Travis and George S. Davis. I have credited Tennessee 'Ernie' Ford, whose version I know best.
3. The poem that introduces chapter thirteen is attributed to the late Yvonne Roy, from a copy in my possession. I have contacted her daughter, Professor Lucinda Roy, but at the time of publication she is unable to positively confirm or deny her mother's authorship. My thanks to her and my apologies if this attribution turns out to be incorrect.
4. Chapter 2, 'The Priory', first appeared as a short story under the title 'Fishing With Harry' in *Waterlog*, published by The Medlar Press.